# Determining [ from Disability

This essential book offers clear guidelines for determining if the Culturally Linguistically Diverse (CLD)/ English Language Learners (ELL) students in your general education classroom are experiencing typical language differences, learning disabilities, or both. By combining helpful case-studies with insightful research, the authors provide a framework for differentiating instruction that uses culturally appropriate interventions to build upon student strengths while creating a foundation for further learning and achievement. You will discover how to:

♦ Connect your own and your students' cultural assets to classroom content;
♦ Review language acquisition stages and design corresponding instruction;
♦ Collaborate with peers and discuss the realities of reaching out for support and problem solving;
♦ Choose effective and appropriate instructional strategies based on documentation of data through progress monitoring;
♦ Move from a traditional behavioristic perspective to a more culturally responsive perspective;
♦ Identify patterns in formal assessments and informal instruction in order to distinguish between language differences and learning disabilities.

In addition, the book includes a number of activities and graphs that can be implemented immediately in any classroom. Many of these materials can be downloaded for free from the book's product page: www.routledge.com/9781138577756.

**Gerry McCain**, PhD, is a professor of education at Southern Oregon University. He taught Bilingual Special Education in Las Cruces, New Mexico, prior to earning his doctorate in Bilingual Special Education.

**Megan Farnsworth**, PhD, is an associate professor of special education at Southern Oregon University.

## Also Available From Routledge
## Eye On Education
(www.routledge.com/eyeoneducation)

**An Educator's Guide to Dual Language Instruction:**
**Increasing Achievement and Global Competence, K–12**
Gayle Westerberg and Leslie Davison

**Partners for Special Needs:**
**How Teachers Can Effectively Collaborate with Parents and Other Advocates**
Douglas J. Fiore and Julie Anne-Fiore

**Let's Get Real:**
**Exploring Race, Class, and Gender Identities in the Classroom**
Martha Caldwell and Oman Frame

**Teacher Agency for Equity:**
**A Framework for Conscientious Engagement**
Raquel Rios

**Teaching ELLs to Read:**
**Strategies to Meet the Common Core, K–5**
Paul Boyd-Batstone

**Helping English Language Learners Meet the Common Core:**
**Assessment and Instructional Strategies K–12**
Paul Boyd-Batstone

# Determining Difference from Disability

## What Culturally Responsive Teachers Should Know

Gerry McCain and Megan Farnsworth

Routledge
Taylor & Francis Group

NEW YORK AND LONDON

First published 2018
by Routledge
711 Third Avenue, New York, NY 10017

and by Routledge
2 Park Square, Milton Park, Abingdon, Oxon, OX14 4RN

*Routledge is an imprint of the Taylor & Francis Group, an informa business*

*Library of Congress Cataloging-in-Publication Data*
Names: Farnsworth, Megan, author. | McCain, Gerry, author.
Title: Determining difference from disability : what culturally
   responsive teachers should know / by Megan Farnsworth and
   Gerry McCain.
Description: New York : Routledge, 2018. | Includes bibliographical
   references.
Identifiers: LCCN 2017059610 | ISBN 9781138577749 (hardback) |
   ISBN 9781138577756 (pbk.)
Subjects: LCSH: Children with disabilities—Education | Linguistic
   minorities—Education. | Multicultural education. | English
   language—Study and teaching (Elementary)—Foreign speakers. |
   Students with disabilities.
Classification: LCC LC4031 .F38 2018 | DDC 371.9—dc23
LC record available at https://lccn.loc.gov/2017059610

ISBN: 978-1-138-57774-9 (hbk)
ISBN: 978-1-138-57775-6 (pbk)
ISBN: 978-1-351-26619-2 (ebk)

Typeset in Palatino
by Apex CoVantage, LLC

Visit the eResources: www.routledge.com/9781138577756

We would like to dedicate this book to all teachers who go the extra mile for their Culturally and Linguistically Diverse students and recognize the unique challenges and gifts they bring to their classrooms.

# Contents

# Foreword

Every week, educators write me asking how to determine if the struggles of a culturally or linguistically diverse student or an English Language Learner are due to learning an additional language or a learning disability of some sort. It seems that though the populations change, these issues do not. Their concerns are not being adequately addressed within the usual Response to Intervention or multi-tiered support systems prevalent in today's schools. These processes, though extremely helpful with most challenged and challenging students, often do not reflect what we know about layered language and literacy development or offer culturally and linguistically responsive interventions that account for the diverse learners' unique combination of linguistic and sociocultural adaptation needs. These systems are frequently designed for native English speakers who are proficient in English and familiar with U.S. cultural norms, values, and experiences and then applied with few or no meaningful modifications to Culturally and Linguistically Diverse learners. Caution must be exercised because the side effects of language and culture transition often appear as specific learning and language disabilities. Additionally, the decision to refer a Culturally and Linguistically Diverse learner to special education services may come as a result of these multi-tiered systems of support. These systems are usually not constructed for second-language learners or based on the research concerning language and literacy development of Culturally and Linguistically Diverse learners.

This book addresses linguistic and cultural assumptions and proposes a clear alternative that will assist all educators in achieving responsive, appropriate, and effective education for diverse learners. Gerry McCain and Megan Farnsworth do this within a culturally responsive pedagogy that is clear and practitioner based. They provide step-by-step guidance with classroom examples for each element under consideration.

As someone who has focused upon separating difference and disability issues and working on appropriate integration of multilingual and cross-cultural special education services for over 50 years and knows firsthand the complexities involved in the decisions educators must make for challenged and challenging Culturally and Linguistically Diverse learners, this well-focused, practical, and timely book is a welcome addition to educators everywhere. The authors understand what matters in serving diverse learners well and the foundation issues that are often overlooked in the process.

*Determining Difference from Disability: What Culturally Responsive Teachers Should Know* represents best practice and uses a research-based approach as it provides a detailed step-by-step process for serving all Culturally and Linguistically Diverse learners effectively from the start. Founded on the Funds of Knowledge paradigm, the authors identify the essential information that needs to be gathered and provide the means of gathering that information so that educators can distinguish difference and potential disabling conditions. They show practitioners how to deliver responsive interventions to ALL learners.

Catherine Collier,
PhD

# Meet the Authors

**Gerry McCain** is a professor of education at Southern Oregon University in Ashland. He earned his PhD in Bilingual Special Education from New Mexico State University. Gerry taught Special Education in southern New Mexico where the majority of his students were new arrivals to the U.S. with little or no English. Gerry has published several articles in the areas of critical theory, multicultural education, special education, and bilingual education. He has authored, co-authored and served as Director of multiple U.S. Dept. of Education Professional Development grants for indigenous and other underrepresented populations throughout his academic career. His research interests are indigenous languages and comparisons of indigenous education programs in the U.S. with countries around the globe. Dr. McCain has taught at the university level for over 25 years and currently teaches Educational Research, Special Education, and oversees the ESOL/Bilingual endorsement program at Southern Oregon University.

**Megan Farnsworth** is an associate professor of special education at Southern Oregon University in Ashland. She earned her PhD in Bilingual Special Education from the University of Arizona, Tucson. She has over a decade of K-12 teaching experience in General Education, Special Education, and English as a Second Language with students in California, Hawaii, Oregon, and Arizona. Dr. Farnsworth's research interests include examining the discourse strategies that native Spanish speaking students leverage to acquire complex English structures in groups with native English speakers. She is now examining the need for Emotional Intelligence in education and collecting stories of grief and resilience from teachers around the world. She currently serves as coordinator of *Educate Chombo*, a grassroots organization that seeks to empower women with literacy skills and economic development in Malawi, Africa.

# Acknowledgments

We want to acknowledge Dr. Catherine Collier for her guidance and positive support throughout the completion of this text. Her work and expertise in this area of uncertainty for exceptional students from diverse backgrounds has been truly inspirational.

We would like to acknowledge Ms. Maria Guardino for her "notes from the field" contribution, in which she shared insights into the realities of classroom complexities and creative multicultural problem-solving strategies.

Megan would like to acknowledge her mother, Marianne Campbell Farnsworth for providing her inspiration to support classroom teachers, as they work tirelessly to help their diverse students succeed. She would also like to acknowledge Frederick Martinez for his never-ending support.

# eResources

As you read this book, you'll notice the eResources icon ☎ next to the following charts. The icon indicates that full-size versions are available as free downloads on our website, www.routledge.com/9781138577756, so you can easily print and distribute them to your students.

## Downloads

# Introduction

The following chapters provide guidelines for general education teachers to determine if Culturally and Linguistically Diverse (CLD) and English Language Learner (ELL) students in their classroom are experiencing typical language and cultural differences, or if they have a learning disability, or both. Examples of culturally responsive and appropriate instructional support are provided for CLD/ELL students, and those who possibly have an exceptionality. The authors offer a critical context of supporting CLD and ELL students by describing reasons for overrepresentation of this student population in special education, as well as how teacher education programs have historically been remiss in training classroom teachers in this area.

This book begins by introducing a fourth grade teacher (Ms. Casad) in the beginning of her third year of teaching. After meeting her students, Ms. Casad feels overwhelmed by the cultural and linguistic diversity in her class. Often, there are additional concerns to consider with CLD students; for example, language differences, cultural differences, levels of academic exposure, and unique family experiences. Four students in Ms. Casad's class are introduced as case studies and focused on throughout the text: César, Rosa, Jun, and Trent.

Authors walk you through a process to answer the question many teachers ask, "How do I know if my ELL students have a learning disability or not?"

The authors discuss the process to ensure appropriate identification of CLD/ELL's cultural, linguistic, and socioemotional needs by providing ways to differentiate language differences from learning disabilities. Attention to details in each level of the process is worked through with four case study students in a general education classroom to illustrate a classroom teacher's responsibilities when meeting ELL students' needs.

Authors show the readers how to (1) connect their own and their students' cultural assets (i.e., strengths) to content, (2) review language acquisition stages and design corresponding appropriate instruction, (3) collaborate with peers and discuss the realities of reaching out for support and problem-solving, (4) choose effective and appropriate instructional strategies based on documentation of data through progress monitoring, (5) move from a traditional behavioristic perspective to a more culturally responsive perspective for deeper understandings of behavior, and (6) learn what patterns to look for in formal and informal assessments to determine language differences from learning disabilities.

Appropriate and effective instructional strategies are intended to build upon student strengths and create a foundation for further learning and achievement. It is often assumed that effective and research-based instruction already occurs in the general education classroom for all students. However, for instruction to be "effective and appropriate" for ELL/CLD students, instruction must be both linguistically and culturally appropriate. That is, the teacher who wants to teach ELL/CLD students appropriately and effectively must know students' levels of language proficiency in their first language (L1) and second language (L2) when planning instruction and assessments. Then, the teacher must provide culturally relevant curricula that reflect the background and experiences of the students (Delpit, 1995; Gay, 2010; Macedo & Bartolomé, 1999). In other words, a child's language and culture are never viewed as liabilities but rather as strengths or assets upon which to build from. Differentiating instruction should always be based upon students' strengths, while also using instructional strategies that promote learning in an environment that is specifically designed to minimize or prevent the development of counterproductive learning behaviors. The foundation of the entire book is based on using our students' strengths at every step of the teaching-learning process.

Following through with this process will help you as a teacher, effectively differentiate instruction using culturally responsive and appropriate strategies, interventions, and accommodations which can identify key factors for determining if a CLD/ELL student in your classroom has an exceptionality or not.

## Bibliography

Delpit, L. (1995). *Other People's Children: Cultural Conflict in the Classroom.* New York: The New Press.

Gay, G. (2010). *Culturally Responsive Teaching: Theory, Research, and Practice* (2nd ed.). New York: Teachers College Press.

Macedo D., & Bartolomé, L.I. (1999) Dancing with bigotry. In D. Macedo & L. I. Bartolomé, (Eds.), *Dancing with Bigotry.* New York: Palgrave Macmillan.

# 1

# The Role of the *Cultural Self* in Teaching and Learning

## Introduction

In this chapter we look into ways that *culture* and *language* form a lens from which teachers learn and teach. The reader is walked through a conceptual framework designed to help examine his/her individual *self* as a cultural being, and ask the questions, "Why do I believe what I believe? Where did that belief come from?" and "how do my cultural beliefs impact my students' learning?" Developing an understanding of ourselves as cultural beings is the first step in (1) understanding our students as cultural beings and (2) providing ways that understanding will help them reach their potential. The question of "why teach?" is also raised to begin the search for your cultural impact on your students.

- ◆ Readers are introduced to the concepts of Funds of Knowledge (Moll, Amanti, Neff, & González, 1992) and Funds of Identities (Moll, 2014) which develop a three-layered model of the *cultural self*.
- ◆ The *cultural self* is a conceptual model of *how* and *why* we do what we do as cultural beings.
- ◆ This concept is intended to help teachers examine how our individual cultural biases, cultural beliefs, and accepted cultural norms impact our teaching and the effects they have on our students; particularly students from CLD backgrounds.

◆ Authors discuss a *cultural mismatch* that contributes to teachers' misunderstandings about student behavior and achievement, which often results in overrepresentation of CLD students in special education.
◆ The reader is guided to reflect on all three layers of the *cultural self* model, and investigate ways your cultural lens informs the way you teach.
◆ The chapter concludes with activities to investigate your *cultural self* in the context of the classroom.

## Why Teach?

Out of all the professions to choose from, why have you chosen to teach? One way to consider this question is to look at aspects of human nature and nurture. Beginning with your heart, search for what aspects in your nature connect you to this profession. Often, teachers say it is their "desire to help" or "give back to their community," due to a strong personal connection made to one of their teachers (or other education professionals) who truly cared about them and brought them to their full potential. Other times it is the opposite experience, in which they did not have teachers who cared; therefore, they want to improve schooling experiences for students like them. At the heart level, often we hear descriptions of passion, empathy, or ethics of care. Take a minute to reflect on what aspects of your heart have brought you to this profession.

In viewing the question of "why teach?" from the "nurture" perspective, examine educational experiences such as trainings or opportunities in which you were given the message that you could be a teacher. This is when you were provided a leadership role that you felt successful and confident in your ability to "teach" others. Often, this opportunity is connected to "social or cultural capital" (see Table 1.3). We will continue to examine aspects of nature and nurture by connecting them to a useful framework called Funds of Knowledge, which helps us see multiple identities that influence the way we teach and learn.

## Funds of Knowledge

We believe that all people possess Funds of Knowledge, which are resources developed to complete the tasks required in everyday life (Moll et al., 1992). Funds of Knowledge are seen as cultural household practices or daily activities, and how people think about what they do. Families accumulate bodies of beliefs, ideas, skills, and abilities based on their experiences in response to larger societal forces (e.g., social class, gender, religion), that affect the situations of their families (Moll, 2014). This research is driven by an equity agenda that advocates for educators to build on students' and their families' knowledge and experiences as resources for connecting to curricula and teaching practices.

Rather than focusing on within-group coherence or static ideas of how people view the world (i.e., the "Islamic Culture"), Funds of Knowledge focus on the specific adaptations that families have developed over time in response to larger social, historical, and political forces. An example is looking at the ways adults' social or living conditions changed based on the use of digital media by their children. Funds of Knowledge are not always visible but are processes involving interaction with the environment, tools, and people, which teachers can utilize as resources for learning.

Funds of Knowledge are identified based on adults/parents leading the household; however, this limitation ignores the independence of children, who actively create specific identities for themselves through social actions. Therefore, the new term Funds of Identities (Moll, 2014) denotes the individual's agency or resources that are transported throughout one's life, changing and adapting, and may or may not reflect those of the family. Funds of Identities include attitudes, abilities, interests, beliefs, skills, and dispositions which affirm students' home languages and cultural practices as cultural capital available in the community. This capital can be used as resources for establishing connections within schools and building healthy communities. By connecting learning environments (such as schools and museums) to families' Funds of Knowledge, educators can create hybrid spaces in which power is distributed.

To illustrate educators' cultural lenses, we have adapted both Funds of Knowledge (Moll et al., 1992) and Funds of Identities (Moll, 2014) to include linguistic, social, cultural, and emotional capital, illustrated in Figure 1.1.

## Culture

Culture becomes an invisible script that directs our daily decision-making processes. Culture enables or constrains us, by blinding us to those who are different than us (Hollins, 2008; Varenne & McDermott, 1999). Culture permeates human behavior and affects everyday activities and can be considered a form of adaptation to the environment (Cheng, 2004). People in different places confronted with similar challenges (e.g., providing food, shelter and finding meaning) have created different repertoires of culturally acceptable solutions. These diverse approaches are influenced by patterns transmitted

**Figure 1.1** Funds of Identities

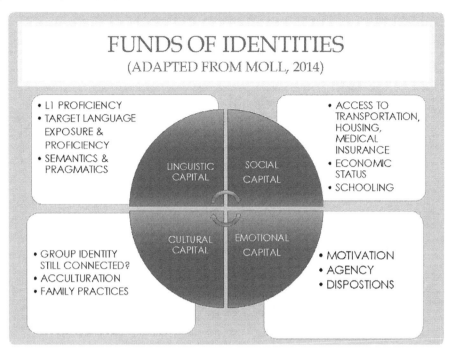

FUNDS OF IDENTITIES
(ADAPTED FROM MOLL, 2014)

- L1 PROFICIENCY
- TARGET LANGUAGE EXPOSURE & PROFICIENCY
- SEMANTICS & PRAGMATICS

LINGUISTIC CAPITAL

SOCIAL CAPITAL

- ACCESS TO TRANSPORTATION, HOUSING, MEDICAL INSURANCE
- ECONOMIC STATUS
- SCHOOLING

CULTURAL CAPITAL

EMOTIONAL CAPITAL

- GROUP IDENTITY STILL CONNECTED?
- ACCULTURATION
- FAMILY PRACTICES

- MOTIVATION
- AGENCY
- DISPOSTIONS

through generations, and vary by age, gender, learning style, religion, geographic region, socioeconomic status, language, ability, education, prior experience, motivation, intelligence, among others (Cheng, 2004). Cultures and languages are dynamic, constantly being invented or improved, and often borrowed from other societies. With such a diversity of languages and cultures in the world, it is often overwhelming to locate a beginning point for identity formation.

In an effort to understand the world around us, we can begin with one aspect of cultural competence, which is looking at ourselves. If we look at what our culture means to us as individuals, then we can make meaning of who we are. It is our own beliefs, biases, and experiences that shape the lens that we view the world with. By questioning and reflecting on these perceptions, we can begin to open our minds to other perspectives. Vygotsky (1978) helps describe this perception in two layers: the intrapersonal (i.e., private, individual level) and the interpersonal (i.e., public and social level) involving social and cultural capital. The intrapersonal level is divided into *self and family*. This way we can assess personal dispositions, cognitive strategies and ability levels, and then view the family's influence that affect these individual qualities. Below is a diagram (Figure 1.2) of ways to think about your Funds of Knowledge and Funds of Identities, which create your *cultural self*.

**Figure 1.2** The *Cultural Self*

# The Cultural Self

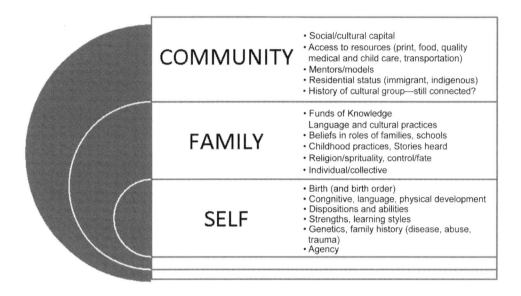

| COMMUNITY | • Social/cultural capital<br>• Access to resources (print, food, quality medical and child care, transportation)<br>• Mentors/models<br>• Residential status (immigrant, indigenous)<br>• History of cultural group—still connected? |
|---|---|
| FAMILY | • Funds of Knowledge<br> Language and cultural practices<br>• Beliefs in roles of families, schools<br>• Childhood practices, Stories heard<br>• Religion/sprituality, control/fate<br>• Individual/collective |
| SELF | • Birth (and birth order)<br>• Congnitive, language, physical development<br>• Dispositions and abilities<br>• Strengths, learning styles<br>• Genetics, family history (disease, abuse, trauma)<br>• Agency |

## Layer One: Self

In beginning with the *self* (Figure 1.2), the first layer represents your individual dispositions, physical, cognitive, and emotional development. Many factors affect who you are, beginning with genetics and family history. If you experienced a typical birth (pre-natal, peri-natal, and post-natal), then often your cultural lens may view other people as experiencing a typical birth. If your genetic make-up included disease or atypical development, then this would shape the way you view the physical body or ability/cognition of others. For example, if you were born with a hearing impairment, then your world would be shaped by specific choices and opportunities available to you that affect where you go to school, how you earn an income, and how you participate with technology. Because the dominant culture is based on characteristics of people born with typical physical development (e.g., hearing), you may feel excluded from the way communities are organized and ways people communicate within the community.

Cognition includes executive thinking skills such as ways one plans, implements, and follows through with a task. This is related to learning styles, strategies, and ways you work through problems in different contexts.

**Table 1.1** *Self*

| Factors | Teacher-Self |
|---|---|
| Dispositions (extrovert, empathetic, mindset) | |
| Cognitive, physical, and language development | |
| Strengths, interests, learning styles, mission, agency | |
| Genetics, family history of disease, or trauma | |

Recent research shows that cognition also plays a role in how flexible your thinking is with a growth or fixed mindset (Dweck, 2010). *Agency* is a term that shows your resiliency to act as an individual regardless of dominating cultural factors explored in layer two of the *cultural self* model (Figure 1.1). Reflect on the factors influencing your *self*, and write them in the Teacher-Self column in Table 1.1.

## Layer Two: Family Cultural Assets

The next layer (layer two) in the *cultural self* model illustrates relationships to your family or social group. Here we see the role that social interaction plays in our cognitive, emotional, and cultural development. Culture and cognition are inextricably wound (Chick, 1997) and are also negotiated through social interaction (Rogoff, 2003).

In viewing culture as an iceberg, the Indiana Department of Education has identified the top or surface layer of the iceberg to represent visible aspects of culture such as food, dress, and language (see Figure 1.3). These visible aspects of culture are manifestations of deeper cultural beliefs and values that lie below the surface. We often focus on the surface layer of cultural traditions and celebrate holidays with food, dress, dance, games, music, and crafts (e.g., Cinco de Mayo). This is a beginning step; however, if we stay at the surface, we may form assumptions that lead to stereotypes without exploring deeper layers. Most elements of culture are below the surface and often invisible. As you can see, many of our thoughts and behaviors are governed by the cultural norms we were raised with!

In examining the deeper layers of the iceberg, we can see how everyday practices are passed on through generations (i.e., transmission of culture). We have chosen a few cultural factors from the iceberg that we believe influence teacher practices, including concepts of fate and control, family structures and gender roles, individualism, attitudes towards elders, patterns of cognition, emotion management, and theories of disease (see Table 1.2).

**Figure 1.3** Iceberg of Culture

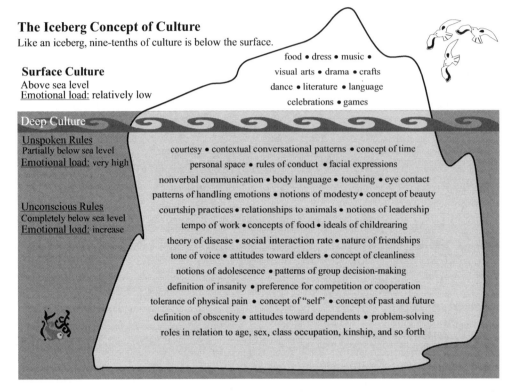

## The Iceberg Concept of Culture
Like an iceberg, nine-tenths of culture is below the surface.

**Surface Culture**
Above sea level
Emotional load: relatively low

food • dress • music •
visual arts • drama • crafts
dance • literature • language
celebrations • games

Deep Culture

Unspoken Rules
Partially below sea level
Emotional load: very high

Unconscious Rules
Completely below sea level
Emotional load: increase

courtesy • contextual conversational patterns • concept of time
personal space • rules of conduct • facial expressions
nonverbal communication • body language • touching • eye contact
patterns of handling emotions • notions of modesty • concept of beauty
courtship practices • relationships to animals • notions of leadership
tempo of work • concepts of food • ideals of childrearing
theory of disease • social interaction rate • nature of friendships
tone of voice • attitudes toward elders • concept of cleanliness
notions of adolescence • patterns of group decision-making
definition of insanity • preference for competition or cooperation
tolerance of physical pain • concept of "self" • concept of past and future
definition of obscenity • attitudes toward dependents • problem-solving
roles in relation to age, sex, class occupation, kinship, and so forth

Sources: www.doe.in.gov/englishlanguagelearning; www.overcomingracism.org/resources/Culture-Iceberg.pdf

**Table 1.2** Cultural Assets

| Cultural Assets | Self as Child | Teacher-Self as Adult |
|---|---|---|
| Dress, celebrations, food, and language | | |
| Patterns of friendship and social structure | | |
| Patterns of handling emotions and self-esteem | | |
| Family structure (nuclear or extended), family responsibilities, and gender roles | | |
| Individualism, independence, and competition, or collaboration | | |
| Relationship to plants, animals, or land | | |
| Body language (eye contact, personal space, tone of voice, nonverbal, facial expressions), linguistic and communication style | | |

## Control and Fate; Theories of Disease

Religious or spiritual ideals often inform people of their place and hierarchy in the universe, in life, and/or afterlife. This central concept guides human behavior relating to the amount of control a person perceives s/he has over choices and outcomes (of people, environments, and inanimate objects). In contrast, some people believe that a supernatural power (i.e., God) controls actions, outcomes, fate, and destiny. Control and fate are at opposite ends of a continuum. People fall all along this continuum, with varying beliefs of the amount of control they have over their lives. Beliefs of control and fate may influence beliefs about the origins of diseases and medical conditions. Some people believe that one can control the outcome of a disease with medical intervention (i.e., vaccinations). Other cultural beliefs place the fate of a disease in the hands of a supernatural being to decide the outcome (i.e., people who do not vaccinate their children), with varying degrees in between these two views. Reflect on implicit or explicit messages given to you about control and fate, and record on Table 1.2. Recognize your beliefs have the potential to marginalize those who hold different beliefs than you (see Reflection activity #3).

## Family Structures and Gender Roles; Child-Rearing and Attitudes Towards Elders

Varying family structures exist, although the dominant cultural norm in education remains two-parent, heterogeneous households. This norm often reinforces traditional gender roles and expectations for children. Some cultural beliefs place grandparents or community elders alongside the hierarchy as parents with parental duties. For example, Pewewardy (2002) informs us that many American Indian/Alaska Native (AI/AN) groups hold high respect for elders, have extended family structures, follow matrilineal clans, and view learning as rooted in the teachings of elders. Other values include: noninterference, cooperation, coexistence with nature, following flexible time frames, holding high tolerance for ambiguity, and learning through oral storytelling. Many of these cultural practices are in conflict with dominant Western cultural norms, including schooling practices. For example, if a teacher gives students a due date with a quick turnaround time for an assignment, AI/AN students may need longer time to consider multiple viewpoints and process information. Reflect on your own cultural beliefs and practices in family structures and gender roles, child-rearing, and attitudes towards elders.

## Individualism/Collectivism

Another aspect of your cultural lens that affects your teaching and learning is the value placed on independence, individualism, and collectivism. Do you live independently from your parents or siblings? Was individual achievement valued and rewarded by your family? Did you play family games where someone won and someone lost? One example of placing high value on independence is the writing of Individual Education Plan (IEP) goals, which often include the criteria "independently" (e.g., Sue will write a topic sentence with three key events independently). Western cultures value personal achievement and individual feelings, whereas Eastern cultures value the interdependence of the *self* and its group (Markus & Kitayama, 1991). Cultural values influence the significance and interpretation of events and relationships, including the way one plans and carries out a task, and evaluates or reflects upon it (e.g., cognitive processes). If you expect students to always perform independently, then you hold the potential of marginalizing students who value and practice community/collectivism. Examples of activities rooted in collectivism include: buddy reading, choral reading, cooperative learning groups, "Think-Pair Share," "Phone a Friend," and many more.

After you reflected on the beliefs and practices you were raised with in your family (Funds of Knowledge, Moll, Amanti, Neff, & González, 2005), reflect on your beliefs and daily practices as an adult (Funds of Identities, Moll, 2014), and then fill out the Teacher-Self column in Table 1.2.

## Layer Three: Sociocultural Capital, Socioeconomic Status, and Privilege

The external layer in Figure 1.1 symbolizes your relationship to your community, including mobility and power, often referred to as *social and cultural capital*. If you are Euro-American, can you trace where your family roots are from? When, where, and why did your ancestors come to America? By reflecting on this response, your understanding of the reasons immigrants migrate(d) to America may broaden, and you may locate yourself among them. If your history includes being brought to the U.S. against your will, then you may find empathy and understanding for those students who also came for the same reason (i.e., refugees or asylum seekers).

How is your family connected to group identity and support structures that strengthen them? Often supportive structures to maintain group identity allow access to resources. Some examples are increased opportunities

**Table 1.3** Socioeconomic Status, Privilege, and Capital

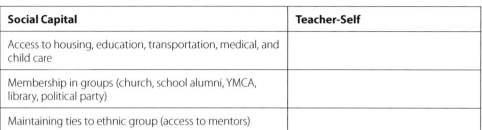

| Social Capital | Teacher-Self |
|---|---|
| Access to housing, education, transportation, medical, and child care | |
| Membership in groups (church, school alumni, YMCA, library, political party) | |
| Maintaining ties to ethnic group (access to mentors) | |

to/for: high quality mentors, private schools, child care, food and medical care; business partnerships, alternative lending options, stable housing, and reliable transportation. What is your family's social mobility status and access to economic resources? If you are a member of the dominant culture that favors a specific skin color, gender, ability, education, religion, socioeconomic status, and sexual orientation, then you probably have high mobility and increased access to resources, which is connected to privilege and power. Social and cultural capital (including political power) affects our values, practices, and perceptions. Methods to uncover these adaptations include observations and interviews that examine family history, structure, labor distribution, parents' attitudes, financial situations, religion, and level of education. After reflecting on your social/cultural capital, fill out the Teacher-Self column in Table 1.3.

## Culturally Competent Behaviors

To help educators prepare students for effective citizenship in a multicultural world, an understanding of cultural differences can help, which creates "cultural competence." Many definitions exist for cultural competence, but most have similar foundations based on a set of congruent behaviors, attitudes, and policies that come together in a system, agency, or group of professionals, enabling them to work effectively in cross-cultural situations. Paige, Jorstad, Siaya, Klein, and Colby (2003) state that cultural competence is, "the process of acquiring the culture-specific and culture-general knowledge, skills, and attitudes required for effective communication and interaction with individuals from other cultures" (p. 177).

Culturally competent educational systems must begin with a set of unifying values, based on the premise that cultural difference is positive and education must be responsive to diverse cultural needs (Diller & Moule, 2005). Another premise is based on the impact of cultural differences on education, the family, and community as a beginning point for teaching, and does not view the individual in isolation. Aspects of a culturally competent system (Cross's study, cited in Diller & Moule, 2005):

- Respect the unique, culturally defined needs of diverse populations;
- Acknowledge culture as a predominant force in shaping behaviors, values, and institutions;
- View natural systems (family, community, healers) as primary mechanisms of support and differ for various cultures and subgroups within cultures;
- Recognize cognitive dimensions of CLD peoples are equally valid and influence how students solve problems;
- Respect preferences that value process over product and harmony rather than achievement;
- Recognize the struggle of CLD people and which elements are most often in conflict with dominant society.

Acquiring cultural competence is a gradual process that does not occur as the result of a reading a book, attending training, or even taking a course. It is a developmental process that involves a reflective and ongoing process of acquiring new knowledge and developing skills, then reflecting on ways they can be incorporated into an existing perspective. As a result, the new perspective can then be put into practice with people, which sparks the reflective process to begin again.

Many skills and dispositions have been identified for culturally competent teachers. One such skill is that teachers are able to overcome differences in cultural backgrounds, expectations, educational needs, and academic traditions (Duckworth & Seligman, 2005; Schuerholz-Lehr, 2007), which involve cognitive, affective, and behavioral components. For example, someone who is culturally competent "has achieved an advanced level in the process of becoming intercultural and whose cognitive, affective and behavioral characteristics are not limited but are open to growth beyond the psychological parameters of only one culture" (McAllister & Irvine, 2000, p. 4). van der Zee and van Oudenhoven (2000) identified four critical dispositions that contribute to successful functioning across cultures: cultural empathy, open-mindedness, social initiative, and flexibility. *Cultural empathy* refers to one's ability to empathize with the feelings, thoughts, and behaviors of those from a different cultural background. Being *open-minded* demonstrates an open and unprejudiced attitude toward different groups and different cultural norms and values. Teachers showing *social initiative* approach social situations in an active way and take initiatives as leaders.

Finally, *flexible* individuals have a tendency to regard new and unknown situations as a challenge, and they manage to adjust their behavior to the demands of such new and unknown situations.

Several professional organizations have identified key aspects of demonstrating cultural competence, such as the Oregon Teacher Standards and Practices Commission (2011) who identified several necessary behaviors and characteristics for teachers:

- ◆ Capacity to promote equity of student access and outcomes;
- ◆ Advocacy for social justice;
- ◆ Awareness of laws and policies affecting learners;
- ◆ Creating a respectful and collaborative environment;
- ◆ Ability to navigate conflicts around race, ethnicity, religion, class, and language in a safe and productive manner;
- ◆ Demonstrating respectful and welcoming verbal and nonverbal interaction skills.

Culturally competent teachers are more likely to create inclusive communities where diverse families feel part of their children's educational experience.

Critical dispositions for teachers working with Culturally and Linguistically Diverse students in George Washington Bilingual Special Education program are cited in Table 1.4.

**Table 1.4** Critical Dispositions in Teacher Preparation Program

| |
|---|
| Critically examine one's own personal history, values, beliefs, and biases toward race, ethnicity, socioeconomic status, culture, language, religion, gender, gender identity, sexual orientation, disability, and other characteristics and life experiences of students, their families, and communities. |
| Reflect on the history and experiences of CLD/Exceptional students and their families in the context of teaching and learning. |
| Demonstrate acceptance toward diverse communication styles, languages, physical appearances, attitudes, values, and beliefs. |
| Affirm the value of and recognize the depth of the knowledge that students' families and communities have as assets for promoting their own children's learning and healthy development. |
| Actively seek to understand and appreciate how students' cultures, languages, and family backgrounds intersect with their academic and social abilities, values, interests, and future aspirations. |
| Affirm a belief in a 'whole child' approach to education that addresses students' cognitive, social, emotional, and physical development. |
| Demonstrate empathy, caring, compassion, leadership, humor, and flexibility in relating with CLD/Exceptional students. |
| Recognize that students learn best when their experiences, interests, and cultural heritages serve as the basis for curriculum connections, and when learning is made relevant to their lives. |
| Source: https://gsehd.gwu.edu/programs/masters-special-education-culturally-linguistically-diverse-learners |

## Conclusion: Our Cultural Lens and the Impact on Teaching

In the classroom, culture affects how learning is organized, how school rules and curricula are developed, and how teaching methods and evaluation procedures are implemented. Teachers play a pivotal role in determining the quality of opportunities, experiences, and outcomes students receive in schools (Gay, 1997, 2010). Research shows that teachers bring their own beliefs into the classroom and may attempt to encourage students to conform to their own perceptions and values (Hollins, 2008). As teachers, it is important to recognize when we do this because classroom communities created by our own belief systems have the potential to marginalize students who do not know or share the same beliefs (Winkelmann, 1991). Therefore, we must critically examine our own beliefs and attitudes towards diverse students, as well as our beliefs in the role that schools play as assimilationists or protecting acculturation processes.

Teachers and students from the dominant culture (i.e., Euro-American, middle class, monolingual standard English speaking) tend to be field independent (detail oriented, analytically inclined), value competition and individual accomplishment (Banks, 2009). CLD students tend to be field dependent, approach learning intuitively rather than analytically and logically, and tend to perform better in cooperative learning contexts (Gollnick & Chinn, 2009). This cultural mismatch contributes to teachers' misunderstandings about student behavior and achievement, which has resulted in overrepresentation of CLD groups receiving SPED services. Artiles, Trent, and Palmer (2004) have found that African American boys are overrepresented in the categories of Intellectual Disability and Emotional Disturbance, and American Indians/Alaskan Natives in category of Intellectual Disability. These two groups are also one and one-half times more likely to receive services for Specific Learning Disabilities than White students, and twice as likely to receive special education for developmental delays as other CLD groups (U.S. Department of Education, 2006).

## Reflection Activities

### Reflection Activity #1: Self-Assessment of Cultural Competence

We want to give you the opportunity to assess your own attitudes, abilities, beliefs, and privileges that you bring to this learning experience. By reflecting your attitudes and beliefs you already possess, you are taking the first step in the teaching and learning cycle. We invite you to think about each statement, consider experiences that may apply to each situation, and rate yourself authentically (using the Likert Scale). Upon reflection, look at the statement you rated the lowest, and create a concrete plan to increase this score (with a date to assess the plan).

**Rating Scale:**
**1 Strongly Disagree.  2 Disagree.  3 Neutral.  4 Agree.  5 Strongly Agree.**

1. I know about my own cultural history and it plays a prominent role in my life.

   1———2———3———4———5

2. I seek to acknowledge cultural norms, and am sensitive to them.

   1———2———3———4———5

3. Diversity is valuable and different perspectives help me think critically.

   1———2———3———4———5

4. I understand learning varies among individuals and does not follow one pattern.

   1———2———3———4———5

5. I have studied firsthand accounts of minority groups' experiences in the U.S.

   1———2———3———4———5

6. I understand that the dominant culture's exclusive laws and practices have limited minority groups' participation in U.S. schools.

   1———2———3———4———5

7. I am aware of different communication/behavior patterns among different groups.

   1———2———3———4———5

8. I am aware of images or words that portray all members of an ethnic group as the same (e.g., All Asians are smart).

   1———2———3———4———5

9. I address stereotypical statements when I hear them used by others.

   1———2———3———4———5

10. I am aware of my membership in groups that carry different power and privilege.

   1———2———3———4———5

### Reflection Activity #2: Autoethnographic Study

This is a personal reflection in which you are the case study teacher. The focus is to discover your cultural impact on students, parents of your students, your peers and colleagues, as well as yourself. The following prompts are provided for you to reflect on, and then record your observations:

1. BEGINNINGS: What is my cultural background (heritage, ethnicity)? Review Figure 1.1. Does it really have an influence on your daily behaviors? How and Why?
2. COMMUNITY AND SOCIETY: Review your cultural assets and social/cultural capital (Tables 1.2 and 1.3). Are you really a product of a larger culture that you have accepted, or does your cultural embodiment drive your philosophical understandings of the everyday?
3. TEACHER IDENTITY: How do your cultural beliefs affect your ways of teaching? How might they impact students and parents? Colleagues?

### Reflection Activity #3: Impact of Culture on Teaching and Learning

Table 1.5 illustrates one way we can organize and then reflect on factors that affect the teaching and learning relationship. First, take the information you wrote in the Teacher-Self columns (Tables 1.1, 1.2, and 1.3) and summarize into the columns below (Physical/Cognitive, Social/Emotional, Cultural/Linguistic, Socioeconomic Status, Privilege, Capital). Then choose one of your CLD students in your classroom and fill out the second column about her/him. By identifying the factors that affect our own development, and then those that affect a CLD student, we can better view how our own biases may affect students' learning. Next, look at the two columns side by side, and reflect on the similarities and differences of your experiences. By reflecting

Table 1.5 Reflection Activity: Factors Influencing Teaching and Learning

| Factors Influencing Teaching and Learning | Teacher | Student | Implications:Due to my belief in_____, I may marginalize those who believe_____. |
|---|---|---|---|
| Physical/Cognitive | | | |
| Social/Emotional | | | |
| Cultural/Linguistic | | | |
| Socioeconomic Status, Privilege, Capital | | | |

and analyzing ways our backgrounds and perspectives affect our teaching we can then view our students' backgrounds and perspectives that affect their learning (Implications). A one-sentence frame that allows you to view these implications is, "Due to my belief/practices in_____, I may marginalize those who believe/practice_____." Only when we can learn to navigate both these perspectives can we fully invest in teaching and learning relationships.

## Bibliography

Artiles, A. J., Trent, S. C., & Palmer, J. (2004). Culturally diverse students in special education: Legacies and prospects. In J. A. Banks & C. A. McGee Banks (Eds.), *Handbook of Research on Multicultural Education* (pp. 716–735). San Francisco: Jossey-Bass.

Banks, J. (2009). Diversity and citizenship education in multicultural nations. *Multicultural Education Review, 1*(1), 1–28.

Cheng, V. J. (2004). *Inauthentic: The Anxiety over Culture and Identity*. New York: Rutgers University Press.

Chick, G. (1997). Cultural complexity: The concept and its measurement. *Cross-Cultural Research, 31*(4), 275–307.

Delpit, L. (1995). *Other People's Children: Cultural Conflict in the Classroom*. New York: The New Press.

Diller, J. V., & Moule, J. (2005). *Cultural Competence: A Primer for Educators*. Belmont, CA: Thomson/Wadsworth.

Duckworth, A. L., & Seligman, M. E. (2005). Self-discipline outdoes IQ in predicting academic performance of adolescents. *Psychological Science, 16*(12), 939–944.

Dweck, C. S. (2010). Even geniuses work hard. *Educational Leadership, 68*(1), 16–20.

Gay, G. (1997). Multicultural infusion in teacher education: Foundations and applications. *Peabody Journal of Education, 72*(1), 150–177.

Gay, G. (2010). *Culturally Responsive Teaching: Theory, Research, and Practice* (2nd ed.). New York: Teachers College Press.

Gollnick, D. M., & Chinn, P. C. (2009). *Multicultural Education in a Pluralistic Society*. Upper Saddle River, NJ: Merrill Pearson.

Hollins, E. R. (2008). *Culture in School Learning: Revealing the Deep Meaning*. New York: Routledge.

Macedo D., & Bartolomé L. I. (1999) Dancing with bigotry. In D. Macedo & L. I. Bartolomé (Eds.), *Dancing with Bigotry*. New York: Palgrave Macmillan.

Markus, H. R., & Kitayama, S. (1991). Cultural variation in the self-concept. *Multidisciplinary Perspectives on the Self*, 18–48.

McAllister, G., & Irvine, J. J. (2000). Cross cultural competency and multicultural teacher education. *Review of Educational Research, 70*(1), 4.

Moll, L. C. (2014). Funds of identities: A new concept based on the Funds of Knowledge approach. *Culture & Psychology, 20*, 31–48.

Moll, L. C., Amanti, C., Neff, D., & González, N. (1992). Funds of Knowledge for teaching: Using a qualitative approach to connect homes and classrooms. *Theory into Practice, 31*(2), 132–141.

Moll, L. C., Amanti, C., Neff, D., & González, N. (2005). Funds of Knowledge for teaching: Using a qualitative approach to connect homes and classrooms. In *Funds of Knowledge: Theorizing Practices in Households, Communities, and Classrooms* (pp. 71–88). Mahwah, NJ: Lawrence Erlbaum Associates.

Oregon Teacher Standards and Practices Commission (2011). Professional Standards Manual. Retrieved from: www.tspc.oregon.gov/publications/TSPC_Prof_standards_manual_3.pdf

Paige, R. M., Jorstad, H. L., Siaya, L., Klein, F., & Colby, J. (2003). Culture learning in language education. *Culture as the Core: Perspectives on Culture in Second Language Learning*, 173–236.

Pewewardy, C. (2002). Learning styles of American Indian/Alaska Native students: A review of the literature and implications for practice. *Journal of American Indian Education*, 22–56.

Rogoff, B. (2003). *The Cultural Nature of Human Development*. New York: Oxford University Press.

Schuerholz-Lehr, S. (2007). Teaching for global literacy in higher education: How prepared are the educators? *Journal of Studies in International Education, 11*(2), 180–204.

U.S. Department of Education. (2006). 26th Annual Report to Congress on the Implementation of the Individuals with Disabilities Education Act, 2004. Jessup, MD: Ed Pubs. (ERIC Document Reproduction Service No. ED494709).

van der Zee, K. I., & van Oudenhoven, J. P. (2000). The Multicultural Personality Questionnaire: A multidimensional instrument of multicultural effectiveness. *European Journal of Personality, 14*(4), 291–309.

Varenne, H. & McDermott, R. (1999). *Successful Failure: The School America Builds*. Boulder, CO: Westview Press.

*Vygotsky*, L. S. (1978). *Mind and Society: The Development of Higher Psychological Processes*. M. Cole, V. John-Steiner, S. Scribner, & E. Souberman (Eds.). Cambridge, MA: Harvard University Press.

Winkelmann, C. L. (1991). Social acts and social systems: Community as metaphor. *Linguistics and Education, 3*(1), 1–29.

# 2

# File Review: Get to Know Your Students' Culture(s) and Language(s)

## Introduction

Chapter 2 focuses on getting to know your students and the importance of their language skills and educational backgrounds. You are introduced to a classroom teacher (Ms. Casad) and her four Culturally and Linguistically Diverse (CLD) students. We walk the reader through the process for finding information that is critical when getting to know your students' cultural and language needs.

- ◆ Cumulative files are reviewed on each of the CLD students to gather a comprehensive picture of their strengths and needs.
- ◆ An About Me survey is introduced to gather information on the four students' cultural assets, which will assist you when developing appropriate instruction.
- ◆ The authors discuss the importance of knowing language acquisition stages, language assessments, and English Language Development (ELD) programs when working with CLD students.

The chapter concludes with activities for you to complete an About Me survey on yourself and create a culturally responsive lesson using student cumulative file information.

## Meet Ms. Casad

Ms. Casad is a fourth grade teacher at Valley Elementary and in her third year of teaching. Although she had Culturally Linguistically Diverse and English Language Learner students last year, she still wonders whether or not she met their needs. This year, she has four CLD/ELL students. During the morning session, she asked students to introduce themselves. Most students spoke their names clearly and maintained eye contact with her or with other students. She noticed that three students did not respond like the others. César looked down and mumbled his name. Rosa screamed out loudly "Rosa!" and sat down quickly. Jun responded that his name was "Cheng Jun," saying his last name first according to the way it was listed in Ms. Casad's roster. She told him that in the U.S., people use their first names in an introduction. Jun refused to say his first name first. She immediately thought something was different about him, and felt unprepared in what to do. She needed to keep the rest of the class engaged, so decided to sit Rosa, Jun, and César at the same table for the rest of the day. After dismissal, she felt overwhelmed.

Standing at the door, Ms. Casad saw Mrs. M. walking down the hall and began talking to her. "How do I meet all these students' needs, including my students learning English and one on an IEP?" She described César: "He is from Honduras and speaks a little English, but not very much. He seems to be sad, and I noticed that he is here at school way before I am in the morning. I wonder if he is getting enough sleep?"

Ms. Casad then began talking about Rosa. "She knows some English, but can talk up a storm in Spanish. She dresses so cute everyday with bows in her hair, all clean and neat, but by the end of the day she looks like she has been rolling in the dirt. She can get so angry with the other kids! I like her, she can be sweet, I just don't want her to get in trouble like her brother. My friend who teaches middle school told me one of Rosa's brothers is in a gang." Mrs. M. responded, "What are your plans for her?"

"Well, I guess I will just try to get to know her and keep an eye on her so she doesn't fall through the cracks. She may be challenging! Then there is this other kid, Jun. He seems nice so far. He is from China and I am not sure what language he speaks. He has some odd behaviors too. He just gets up and starts wandering around the classroom, and looks at me with this strange expression on his face. When I asked him his name, he insisted on saying his last name first. I thought that was kind of strange."

Mrs. M. said, "I read somewhere that people from Chinese cultures do that, they say their last name first then their first name last. It is a cultural thing. What is the big deal with that?"

Ms. Casad chuckled and said, "I told him that in America, we say our names with the first name first and our last name last. For example, my name is Lori Casad, not Casad Lori. I don't think he understood. I also have one student, Trent, on an IEP (Individualized Education Plan). I have had several students on IEPs before, but now that I think about it, I have never had a male African American student before."

"Remember to utilize the PLC for support, that is what they are here for," Mrs. M. said encouragingly.

"Thanks for all the help. I think I am going to try some strategies from a workshop I took this summer on 'culturally responsive pedagogy.' The presenters talked about specific instruction for CLD students. They even talked about what to do if you think one of your ELLs might need special education services. I just hope it is better than what I did last year!" Ms. Casad said. "Good plan and good luck!" Mrs. M. said as she walked down the hall.

## Getting to Know Your Students

Ms. Casad decided she would take home her CLD students' cumulative files to get a better picture of who they are, and located the district's Student Profile form (See Table 2.1) to record students' information.

All students have several factors that make them unique as individuals. Looking into their cumulative file is one good way to begin finding out about those factors. CLD students as well as students receiving special education (SPED) services often have various kinds of factors that require teachers to look deeper into their files. The four case study students in Ms. Casad's classroom are all considered Culturally and Linguistically Diverse. CLD students are those who speak a language other than English, and who bring diverse cultural heritages and assets to the school (Herrera & Murry, 2011). This term references students who are "different" than the mainstream student in American public schools. A "mainstream" student belongs to normative groups (i.e., holding power in the U.S.), which may include: being monolingual, standard-English-speaking, Caucasian or White, middle class, heterosexual, and abled-bodied. CLD students belong to one or more minority groups (i.e., lack power) due to language (non-native standard-English speaker) or ability status (disabled), gender identity (LGBTQ), and cultural, racial, or ethnic status (other than White or Caucasian).

**Table 2.1** Student Profile Form

| File Review | Physical | Cultural-Linguistic | Social-Emotional | Cognitive |
|---|---|---|---|---|
| Name Caregiver name Contact info (email/ph/ address) | Health screening, Identified accommodations | Home Language Survey, ELPA score/ LAS, ELD previous services, Previous teachers, Parent English level, Length of time in U.S. schools | Behavior concerns or strengths, Identified accommodations | Smarter Balance (or equivalent), State test score, DIBELS (Reading fluency assessment), Identified accommodations |

Ms. Casad looked at each of the four CLD students' cumulative files for background information and felt overwhelmed! Therefore, she decided to focus on César, Rosa, and Jun's cultural and language background as a starting point. She will look closer at Trent's IEP; Trent qualified for SPED services under the IDEA (Individuals with Disability Education Act, 2004) categories of Specific Learning Disability and Communication Disorder. She transferred cultural-linguistic information from their cumulative files to a Student Profile form (see Table 2.1) provided by her district office. Gathering as much background information as possible is critical for teachers to get to know CLD/ELL students.

When looking at students' cumulative files, we recommend to look for items to develop a profile of students' needs and backgrounds: (1) previous academic progress, (2) state assessment scores, (3) language assessment scores, (4) cultural information, and (5) a behavior rating scale or kind of behavior analysis. If a student is a native English speaker, then you probably will not pay much attention to his/her *Home Language Survey* (HLS). However, when a student is considered CLD, or speaks a language other than English, you would look at the information above, and also pay close attention to the language of the student as indicated on the HLS.

Federal Law Section 3127 Title VI—Office of Civil Rights (OCR) Guidelines require public schools who receive federal funding to determine the language(s) spoken at home by every student. The HLS is the tool recommended by the OCR to (1) establish the home language (i.e., dominant or primary) of every student and (2) find out if there are additional languages other than English spoken in the home. The Home Language Survey (HLS) is a questionnaire included in registration packets for new students (based on federal policy, see link below). This form is given to parents or guardians that inform schools and local education agencies which students may require formal assessment of their English language proficiency to determine whether or not they are eligible for English Language Development (ELD) services ("ELD" is a program that has replaced the term "ESL" in many states). See the following link for more information on HLS requirements (www2.ed.gov/about/offices/list/oela/english-learner-toolkit/chap1.pdf).

## Home Language Survey

According to Linquanti and Bailey (2014), when a student's HLS shows a language other than English spoken in the home, that student may qualify for English Language Development (ELD) services. The HLS is the first tool or indicator that institutions use to establish language preferences or dominance, and to determine if further assessments are needed to qualify a student to receive ELD services. Home Language Surveys vary across the nation but all attempt to find out language dominance. Only three questions are required on the HLS by federal law: (1) What is the primary language used in the home, regardless of the language spoken by the student? (2) What is the language most often spoken by the student? and (3) What is the language that the student first acquired? (Linquanti & Bailey, 2014). Below is an example of a typical Home Language Survey sent out in registration packets, and then placed in students' cumulative files. (See Table 2.2.)

**Table 2.2** Home Language Survey

---

Encuesta sobre el lenguaje en el hogar

School: _____ Date: _____
Escuela                                    Fecha

**Valley School District No. 7 wants to determine the language(s) spoken in the home of each student. This information is essential in order to provide meaningful instruction for all our students. This survey will be used to help us determine what instructional programs will best serve your child.**

El Distrito Escolar de Valle No. 7 quiere determinar qué idioma(s) se habla(n) en el hogar de cada estudiante. Esta información es esencial para proveer enseñanza significativa a todos nuestros estudiantes. Esta encuesta se utilizará para determinar cual programa de instrucción le ayudará efectivamente a su hijo/a.

**Your cooperation is requested. Please answer the following questions and return this survey to his/her school as soon as possible. Thank you for your help.**

Se solicita su cooperación. Por favor, conteste las preguntas y devuelva esta encuesta a la escuela. Gracias por su cooperación.

**Name of Student:** _____

Nombre del Estudiante    **Last** (Apellido)    **First** (Nombre)    **Middle** (2do. Nombre)

1.  **Which language did your child learn when he/she first began to talk?** _____
    ¿Cuál fue el idioma que su hijo/a aprendió cuando empezó a hablar?

2.  **Which language does your child use most frequently at home?** _____
    ¿Qué idioma habla su hijo/a con más frecuencia en el hogar?

3.  **Which language do you use most frequently to speak to your child?** _____
    ¿Qué idioma habla usted con más frecuencia con su hijo/a?

4.  **What language(s) is/are spoken in the home?**
    ¿Que idioma(s) hablan en el hogar?
    a. _____        b. _____        c. _____

5.  **Name the language most often spoken by the adults at home.** _____
    Anote el idioma que hablan con más frecuencia los adultos en el hogar.

6.  **In which language would you like to receive school-to-home communication?** _____
    ¿En qué idioma prefiere recibir comunicación de la escuela?

---

**Parent/Guardian Signature:** _____    **Date Received:** _____
Firma del Padre/Tutor                                              Fecha recibido

**The Home Language Survey is administered to meet requirements of the U.S. Office of Civil Rights.**
La "Encuesta sobre el lenguaje en el hogar" es administrada para cumplir con los requisitos de La Oficina de los Derechos Civiles de EEUU.

## Language Assessment

Students who are raised in homes where English is not spoken come to schools with unique strengths that can become the foundation of instruction. Research shows that these students have cognitive and linguistic capacities that can facilitate learning (Herrera & Murry, 2011). Language is difficult to assess; therefore, many types of language assessments are needed to draw comprehensive pictures of children's language development (Gottlieb, 2006). Best practices begin with locating information about the child's native-language development and proficiency, and proficiency in English with both formal (e.g., standardized) and informal (e.g., authentic) measurements (August & Hakuta, 1997). However, few standardized tests are available for every language, resulting in the need for alternative assessment (i.e., nondiscriminatory or authentic assessments). In conducting nondiscriminatory assessments, educators can discover alternate understandings of CLD behaviors in the context of their cultural and linguistic backgrounds, rather than attributing behaviors to a learning disability (Baca & Cervantes, 2006). Examples of alternative assessment include: observation, interviews, interactive inventories, dynamic assessment, and portfolios.

Each state has an official English language assessment (e.g., Mountain State Consortium adopted the ELPA [English Language Proficiency Assessment]) that assesses a student's English language proficiency in reading, writing, speaking, and listening. Results identify a student's stage of language acquisition in levels 1, 2, 3, 4, 5 (see Table 2.3). Often, when students have not received formal native-language instruction, they score low on standardized tests that assess proficiency in the native language. If they have not acquired developmentally appropriate proficiency in their native language, it may be due to family circumstances (e.g., trauma, genetics), or the presence of an undiagnosed disability, which can delay English language acquisition. Thus, low levels of native-language proficiency, and English language proficiency, can look like there is some language disability (Collier, 2010).

## What Do I Need to Know About Second-Language Acquisition?

Students progress through predictable stages of language (see Krashen, 2000, 2012) with varying time spent in each stage depending on aptitude, native-language proficiency, personality, motivation, previous

**Table 2.3** Language Acquisition Stages

| Official Name | Beginning | Early Intermediate | Intermediate | Early Advanced | Advanced |
|---|---|---|---|---|---|
| Other Names | Silent Period, Newcomer Preproduction | Early Production, Emergent/Beginner | Social Language Stage | Intermediate Fluency, Transitional Academic Language Stage | Academic Language |
| Student Behaviors | ◆ Minimal comprehension of general meaning; <br>◆ Gaining familiarity with sounds, rhythms, and patterns of English; <br>◆ Responses range from no verbal response, one to two words, single words, phrases; <br>◆ Speech errors observed | ◆ Increased comprehension of general and some specific meaning; <br>◆ Using routine expressions independently; <br>◆ Responding using phrases and simple sentences; <br>◆ Basic errors in speech | ◆ Good comprehension of general meaning and increased comprehension of specific meaning; <br>◆ Responding in more complex sentences with more detail using newly acquired vocabulary to experiment and form messages | ◆ Consistent comprehension of general meaning and good understanding of implied meaning; <br>◆ Sustaining conversation and responding with detail; <br>◆ Participating using more extensive vocabulary; <br>◆ Using standard grammar with few random errors | ◆ Comprehension of general and implied meaning, including idiomatic and figurative language; <br>◆ Initiating and negotiating using appropriate discourse, varied grammatical structures, and vocabulary; <br>◆ Using conventions for formal and informal language |
| Language Samples | *bear, brown* | *The bear is brown. He is eating.* | *The brown bear lived with his family in the forest.* | *Can bears live in the forest if they find food there?* | *Would you like me to bring pictures of the bear that I saw last summer?* |
| Timeline | 0–6 months in U.S. schools | 6 months–1 year in U.S. schools | 1–3 years in U.S. schools | 3–5 years in U.S. schools | 5–7 years in U.S. schools |
| Teaching Strategies | Use manipulatives, visuals, realia.Create climate of acceptance/ respect. Use cooperative learning groups. Use physical response to check comprehension. Display print model activities. Use hands-on activities. Ask yes/no questions. | *Continue Stage 1 strategies PLUS:* Simplify language not content. Lessons designed to motivate students to talk. Ask questions that require one or two word responses. Expand vocabulary. | *Continue Stages 1 and 2 PLUS:* List and review instructions step by step.Build on students' prior knowledge. Incorporate more reading and writing. Encourage students in producing language. | *Continue Stages 1–3 PLUS:* Have students brainstorm, list, web, use graphic organizers.Ask questions soliciting opinions, judgment, explanation (more why and how questions). Introduce figurative language. Develop more academic language (oral and written). | *Continue Stages 1–4 PLUS:* Incorporate note-taking skills. Expand figurative language (idioms).Teach study skills and test-taking skills. |

Source: Synthesis of the *Language Acquisition Chart* developed by the ESL/Bilingual Department of the Portland Public Schools.

exposure to content in native language, and quality of instruction (Fill-more, 1991). Typical second-language acquisition can take between five to seven years (Roseberry-McKibbin & Brice, 2000) and eight years to achieve cognitive academic English proficiency, which is dependent on the quantity and quality of the English language instruction the student receives.

When conducting standardized language assessments, best practices inform educators to choose those that are normed and standardized for Spanish- and English-speaking bilingual children (e.g., *Clinical Evaluation of Language Fundamentals*, 4th Edition; *Spanish and the Preschool Language Scales*, 5th Edition, Spanish) (Farnsworth, 2016). According to Gottlieb (2006), standardized tests produce reliable data, rank students at a national level, are easily scored, and easy to train practitioners on how to give these tests. However, these test scores often are deciding factors on whether or not students will be entered or exited from English Language Development classes. Even with assessments normed on Spanish- and English-speaking bilingual children, test construct may not be valid (Farnsworth, 2016). For example, the *Picture Vocabulary* subtest on the Woodcock-Muñoz Language Survey contains pictures such as an igloo, pyramid, tourniquet, a person panning for gold, candelabra, and a magnet (Woodcock & Muñoz-Sandoval, 1993). These pictures may be unfamiliar to CLDs/ELLs due to their cultural backgrounds and/or length of time spent in the U.S.; therefore, the test is inaccurately assessing background knowledge, and not language proficiency (Farnsworth, 2016).

## English Language Proficiency Assessment (ELPA)

ELPA is Oregon's English Language Proficiency Assessment that includes writing, listening, speaking, and constructed response items. Any student who qualifies for ELD services or has exited ELD at some point during the school year must take the ELPA (Oregon Department of Education, 2015). The ELPA21 assessment is based upon the new Oregon English Language Proficiency Standards and measures four language domains: reading, writing, listening, and speaking. These domains are also known as reading comprehension, written production, listening comprehension, and oral production skills.

### How Are the Results Used?
The test results are used to measure English proficiency of students and determine if a student is ready to exit the ELD or ESL Program. Results are also used for state and federal accountability purposes including

reporting on Annual Measurable Achievement Objectives. Results are mailed to families once a year, late summer or early fall. Teachers may also share results with families during parent conferences and other meetings.

### Who Requires It?

Students in kindergarten through grade 12 whose home language is not English are required by both federal and state laws to be assessed in English language proficiency.

The ELPA21 assessment measures and reports on students' English language proficiency overall, as well as in reading, writing, speaking, listening, and comprehension. Delivered online, ELPA21 is designed to be interactive and includes questions that reflect real-world scenarios. Its main purpose is to qualify students for appropriate language services and help guide schools to best support student needs (Oregon Department of Education, 2015).

When language assessment results determine a need for ELD services, the student now is considered an English Language Learner (ELL) and is placed in a program best suited for his/her needs. ELLs (students who scored in levels 1–4) must be provided with federally required ELD services until they obtain English fluency, as measured on their annual assessment (see Table 2.3). Literacy screening would be instructionally meaningful only for students who have received prior instruction in English, or who are demonstrating some signs of a disability. Some students speak enough English to not qualify for ELD services, but have limited classroom language foundations so they may perform similar to students with a learning disability. A structured intensive intervention in English, including basic phonics and literacy readiness would serve two purposes in helping determine a possibility for ELD services: (1) profile the student's proficiency and (2) establish whether the score is learning based or language based.

## English Language Development (ELD) Services

All federally funded Title III programs require teachers of those programs to be state certified in English for Speakers of Other Languages (ESOL) or Bilingual Education (BE). Some of the Title III programs in public schools include (1) Dual Language Program, which provides integrated language and academic instruction for native English and native speakers of another language with the goals of high academic achievement, first- and second-language proficiency, and cross-cultural understanding; (2) Developmental Bilingual Education or Late-Exit Developmental bilingual education which is designed to educate English Language Learners (ELLs) using both English and their first language for academic instruction. This type of program focuses on promoting high levels of academic achievement in all curricular areas and full academic language proficiency in the ELL's first and second languages; (3) Transitional Bilingual Education or Early-Exit Transitional Bilingual Education is designed to provide academic instruction in English Language Learners' primary language as they learn English; (4) the Newcomer program which is designed to help students acquire beginning English language skills along with core academic skills and knowledge, and to acculturate to the U.S. school system; and (5) Sheltered English Instruction also referred to as Content-Based ESL/ELD or Pull-Out, which is the most common and most widely used approach in public schools. This approach is designed for teaching content to ELLs in strategic ways that make academic subject matter concepts comprehensible while promoting students' English Language Development (Echevarria, Vogt, & Short, 2000).

All public schools receiving Federal Title III dollars must have a program in place for supporting ELL students. Federal laws for serving students with languages different than English are in place to ensure non-biased and or nondiscriminatory education practices are taking place for all students. (For historic information see the Civil Rights Act of 1964 which banned race, sex, and national origin discrimination in public facilities and the Elementary and Secondary Education Act of 1965). Ms. Casad began recording information on the Student Profile forms, starting with César.

## Case Study Students' Cumulative File Information

### César: Cumulative file information (Responses shown in parentheses)

1. *Home language*
   a. What is the primary language used in the home, regardless of the language spoken by the student? (Limited English, everyone in home speaks Spanish)
   b. What is the language most often spoken by the student? (Spanish)
   c. What is the language that the student first acquired? (Spanish)

2. *Language Assessment scores*
    a. English Language Proficiency Assessment (ELPA): Level 2 (Early Intermediate). For example, "Uses routine expressions independently, responds using phrases and simple sentences, and basic errors in speech." (See Table 2.3.)
    b. Native-language proficiency (based on Woodcock-Muñoz Language Survey assessment in Spanish): Level 4 (Early Advanced).
3. *Past and recent behavior issues/concerns*
    a. Are there any concerns at school or home? (Not known)
4. *Academic performance*
    a. Academic concerns (Low reading and language arts scores)
    b. Was student ever referred for testing for disability? (Unknown)
    c. Records from previous school? (No, he attended school in Honduras)
5. *Home life and interests*
    a. Original home country (Honduras)
    b. Aspects of hometown (farming town)
    c. Family dynamics (4 older brothers and father in Honduras, mother and younger sister came to U.S. with him. Younger sister is at the same elementary school.)
    d. Success (Feels more comfortable in pull-out class due to more native-language instruction, smaller class size.)
    e. Academic interests (Likes math, does not like reading. Likes learning but is shy to ask questions)
    f. Are parents/guardians literate? (Not known)
6. *Attendance*
7. *Custody paperwork (N/A)*
8. *IEP/504 (N/A)*
9. *RTI team documentation*
    a. Interventions used and effectiveness? (No)

## Summary of César

The town where César grew up was considered an agricultural town with a very small population. Most of the families there relied on farming and raising cattle for their income. He has four older brothers and one younger sister. He and his younger sister along with the mother are the only family members that made the trip to the U.S. His older brothers and father stayed in Honduras to carry on with the family farm. César's mother has some relatives in

Table 2.4 Students' Cultural-Linguistic Profiles

| César | Rosa | Jun | Trent |
|---|---|---|---|
| **Home Language Survey** (Spanish only) **ELD previous services** (none) | **Home Language Survey** (Spanish and English) **ELD previous services** (ELD grades 2 and 3) | **Home Language Survey** (Chinese-Mandarin) **ELD previous services** (No) | **Home Language Survey** (English) **ELD previous services** (N/A) |
| **Previous teachers** (unknown in Honduras, placed in Mr. S. class end of third grade) **ELPA score/LAS** (Level 2) | **Previous teachers** (Mrs. Young grade 2, Mr. Bliss grade 3) **ELPA score/LAS** (Level 4) | **Previous teachers** (?) **ELPA score/LAS** (Level 3) | **Previous teachers** (SPED teacher and previous grade-level teachers in building) **ELPA/LAS** (N/A) |
| **Parent language level** (Spanish only) | **Parent English level** (Basic English and Spanish) | **Parent English level** (Fluent Mandarin and some English) | **Parent English level** (Fluent English speakers) |
| **Length of time in present school** (6 months) | **Length of time in U.S. schools** (2.5 years) | **Length of time in U.S. schools** (2 years) | **Length of time in U.S. schools** (4 years) |

New Mexico so she brought the youngest to try for a better future and better education. No one in the family speaks English. The sister has also enrolled in the same elementary school.

Looking at César's cultural-linguistic background information in his cumulative file, Ms. Casad noticed his language preference is Spanish (from HLS), in which he scored in Early Advanced (level 4) on the Woodcock-Muñoz Language Survey assessment in Spanish. César was given the ELPA-English language assessment after enrolling in Valley Elementary in May (end of third grade), and scored at level 2, in the Early Intermediate level or early stage of language production and comprehension. She recorded this information on the Student Profile form (see Table 2.4).

### Rosa: *Cumulative file information (Responses shown in parentheses)*

1. *Home language*
   a. What is the primary language used in the home, regardless of the language spoken by the student? (Spanish and some English)
   b. What is the language most often spoken by the student? (Spanish)
   c. What is the language that the student first acquired? (Spanish)
2. *Language Assessment scores*
   a. English Language Proficiency Assessment (ELPA):
      Level 3–4 (Intermediate-Early Advanced). For example,

"Good comprehension of general meaning and increased comprehension of specific meaning." (See Table 2.3.)
   b. Native-language proficiency: (Based on Woodcock-Muñoz Language Survey assessment in Spanish): Level 3 (Intermediate; similar to ELPA results).
3. *Behavior issues/concerns*
   a. Concerns at school or home? (Anger outbursts and physical aggression. Brother in local gang.)
4. *Academic performance*
   a. Academic concerns (low math performance)
   b. Was student ever referred for testing for disability? (Not known)
   c. Records from student's previous school? (No)
5. *Home life and interests*
   a. Original home country (Mexico)
   b. Aspects of hometown (small rural town)
   c. Family dynamics (2 older brothers, mother, and Rosa came to U.S. together. Older brothers attended the same elementary school.)
   d. Success (Feels more comfortable in small class with more native-language instruction, smaller class size. Likes reading and learning new vocabulary, and does not like math. Hesitant to show she does not understand.)
   e. Are the parents literate? (Not known)
6. Attendance
7. Custody paperwork (N/A)
8. IEP/504 No
9. RTI team documentation
   a. Documentation of interventions used and effectiveness

## Summary of Rosa

Rosa is 9 years old. At the age of 6 she and her mother crossed the Rio Grande on an inner tube to come to the United States. She is a very spirited girl who is unrestrained when telling you *exactly* how she feels. Rosa is average in size for her age and has long dark brown hair. She comes to school every day wearing a dress with ribbons or bows in her hair. However, she is very much a tomboy, and by the end of the day her clothes will be soiled and her hair disheveled from playing or fighting. Rosa is the youngest, and has two older brothers. One brother is in a local gang.

Ms. Casad saw in the cumulative file that Rosa is a native Spanish speaker (on HLS) and also has been assessed to find her native-language proficiency level. She is a level 3 in Spanish (Intermediate), which indicates strong social language skills and a true balanced bilingual. Rosa's oral and Reading-Writing English proficiency is level 3–4, which indicates some academic fluency, and she is receiving ELD services. The file also indicated that Rosa's previous teachers had some behavioral concerns. Ms. Casad will follow up on with the ELD teacher about how she can academically support Rosa. She records this information on the Student Profile form (see Table 2.4).

### Jun: *Cumulative file information (Responses shown in parentheses)*

1. Home language
   a. What is the primary language used in the home, regardless of the language spoken by the student? (Chinese-Mandarin)
   b. What is the language most often spoken by the student? (Chinese-Mandarin)
   c. What is the language that the student first acquired? (Chinese-Mandarin)
2. Language Assessment
   a. English Language Proficiency Assessment (ELPA): Level 2–3 (Early Intermediate-Intermediate). For example, "Uses routine expressions independently, responds using phrases and simple sentences. Basic errors in speech with some good comprehension of general meaning and increased comprehension of specific meaning (see Table 2.3: level 2 and 3).
   b. Was student tested in native language? (Yes, see Appendix D)
3. Past and recent behavior issues/concerns (some behavior concerns. Outbursts of odd behavior)
   a. Are there any concerns at school or home? (Not known)
4. Past academic performance
   a. Academic concerns (Language arts, reading)
   b. Was student ever referred for testing for disability? (Not known)
   c. Records from previous school (Not known)
5. Home life and interests
   a. Original home country (China)
   b. Aspects of hometown (Rural village)
   c. Family dynamics (1 sister, 1 brother, mother and father at home. Older sister attends the middle school)
   d. Success (Likes math)
   e. Are parents literate? (Yes, based on prior conversations with teachers.)
6. Attendance
7. Custody paperwork (N/A)
8. IEP/504 (Not known)

9. RTI team documentation
    a. Documentation of interventions used and effectiveness (No)

## Summary of Jun

Jun came to Valley Elementary at the beginning of this year (fourth grade), and attended a nearby elementary school in third grade. He is 10 years old and has been in the U.S. for two years. He is a native Mandarin speaker. His English language proficiency level is 2–3, and qualifies for ELD services. The file also suggests that there may be some concerns with "odd" behavior. Ms. Casad records this information on the Student Profile form (see Table 2.4).

## Trent: *Cumulative file information (Responses shown in parentheses)*

1. Home language (English)
2. Past and recent test scores
    a. ELPA (N/A)
3. Past and recent behavior issues/concerns
    a. Concerns at school or home? (No)
4. Past academic performance
    a. Academic concerns (meets criteria for Specific Learning Disability, found eligible using *Strengths and Weaknesses* model)
    b. Was student referred for testing for disability? (Yes, and qualified for SLD).
    c. Are there records from his previous school? (Yes)
5. Home life and interests
    a. Original home country (U.S.A.)
    b. Aspects of hometown (Metropolitan city)
    c. Family dynamics (one younger brother, who attends the same elementary school.
    d. Success (Likes math and sports).
    e. Are the parents literate? (Yes).
6. Attendance (100%)
7. IEP (Yes, Trent is on an IEP for primary category of Specific Learning Disability, secondary disability as Communication Disorder)
8. RTI team documentation (Yes, data available in IEP)
    a. Documentation of interventions used and what was effective? (In IEP under classroom accommodations: Give more time to complete tasks, reduced assignment size, task and concept analysis used for staying on task (Appendix A).
    b. Notes from monitoring? (In SPED file)
    c. Parent communication? (Yes, both parents are supportive and attend all meetings)

**Table 2.5** Trent's IEP Excerpt

| **PRESENT LEVELS OF ACADEMIC ACHIEVEMENT AND FUNCTIONAL PERFORMANCE** |
|---|

Present level of academic achievement (i.e., reading, writing, mathematics, etc.), including most recent performance on state- or district-wide assessments:

◆ Strengths of the student
◆ Needs of the student
◆ How the student's disability affects involvement and progress in the general education curriculum *34 CFR 300.320(a)(1); 300.324(a)(iii)*

---

Reading:

On 9/19/15 in a classroom setting and taken individually on a Chromebook, Trent took an iReady assessment (district-wide assessment used for reading and math) and tested out of the following areas: Phonological awareness and high-frequency words. Trent scored in the 1st grade level for phonics, 3rd grade level for vocabulary, 2nd grade level for comprehension and 2nd grade level for informational text. Trent is able to understand organization and basic features of texts, decode regularly spelled one-syllable words with short vowels. Trent is also able to identify facts and details or cite explicit statements from 2nd grade texts, and explain what the text says. Trent is also able to recognize characters and story elements in a text such as setting, and plot in 2nd grade level texts. Trent will continue to work on reading and comprehending literature and informational text at the 2nd grade level. Trent will continue to work on recognizing characters and story parts at the 2nd grade level.

Math: N/A

Written Language:

On 9/19/15 in a classroom setting and taken individually and hand-written, Trent responded to a narrative writing prompt asking him to describe his dream home if money were not an issue. Trent spelled 46/87 words correctly, and is able to demonstrate basic organizational skills in his writing. He stayed on topic throughout his entire response. Trent's sample had 1/9 sentences written completely (containing subject, verb, and object). Trent will continue to work on writing complete sentences (containing subject, verb, and object), while checking for punctuation errors at the 2nd grade level.

How the student's disability affects involvement and progress in the general education curriculum: Trent's disability in Specific Learning Disability affects his ability to make progress at the same rate and speed as his same grade nondisabled peers. Due to organizational issues, Trent struggles with multi-step tasks and will benefit from a specially designed instruction and accommodations. He also requires specially designed instruction in academics to make progress in the classroom.

---

Present level of functional performance (not limited to, but may include communication, social skills, behavior, organization, fine/gross motor skills, self-care, self-direction, etc.), including the results of initial or most recent formal or informal assessments/observations:

◆ Strengths of the student
◆ Needs of the student
◆ How the student's disability affects involvement and progress in the general education curriculum *34 CFR 300.320(a)(1)*

---

Narrative and supporting data:

Study Skills:

As of 10/13/2016 Trent is passing the majority of his subjects. He is currently not passing in Language Arts. Trent will continue to work on completing assignments and turning them in when they are due. Trent will ask for help when needed from his teachers.

How the student's disability affects involvement and progress in the general education classroom:

Trent's disability in Specific Learning Disability affects his ability to make progress at the same rate and speed as his same grade nondisabled peers. Due to memory issues, Trent struggles with multi-step tasks and will benefit from a specially designed instruction and accommodations. He also requires specially designed instruction in academics to make progress in the classroom.

## Summary of Trent

Trent's cumulative file shows that he qualified under the IDEA (2004) categories of (1) Specific Learning Disability and (2) Communication Disorder to receive special education services (See Full IEP in Appendix A). Trent is 9 years old and qualified for SPED services in second grade at Valley Elementary at the age of 7. He is a bright young man but has difficulty staying on task and displays number and word reversals. He has one younger brother. Trent's father is an auto-mechanic, and his mother is a medical doctor. Trent is one of approximately 2% of African American students in the district. Ms. Casad will meet with the special education teacher Mr. Hill to follow Trent's IEP instruction methods and goals (see Table 2.5 for an excerpt of IEP including Present Levels of Academic Achievement and Functional Performance [PLAAFP]). Trent receives academic services for Reading and Language Arts. Trent's goals and objectives written in his IEP are implemented in the Resource Room with the SPED teacher, Speech Language Services from the Speech Language Pathologist, and in Ms. Casad's general education fourth grade classroom. (See Appendix A for full IEP.)

# Collecting More Information on Students' Cultural Assets

Ms. Casad sees basic information in students' cumulative files. However, critical information is missing. She felt there was more information needed before designing appropriate lessons for her CLD/ELL students, so she decided to send a survey home to gather information on students' families. She wanted to discover their Funds of Knowledge and cultural assets (see Chapter 1); therefore, she added a question about child-rearing and elders, "Do you take care of anyone or anything?" (e.g., sibling or parent, pets, or a garden; see Table 2.6). "Pets or garden" was specific to her students' geographic region to discover relationships to plants, animals, and land (see Chapter 1, Table 1.2). She noticed that in the Pacific Northwest, many families discuss their cultural values in relation to the land (e.g., farming, ranching, fishing, river rafting, kayaking, gardening, composting, etc.). Satisfied with the survey as a balance between getting a bigger picture of cultural backgrounds and respecting privacy, Ms. Casad made copies of the About Me survey (see Table 2.6) and sent them home.

Students' cumulative files and About Me surveys provided Ms. Casad with information on students' strengths, interests, and needs, to help her design lessons and activities that are culturally relevant and meaningful.

**Table 2.6** About Me Survey

| About Me! Survey |
|---|
| This survey will help me teach you, and is sent out with respect. |

1. **My favorite food is:**
2. **My interests or hobbies are:**
3. **My favorite kind of music is**

   ◆ Rock or indie
   ◆ Rap or hip hop
   ◆ Classical
   ◆ Blues
   ◆ Country
   ◆ Folk

4. **The people who live in my home are:**
5. **Something I like about school is:**
6. **Three of my strengths are: (e.g., "I'm a good listener", "I am kind.")**
7. **My family has a tradition of:**
8. **I prefer to work alone, or work with peers (circle one)**
9. **If I could visit any place, I would choose to go _____ because**
10. **Do you take care of anyone or anything? (sibling or parent, pets, or garden)**
11. **I learn best by: (check all that apply)**

   ◆ Listening
   ◆ Reading
   ◆ My teacher lecturing
   ◆ Watching a video
   ◆ Taking notes
   ◆ When moving my body
   ◆ Interacting with others
   ◆ Drawing

## Services Available at Valley Elementary School

At Valley Elementary, there is only a Sheltered English Instruction Pull-Out program (i.e., ELD program). Mrs. Tellez is a native Spanish speaker and the ELD teacher, who has worked with ELL students for six years. Teachers feel that Mrs. Tellez effectively collaborates with them and students' families to help them understand the cultural-linguistic needs of CLD/ELL students. Mr. Hill is the SPED teacher at Valley Elementary with 12 years' experience. He knows Trent quite well and has worked with plenty of general education teachers who have students receiving SPED services in their classrooms. Trent will be in Ms. Casad's classroom for most of the day and go to Mr. Hill's resource room for Language Arts.

## Conclusion

Looking into students' cumulative files is a great place to get to know your students. Cumulative files provide a big picture of students' academic and educational backgrounds with language preferences and proficiencies, academic records, formal and informal assessments, and behavioral concerns. When working with ELL/CLD students you may need to go deeper to *get to know your student* by using tools such as the About Me survey, observations, interviews, profiles, checklists, etc. In Chapter 3 you will see some ways Ms. Casad plans and teaches culturally responsive lessons based on information from Student Profile forms (from Chapter 2) and cultural assets (Chapter 3). Culturally responsive teachers plan with intention, as well as perform intentional reflection on instructional effectiveness.

## Reflection Activities

### Reflection Activity #1: Design an About Me Survey

Now it is your turn to design an About Me survey! Think about what aspects of yourself describe you, including cultural assets (i.e., personality, beliefs, values, daily practices, interest groups, etc.). Reflect on ways to discover these. For example, what questions would a family friend ask you to find out more about you? Design a survey, questionnaire, or observation protocol that might guide you to discover aspects of someone you do not know well, but want to get to know better (without being too direct or intrusive). Then fill it out on that person, and on yourself! Is it an effective tool? Why or why not? What would you change for it to yield more accurate results?

### Reflection Activity #2: Create Culturally Responsive Topics and Plans

1. Start by reviewing the provided information on the four case study students. Do they have any common assets (i.e., strengths, interests, or abilities)? Consider their cultural and linguistic profiles, and cultural assets. Locate one common asset, and then think of topics that could serve as the base for a culturally responsive lesson.
2. Review cumulative file information and any other information available on your own CLD students, including students on IEPs. After locating a common asset, create a lesson plan that builds on these assets. Follow the culturally responsive lesson planning guide (see Chapter 3, Table 3.1).

## Bibliography

August, D., & Hakuta, K. (Eds.). (1997). *Improving Schooling for Language-Minority Students: A Research Agenda*. Washington, D.C.: National Academy Press.

Baca, L. & Cervantes, H. (2006). *The Bilingual Special Education Interface*. Upper Saddle River, NJ: Pearson, Merrill, Prentice Hall.

Collier, C. (2010). *Seven Steps for Separating Difference and Disability*. Thousand Oaks: Corwin Press.

Echevarria, J., Vogt, M.-E., & Short, D. (2000). *Making Content Comprehensible for English Learners: The SIOP® Model*. Boston: Allyn & Bacon.

Farnsworth, M. (2016). Differentiating second language acquisition from Specific Learning Disability: An observational tool assessing dual language learners' pragmatic competence. *Young Exceptional Children*. Advance online publication. doi: 10.1177/1096250615621356

*Federal* Law Section 3127 Title VI—Office of Civil Rights (OCR) Guidelines. Retrieved from: www.hhs.gov/ocr/civilrights/resources/specialtopics/lep/index.html

Fillmore, L. W. (1991). When learning a second language means losing the first. *Early Childhood Research Quarterly*, 6(3), 323–346.

Gottlieb, M. (2006). *Assessing English Language Learners: Bridges from Language Proficiency to Academic Achievement*. Thousand Oaks: Corwin Press.

Herrera, S. G., & Murry, K. G. (2011). *Mastering ESL and Bilingual Methods: Differentiated Instruction for Culturally and Linguistically Diverse (CLD) Students* (2nd ed.) Boston: Allyn & Bacon.

Krashen, S. (2000). What does it take to acquire language? *ESL Magazine*, 3(3), 22–23.

Krashen, S. (2012). Seeking a justification for skill-building. In *Proceedings of the 19th Annual KOTESOL International Conference* (pp. 13–20). Korea Teachers of English to Speakers of Other Languages.

Linquanti, R., & Bailey, A. L. (2014). *Reprising the Home Language Survey: Summary of a National Working Session on Policies, Practices, and Tools for Identifying Potential English Learners*. Washington, D.C.: Council of Chief State School Officers.

Oregon Department of Education. (2015). *ELPA 21*. Retrieved from: www.Oregon.gov/ODEode.frontdesk@ode.state.or.us

*Roseberry*-McKibbin, C., & Brice, A. (2000). Acquiring English as a second language. *ASHA Leader*, 5(12), 4–7.

Woodcock, R. W., & Muñoz-Sandoval, A. F. (1993). *Woodcock-Muñoz Language Survey*. Itasca: Riverside Publishing.

# 3

# Inclusive Classrooms Begin With Culturally Responsive Pedagogy

## Introduction

In Chapter 3, examples of culturally responsive pedagogy (CRP) in the classroom are provided. CRP is an important foundation for CLD/ELLs' success. The general education teacher's role for providing CRP for Culturally and Linguistically Diverse (CLD) students is discussed along with examples of the implementation process by Ms. Casad, as she designs lessons that build on her students' cultural assets in a fourth grade Oregon Trail unit. Examples of CRP include:

- ◆ Connecting topics/subject matter to students' cultural assets and relative experiences, i.e., immigrant journeys;
- ◆ Building positive relationships with students including developing empathy;
- ◆ Encouraging CLD students to speak and read in their native languages, i.e., using relevant vocabulary;
- ◆ Utilizing individual learning styles to engage in the learning unit, i.e., kinesthetic learning style, "walking" the floor map;
- ◆ Including ethnic and cultural perspectives in the learning unit, i.e., Chinese and American Indian perspectives;
- ◆ Connecting content to student identities;
- ◆ Performing Intentional Reflection.

The chapter concludes with a discussion on the individual differences each of the students brings with them to the classroom. The differences in their cultural, linguistic, and social/emotional and behavioral needs bring challenges for educators to consider when deciding how to provide culturally and linguistically appropriate instruction.

Three end-of-chapter reflective activities are provided including a voice from a "Teacher from the field," who discusses the question of "How can I bring cohesiveness into this class?"

## Culturally Responsive Pedagogy

More diverse students in our public schools exist today than any time in history (Kent, 2015). Fifty-six percent of public school teachers in the United States have at least one English Language Learner (ELL) in their class, but less than 20% of these teachers are certified to teach them (Brown & Doolittle, 2008; Waxman, Tellez, & Walberg, 2004). Many pedagogies exist for teaching diverse students; however, culturally responsive pedagogy (see Lee, 2007; Nieto, 2005; Gay, 2010) is a comprehensive pedagogy for Culturally and Linguistically Diverse (CLD) students because it emphasizes the impacts of both culture and language in teaching and learning. Sheltered Instruction Observation Protocol (SIOP; Echevarria, Vogt, & Short, 2007) focuses on language development, but lacks emphasis on the role of culture in learning. Critical pedagogy (see Freire, 1998; Giroux, 1998; McLaren, 2015) focuses on empowerment and social justice, but lacks emphasis on English language development.

In this chapter, you are introduced to four critical components of culturally responsive pedagogy (CRP) that provide a framework for working successfully with CLD/ELLs: (1) collect information on students' cultural assets (e.g., observation); (2) encourage native-language use, a bilingual dictionary, or translator tool; (3) make connections from students' cultural assets to course content (e.g., pioneers' journeys on the Oregon Trail to ELL immigrants' journeys to the U.S.); and (4) perform intentional reflection on the ways one's own cultural assets affect teaching and learning. Ms. Casad reflects on her own family's acculturation process into the U.S., and develops empathy for ELLs by reflecting on her own moving experiences

While reflecting on her interactions with Jun, Rosa, and César, Ms. Casad remembered her two-day workshop on culturally responsive pedagogy (CRP). She located the training materials and looked at the foundational principles. According to Gay (2010), CRP principles include: (1) beliefs about cultural and racial diversity shape teachers' instructional behaviors toward ethnically different students; (2) culture profoundly affects learning;

(3) school achievement involves more than academics; and (4) cultural diversity is a strength, a value, and resource. Teachers implementing CRP use the cultural knowledge, prior experiences, frames of references (i.e., perspectives), performance styles (i.e., communication styles), and heritages of culturally diverse students as vehicles to make learning more meaningful for them (Gay, 2010).

One reason CRP can seem ambiguous to beginning teachers is that it is a mindset, and cannot be reduced to a list of techniques and strategies. It goes beyond having a multicultural day or learning about a different culture from a book. CRP involves being knowledgeable of the cultural assets (i.e., values, strengths, and family practices) represented in your classroom, including your own, acknowledging them every day, talking about their significance, and making multiple daily connections between them and the standard curriculum. In order to build a classroom community based around CRP, educators themselves must understand and respect different beliefs and practices, as well as understand the importance and value of learning about multiple cultures in the classroom every day (Sato & Lensmire, 2009).

## Culturally Responsive Lesson Planning

In looking at the CRP training manual's suggestions for lesson planning (see Table 3.1), Ms. Casad filtered out the strategies that would take too much time and energy, and located a practical suggestion under *Relevance*: collect information on students' cultural assets (e.g., interests, learning styles, family practices), and realized she had already begun doing this with the About Me survey (see Chapter 2, Table 2.5)!

**Table 3.1** Culturally Responsive Lesson Planning Guide

| Environment | Relevance | Language Supports |
|---|---|---|
| ◆ Culturally appropriate role models and messages displayed<br>◆ Universal Design for Learning (UDL): intentional use of space (wide walkways, low lighting, scent free)<br>◆ Inclusive visuals, pictures | ◆ Collect information on students' cultural assets (e.g., interests, learning styles, cultural, or family practices) and make connections to content<br>◆ Allow student choice of topics | ◆ Post vocabulary words, sentence frames, and objectives<br>◆ Oral language development (example: "tell a friend")<br>◆ Encourage native-language use, bilingual dictionary, or translator tool<br>◆ Realia, manipulatives, graphic organizers<br>◆ Interaction: hands-on activities, cooperative learning in small groups |

**Table 3.2** Students' Cultural Profiles

| César | Jun | Rosa | Trent |
|---|---|---|---|
| Good listener, prefers to work in groups or w/ peers. Follows rules. Respectful. Holidays important (Catholic). Would like to visit Honduras because still has family there. Loves animals. Family worked as ranchers and farmers. | Can be independent. Non-competitive. Kinesthetic learner. Likes to play video games. Family came from a farming village in China. Jun has sister and brother. Likes math. Family holds high respect of teachers. | Hard worker. Highly verbal and independent. Lacks social skills due to independence. Strong leader. Moved here from Mexico. Lives w/ mother and brothers (may be in gangs). Attends catechism classes. | Hard worker. Shy. Interested in insects and science. Parents are educated and highly involved in school. Close relationship to younger brother. |

Ms. Casad located Jun, Rosa, César, and Trent's About Me surveys, and recorded a few of their cultural assets on their *Cultural Profiles* (see Table 3.2). She then chose a suggestion from the CRP planning guide (Table 3.1), *make connections from students' cultural assets to content*, and began to think about the upcoming unit on the Oregon Trail.

## Place-Based Education

Looking at her ELL students' cultural assets information (see Table 3.2), Ms. Casad noticed they had arrived in the U.S. from another country, thus have background knowledge and experiences with moving to another place. This was similar to the pioneers on the Oregon Trail! The Oregon Trail is state-required content in fourth grade for Oregon students, in which students learn about their geographic location in the world, and "sense of place." This topic of place-based curriculum appears in other fourth grade curricula where CRP could be successfully implemented. For example, in California, fourth grade students study missions in social studies. In Hawaii, students describe features of early Hawaiian life, such as rules and laws, gods/religion, roles of women/classes of people, sports and games, food, kapu system, land ownership taxes, and/or education (Hawaii Content & Performance Standards, 2007)

In Valley Elementary's fourth grade social studies curriculum, the study of American Indians/Alaska Natives (AI/AN) occurred after the Oregon Trail unit. For the past two years, Ms. Casad taught these two topics in a segregated, linear sequence. However, she now questioned this approach. If we are trying to teach multiple perspectives, why would AI/AN perspectives be omitted in favor of the westward expansion, settler perspective? She wondered how critical thinking could be developed without multiple perspectives. Therefore, she decided to integrate AI/AN perspectives into the Oregon Trail unit and would contact the Indian Education coordinator in the district office for resources.

## Multiple Perspectives

Exploring multiple perspectives is the core element in multicultural education (Banks & Banks, 2010). Often, teachers do not receive guidance on how to explore these multiple perspectives, nor create multicultural classrooms. 2017 Common Core State Standards also expect teachers to teach multiple perspectives (see www.corestandards.org/ELA-Literacy/SL/6/1/d/).

One way for teachers to implement this practice is to research the multiple voices involved in an event and present the voices in student activities. The Sheltered Instruction Observational Protocol (SIOP) emphasizes supplementary reading within activities (Echevarria, Vogt, & Short, 2007). One suggested activity in the SIOP approach is for students to grapple with authentic multiple voices in a "dinner party." Teachers choose different perspectives from the same historic event and assign students to play these various roles at a "dinner party" (Echevarria, Vogt, & Short, 2007). For example, in the Oregon Trail unit, different characters could be chosen (e.g., mother of six children, elder woman, male tracker, tribal elder) and given a prompt such as, "the wheel has fallen off a wagon and you are to discuss possible actions to take." Four students (or various groupings) are assigned to the characters to role-play at the camp dinner. By engaging in this activity, students discuss different perspectives from the same event, which expands understanding of the complexities of human behaviors that influence decision-making that creates history.

Ms. Casad realized that she needed to create an environment where students could feel safe to discuss these diverse perspectives, which required kindness, empathy, and understanding. She now realized her responsibility for creating and maintaining safe environments for students to practice skills to become culturally competent and socially responsible citizens. She returned to the *Self-Assessment of Cultural Competence* (see Chapter 1, Reflection Activity #1) and began planning to help students develop two mindsets of cultural competence: (1) diversity is valuable, and different perspectives help me think critically and (2) understanding that learning varies among individuals, and does not follow one pattern.

## Oregon Trail

Ms. Casad was inspired and wrote notes on ways to connect the Oregon Trail unit to CLD students' cultural assets, and implement multicultural education:

1. Creating the prompt, "Imagine that you are an 11-year-old American Indian who is witnessing the settlement by the 'pioneers.' What might you be thinking about the new people moving in and taking over your land? What should we do when threatened with relocation, fight, flee, or agree to move (to a reservation)?";
2. Providing graphic novels and bilingual books about the Oregon Trail;
3. Finding places to connect the pioneers' journey to immigrants' journeys to the United States (with trials and tribulations, desire to get somewhere to have opportunities, leaving things behind, etc.);
4. Showing a historical documentary of the Oregon Trail that includes Native American and African American perspectives;
5. Providing a large floor map of the U.S and encouraging students to walk the trail.

In addition to connecting content to students' cultural assets, Ms. Casad also wanted to meet Rosa, Jun, and César's unique language needs. Therefore, she returned to the *Language Acquisition Stages* (see Chapter 2, Table 2.3) to view suggested teaching strategies in the different stages: 1–2 (César), 2–3 (Jun), and 3–4 (Rosa). She realized this was going to take some organization, and copied a few strategies onto her students' *Cultural-Linguistic Profiles* (see Table 3.3).

Ms. Casad then returned to the CRP Planning Guide and viewed the *Language Supports* (see Table 3.1). She realized there were so many great suggestions for lesson planning! Using these tools, Ms. Casad planned the first lesson to introduce the Oregon Trail, differentiating instruction to meet students' cultural and linguistic needs (see Table 3.4).

In beginning the Oregon Trail unit, Ms. Casad first elicited information students knew and wanted to know about the Oregon Trail on the K-W chart (see Table 3.5). Many students were curious! Rosa wanted to know where the trail began, and if it went through Mexico or not. Ms. Casad noted this contribution as a significant interest, and would bring in maps to show Rosa trail locations and proximity to Mexico.

**Table 3.3** Cultural-Linguistic Profiles

| César | Jun | Rosa | Trent |
|---|---|---|---|
| Good listener, prefers to work in groups or w/ peers. Follows rules. Respectful. Holidays important (Catholic). Would like to visit Honduras because still has family there. Loves animals. Family worked as ranchers and farmers. | Can be independent. Non-competitive. Kinesthetic learner. Likes to play video games. Family came from a farming village in China. Jun has sister and brother. Likes math. Family holds high respect of teachers. | Hard worker. Highly verbal and independent. Lacks social skills due to independence. Strong leader. Moved here from Mexico. Lives w/ mother and brothers (may be in gangs). Attends catechism classes. | Hard worker. Shy. Interested in insects and science. Parents are educated and highly involved in school. Close relationship to younger brother. |
| **LA Stage 2** Use manipulatives, visuals, realia. Create climate of acceptance/respect. Use physical response to check comprehension. Display print. Model activities. Use hands-on activities. Lessons designed to motivate students to talk. Ask questions that require one or two word responses. | **LA Stage 3** List and review instructions step by step. Build on students' prior knowledge. Incorporate more reading and writing. Have students brainstorm, list, web, and use graphic organizers. Use sentence frames. Use cooperative learning groups. Expand vocabulary. | **LA Stage 3–4** Ask questions soliciting opinions, judgment, explanation (ask why and how questions). Introduce figurative language. Develop more academic language (oral and written). | **Specific Learning Disability** Break up long tasks or assignments into smaller segments. Use prompts and cues to draw attention to important information. Teach to highlight instructions on assignments. Use verbal cues such as using signal words to get student's attention. Ask the student to paraphrase directions. |

**Table 3.4** Bound for Oregon Lesson Plan

| Lesson Title | "Bound for Oregon" Chapters 1–2 Vocabulary Building |
|---|---|
| **Content Area, Time** | Oregon Trail fourth grade Language Arts/Social Studies 60 minutes |
| **Standards** | 4.RL.10 By the end of the year, read and comprehend literature, including stories, dramas, and poetry, in the grades 4–5 text complexity band proficiently, with scaffolding as needed at the high end of the range. |
| **Objectives** | Today I will: 1) List what I know, and want to know about the Oregon Trail 2) Define key vocabulary words 3) Use three vocabulary words in a sentence<br><br>*Differentiation: Post vocabulary words, sentence frames, and objectives* |

(Continued)

**Table 3.4** (Continued)

| Lesson Title | "Bound for Oregon" Chapters 1–2 Vocabulary Building |
|---|---|
| **Assessment** | Students will complete an exit ticket with three vocabulary words defined and written in sentences. |
| **OPEN** | Students will share what they know about the Oregon Trail. Then, they will talk in their table groups about what they want to know. Then list in next column.<br><br>*Differentiation: Find private moment to praise Rosa, "You have great opinions. I know you are going to do great at this activity!" Place graphic novels at Jun and César's tables* |
| **Body** | (1) Explain to students *Find your partner activity*:<br>    Students will find a partner with the same colored card. Together, they will choose four words from list of vocabulary words from "Bound for Oregon" text.<br>(2) Students look up definitions and write down.<br>(3) Decide ways to act out three words, practice.<br>(4) Group A will join with another group (group B) and act out their three words.<br>(5) Group B will guess group A's words.<br>(6) Group B will act out their words and Group A guesses.<br><br>*Differentiation: Suggest words that are better suited for drawing: hearth, paradise, nestled. Allow for more time to finish as needed. Rosa: Partner with Juan (option to discuss concepts in Spanish) Jun: Remind him to use translator tool to find definitions and that he can draw pictures.*<br><br>*César: Show photos and allow him to draw or write definitions in Spanish. He can show his picture, or partner can read the definition.*<br><br>*Trent: Ask him to paraphrase directions.* |
| **Close** | Students will turn in their three sentences (exit ticket) using vocabulary words.<br>*Differentiation for César and Jun: Provide a vocabulary definition matching activity instead. Ask them to match definitions to appropriate words* |
| **Vocab words** | drawback, reluctant, nestled, somber, famine,<br>provisions, shirked, transparent, taunt, monotony,<br>endure, paradise, hearth, abscess |

Note: Differentiation is in italics.

**Table 3.5** K-W Oregon Trail

| What we KNOW about OR Trail | What do we WANT to know about OR Trail |
|---|---|
| It is in Oregon | Was there electricity? |
| They hunted for their food | What did they eat? Did they eat plants and animals along the way? |
| People got sick and died | How long is the trail? |
| It is long and they had to travel for a long time | Where does it begin? Where does it go? |
| The pioneers had wagons and not cars | Are there rivers and did people fish? |
| It was difficult to cross | Why did people go? |
| People made their own clothes | How long has the trail been around? |

## Connections From Cultural Assets to Content: Journeys

One key goal of the Oregon Trail unit was to emphasize multiple perspectives of the historical event. Ms. Casad wanted to connect the Oregon Trail journey that pioneers made, to her ELL students' immigrant journeys, without pointing them out and potentially stigmatizing them. She began the discussion by asking who had moved before, and possible reasons people moved from one place to another. Few hands went up, as many students had never moved before. The community surrounding Valley Elementary is fairly rural with 60% of students qualifying for the Free and Reduced Lunch program (i.e., low socioeconomic status). The town has one active lumber mill, after four mills closed in the past 20 years. Ms. Casad changed to her question to be more inclusive, "who has gone on a long trip, which is also called a *journey*?" Max was the first student who raised his hand. He explained that his family had gone to Disneyland during the summer and their car had gotten a flat tire. He talked about how the family waited by the side of the road while his aunt tried to change the tire. Ms. Casad asked Max how he felt while he waited. He said that he was bored, tired, and impatient because he just wanted to get to the amusement park! Ms. Casad took this opportunity to explain how during a *journey*, many things happen along the way that are not expected or planned on, like a flat tire. She wondered aloud who else had experienced these obstacles during their journeys.

Anna began to speak, but Rosa pushed her aside and yelled that she had been on a very long trip. Ms. Casad expressed that she wanted to hear everyone's voice, but this required students to speak one at a time and be respectful of each other. "We want to hear your story Rosa, but Anna began to speak first, so you can share after Anna finishes." Rosa looked very angry and sat down with her arms folded. After Anna had finished sharing, Rosa stood up and said, "My mom waked me up in the night and I had to stay quiet, and then we went in the water for a long time." Ms. Casad replied by asking Rosa why her family came to the United States. Rosa replied, "U.S. better since not all people get hurt." Ms. Casad thanked Rosa for sharing her story, and explained to the class that many people take a journey because they believe the next place will be better than where they lived.

Ms. Casad then asked how many students had grandparents. Almost all students raised their hands. She taught the children that almost all of their grandparents' parents, including her own, had come into the U.S. from another place, and were called "immigrants." Only American Indians were indigenous to the U.S., and she showed a map of AI/AN territories. She then showed pictures she had taken at the recent pow-wow. Nicole raised her hand and shared her experience of dancing at that pow-wow. Ms. Casad assigned students to ask their families where their ancestors had come from, and then they would mark the places on a world map.

While Ms. Casad was teaching, she noticed that Rosa and César were not participating. She remembered her goal to *encourage native-language use* and encouraged Rosa and César to speak in Spanish to each other during small-group work if they preferred, but they did not seem to be getting along. Rosa was outspoken, and César appeared very tired and disengaged. She recalled from her educational training how important it is to empower outspoken students by placing them in leadership roles; therefore, found a private moment to tell Rosa, "I have noticed that one of your strengths is sharing your opinions. By what you shared earlier with the class, I know you are going to add wonderful information to this unit. I can't wait to hear more about your experience coming to the United States." Although Rosa did not respond verbally, her body appeared to relax and Ms. Casad could feel some tension disappear.

Ms. Casad also introduced two bilingual books written in English and Spanish, and two books written from an American Indian perspective about the Oregon Trail that the librarian had helped obtain. During reading time, she noted that Rosa was reading one of the new bilingual books quietly to herself. Ms. Casad understood that César and Rosa came to the U.S. because their families felt there were safer opportunities here than to remain in their home countries. She wanted to validate their experiences of leaving familiar places, and now knew she could connect these experiences to the pioneers during the Oregon Trail unit. She felt like she needed to get to know them better to help improve their educational outcomes.

In reflecting on César's disengagement, Ms. Casad remembered that on several occasions, César was waiting by her classroom door in the morning before she arrived. This concerned her, so she planned to arrive early the next day. The next morning when Ms. Casad arrived at school at 6:00 AM, she saw a man drop off César at school. She learned this man was César's uncle, but César did not seem to want to talk about him. Now she understood why he seemed so tired by the afternoon. Ms. Casad continued learning about César's cultural assets through observation, conversation, and reflection, building their relationship of care, a critical foundation for success.

## Encourage Native-Language Use, Bilingual Dictionary, or Translator Tool

Ms. Casad viewed speaking a language other than English as a valuable ability in life. She took three years of Spanish courses in high school, and was somewhat confident in her ability; therefore, she looked up two Spanish phrases to use with Rosa and César. Jun was more difficult because she absolutely did not know anything about his language, so she decided to talk with the school librarian, whom she believed was Chinese. When catching up with the librarian Mrs. Trung, Ms. Casad discovered that she did not know any Chinese languages, and was Vietnamese. Ms. Casad remembered that she wanted to help *all* kids, and see *all* native languages as equally valuable, not just those she was familiar with.

During lunch, she asked Jun to help her translate his About Me survey into his native language by using an online translation tool. Jun appeared very excited to help her, as she learned later that his family greatly respected teachers and it was a deep honor that he was asked to help the teacher with a task. She showed Jun how to enter a question in English and press a button to retrieve the Chinese translation. She then asked him copy the characters onto the survey, assuming he could read the characters he wrote down. He did this at a very slow, meticulous pace; his characters looked perfect in form. While she watched him searching for keys, she wondered if it was Jun's first time using a computer. All of her previous fourth graders were comfortable with technology, and she thought, *"Don't most people have access to technology these days?"* Ms. Casad later learned that Jun's older sister had completed the survey for him since he could not understand the English nor the Chinese he had added to the survey. While reading an Internet article about technology, Ms. Casad saw the term "Digital Divide," which refers to the gap between those who have access to technology (and Internet) in contrast with those who do not. She thought she should add the question, "Do you have a computer at home?" to the About Me survey for next year.

## Connections From Students' Cultural Assets to the Text: Relevant Vocabulary

Ms. Casad began discussing the vocabulary from the historical fiction chapter book, *Bound for Oregon* (Van Leeuwen, 1994). "Father had to split rails for work and he got a bad bruise. His bruises turned into *abscesses* and father could not work for several weeks." Ms. Casad began a "think-aloud" to model the process of constructing meaning for the word *abscess*. "I know when I get a bruise on my arm it is painful to write. Last night, the basketball player Stephen Curry fell into the crowd and got a big bruise! He had to come out of the basketball game and rest. We will see if it turns into an abscess. If the bruise is not iced and rested, it may get worse and turn into an abscess, which means a swollen part of the body that has been injured."

Ms. Casad noticed that Jun was looking around the classroom appearing distracted. She approached him and asked, "Do you know what a bruise is?" Jun remained silent and smiled. She thought, how can I help him understand the word "bruise?" She then asked students if anyone had a bruise to show Jun. Several students showed their bruises to Jun. She asked Jun to repeat the word and write it in Chinese next to the written English vocabulary word. He smiled but did not write anything down. She realized that she needed to prepare real-life hands-on examples (i.e., realia) for Jun to maintain his engagement and understanding of the vocabulary.

Ms. Casad continued discussing relevant vocabulary and making connections from Text-to-Self (i.e., cultural assets). "The narrator (a 9-year-old pioneer girl) wondered why her dad could not bring their kiln on the journey. Does anyone know what a *kiln* is?"

One student responded that a kiln is an oven, and that her mom fired clay bowls in their kiln and sold them at the farmers' market on Saturdays. Ms. Casad replied, "Yes, it is an oven. Does it sound like a *kiln* is light enough to carry across the trail? The family already decided to carry a cast iron frying pan in their wagon, so decided to leave the kiln behind. Have you ever had to leave something important behind?"

The students were quiet, and then hands slowly began to rise. César's hand shot up and he began talking, "*Cuando I go from mi country, no have cama, house, ropas, and mi abuela, I no happy porque and I no take mi dog.*" Ms. Casad knew enough Spanish to revoice César's response for the other students, "When I left my country, I left my bed, my house, my clothes, and my grandmother. I was sad because I could not bring my dog."

Ms. Casad felt a lump in her throat and struggled with knowing what to say. She felt sympathy for César because she never had to leave everything behind during her three moves. She always had a choice of what to leave or bring to her new houses. Ms. Casad said, "Thank you for sharing your connection to the story, César; you made a Text-to-Self connection, which makes you a better reader." As students read silently, Ms. Casad circulated around the room to check for understanding, still thinking about César.

## Empathy

Ms. Casad reflected on her interaction with César and Rosa, and felt like she did not meet their needs. She returned to her CRP training materials and read,

> five qualities essential for teachers to be culturally responsive: (1) a
> sense of mission to serve ethnically diverse children to the best of

their abilities; (2) solidarity with, *empathy* for, and value of students' lives, experiences, cultures, and human dignity; (3) courage to question mainstream school knowledge and conventional ways of doing things, and beliefs and assumptions about diverse students, families, cultures, and communities; (4) willingness to improvise, to push the envelope, to go beyond established templates and frameworks, embrace uncertainty and flexibility; and (5) a passion for equality and social justice.

(Nieto, 2005; cited in Gay, 2010, p. 145; emphasis added)

Reflecting on how she felt when César was sad about leaving so much behind, Ms. Casad focused on *empathy*, "solidarity with, empathy for, and value of students' lives, experiences, cultures, and human dignity" (Gay, 2010, p. 145), and wondered, did she hold empathy for César?

Many teachers have sympathy for their students, which holds them at a safe, emotional distance. In order to practice empathy, teachers must seek commonalities of experiences, which create strong relationships. Empathy is defined as the ability to identify what someone else is thinking or feeling, and to respond to her/his thoughts and feelings with an appropriate emotion (Baron-Cohen, 2011) that implies a shared interpersonal experience. Ms. Casad thought, how can I feel empathy for immigrants who faced many challenges if I do not share their experiences? She reflected on events when she felt large challenges, and remembered an assignment in her graduate program titled, "Walk in their shoes." For this project, students chose challenges to experience during an entire day. Some peers chose visual, hearing impairments, or physical challenges. She had chosen to experience a language impairment and did not speak for the day. Coming from the dominant U.S. culture in which independence is highly valued, she remembered being frustrated and dependent on friends, feeling alienated and despondent. She realized it was possible to walk in César's shoes by remembering feelings of sadness, they both had felt when facing challenges, even though they were different challenges.

Ms. Casad also remembered two more events of facing challenges. She had taken beginning Spanish classes in high school, which were very difficult. She felt so lost. She could not follow the teacher, who only spoke in Spanish (i.e., immersion), and she became quiet and frustrated. She wanted to quit the class but needed it for graduation, so sought out resources including a tutor. The third memory of facing a challenge was of having a cat as a child. She loved her cat Otis, and on some days felt Otis was her only friend. One day Otis disappeared. She looked for her and felt responsible for her getting lost. Ms. Casad wondered if César felt responsible for leaving his dog. She would ask him tomorrow, and share with him her story of Otis. "Telling your story is part of the healing of a traumatic event" (Kübler-Ross & Kessler, 2005, p. 62). Teachers must possess skills to navigate their students' as well as their own emotions, which contributes to successful teaching and learning relationships (Bair, Bair, Madera, Hipp, & Hakim, 2010). One skill in relationship-building is possessing Emotional Intelligence, defined as the ability to perceive and express emotions, to understand and use them, and to manage emotions to foster personal growth (Mayer & Salovey, 1997).

The following morning, Ms. Casad found César alone by her door. She asked him to sit with her, and shared her story of losing her cat. César listened and looked down. She asked him how he felt about leaving his dog. He looked at her and said, *"Yes, I have sad porque mi dog es over there and nadia persona to feed him. El es mi best friend en este mundo."* ("Yes, I am sad because my dog is there and no one to feed him. He is my very best friend in all the world.") She apologized for not asking him more about his experience when he shared during class. "Your story was hard for me to hear since it was so sad. Sometimes when people hear others' sadness, they feel discomfort and change the topic. But your story is very important. Many people new to this country have similar stories to yours, and others have very different stories. It is important for everyone to share their story so we can all learn from each other. Do you want to tell students more about leaving your home?" César nodded in agreement, and smiled.

## Connecting Content to Students' Identities

That afternoon when she began the Oregon Trail lesson, Ms. Casad asked students if they knew which countries their families had immigrated from. She helped students locate the country(ies) their ancestors had immigrated from and mark them with a push-pin on the world map. Then on a poster, students wrote the countries names: Honduras, Ireland, Mexico, etc. Ms. Casad asked Jun which country he came from. He smiled and responded, "Fujian." "What's Fujian?" she asked. While pointing to the letters on the map, C-H-I-N-A, she asked him, "What's the name of this big country?" "China" Jun read. "Yes, you immigrated here from China." She handed him a pen, and he neatly added "China" to the poster.

Later, when students discussed settlers leaving their homes, César shared more details about leaving everything behind, and feeling sad about it. Ms. Casad shared her cat story, and explained, "When you leave or lose pets, family, or friends, this is called "loss," and you can feel sadness called "grief." César and I both lost our pets. Please share with your neighbor when you have felt loss." She handed students a list of emotions to help expand their vocabulary of emotions. They chose three and wrote them on a large heart poster. Ms. Casad explicitly made connections between these emotions and those of the migrants on the Oregon Trail, and then explained that many immigrants/pioneers anticipated a new life.

"Often, people leave because their circumstances are difficult, and look forward to new opportunities and hope for a better life. However, when one group of people arrives in a new location, there are large consequences for the people who live in that place, often resulting in confusion. For example, how would you feel if someone appeared on your doorstep and said, 'I am here to live in your yard'? Then she set up her tent near your garden and began unpacking." Ms. Casad then handed out the following prompts to small groups for discussion:

1. How would you feel about this person now living in your yard?
2. What would you need to discuss with him/her?
3. Imagine that you are an 11-year-old American Indian boy who is witnessing the settlement by the "pioneers." What might you be thinking about the new people moving in and taking over your land?
4. What should we do when we feel threatened?
5. How would you feel if you were told you needed to leave and relocate? Fight, flee, or agree to move?

## Intentional Reflection

Ms. Casad felt happy that she had reflected on César's situation, and enacted principles of CRP, "solidarity with, empathy for, and value of students' lives, experiences, cultures, and human dignity" (Nieto, 2005, cited in Gay, 2010, p. 145). She also felt satisfied in helping students understand César's challenges on his journey, which personalized, contextualized, and connected students to each other's stories, and the pioneers' experiences (i.e., Text-to-Self, and Text-to-Text).

Ms. Casad also reflected on her assumption that Mrs. Trung, the librarian, was "Chinese." She wondered if she thought all people that looked "Asian" were Chinese. She vowed to examine her biases by questioning and challenging them. Then, she would gather relevant information and revise her assumptions to include a more accurate, informed portrayal of people and situations, thus reducing stereotypes (Gay & Kirkland, 2003).

During a faculty meeting after school, Mrs. M. asked Ms. Casad, "How is it going with Rosa?"

Ms. Casad wondered aloud how soon she could expect Rosa to become American. Mrs. M. replied, "You mean, how soon do ELLs assimilate?" Ms. Casad heard of the word "assimilate" when her grandfather talked about his parents forbidding him to learn their native language after immigrating to the U.S. Her grandfather said, "My parents just wanted me to become American as fast as I could. They told me to forget our home country's practices and language. They thought that was the best way to get a job, be accepted, and successful."

Ms. Casad smiled and repeated, "Assimilate?" Mrs. M. said, "Yes, when an immigrant comes here they can assimilate, or give up their home language and culture, and adopt 'American' beliefs and practices. Sometimes the term *assimilation* is described with the metaphor, *Melting pot*." She continued, "Or they can acculturate, and adopt some American ways, while still holding onto major beliefs, practices, and language of their home culture as best they can. Sometimes the term *acculturation* is described with the metaphor, *salad bowl*."

Ms. Casad reflected upon the question she asked students to ask their families, "Did your ancestors come from another country?" She thought about how different she might be today if her grandfather had been able to retain his language and culture, and realized that she may have spoken English as a second language, resulting in another identity. She knew that effective culturally responsive educators advocate for ELLs and see "differences" as strengths; therefore, she thought about ways she could help children feel pride in maintaining their cultures. Her mind began to race about ways to acknowledge contributions their cultures added to the "American" way of life. She would ask students, "How is the U.S. better off with immigrants' contributions?"

Ms. Casad wondered, was the U.S. a better country for what her ancestors had contributed?

*Cultural assets* now meant something more personal to her, so she filled out the table to identify her own cultural identities (see Table 3.6). In reflecting on them, she realized how different her beliefs and practices were from César, Rosa, and Jun! She had grown up in such different circumstances. The largest difference was the U.S. political system of democracy, which granted much of her social and cultural capital, and privilege. Her cultural lens focused on the pursuit of democracy, with freedom to choose almost everything, including education, food, social interactions, and ways to spend her time (e.g., leisure, hobbies, vacation, etc.). She grew up very independent, which was supported by her networks (i.e., school, family, societal expectations). However, this independence contributed to her disconnection and distance from her family. Ms. Casad's intentional reflection was the first step in viewing ways power and privilege affected her teaching and learning relationships.

**Table 3.6** Ms. Casad's Cultural Assets

| Cultural Factors Influencing Teaching and Learning | Ms. Casad |
| --- | --- |
| Dress, celebrations, food, and language | Casual professional attire for school and work, casual for days off, formal for official occasions. |
| Patterns of friendship and social structure | Family first, socialize/friends at school and work. |
| Patterns of emotions and self-esteem | Quiet, patient, inwardly self-confident, private/introspective, positive thinking |
| Family structure (nuclear or extended), family responsibilities, and gender roles | Strong familial ties to my daughter and brother. Strong ties to my partner and his children. I am not close to father. I feel strong role of mother. |
| Individualism and independence; or competition and collaboration | Independent and collaborative. |
| Relationship to plants, animals, or land | Feel interconnected to nature, love to camp, fish, walk, organic garden, and meditate. |
| Body language (eye contact, personal space, tone of voice, nonverbal, facial expressions), linguistic communication | Usually adjust to fit who I am talking to. Like personal space. Sometimes loud voice. |
| Access to housing, transportation, and medical care | Rent house, own car. Health insurance through work. |
| Membership in groups (church, school alumni, YMCA, library, etc.) | College alumni, YMCA, Delta Kappa member, library card, member National Education Association. |
| Maintaining ties to ethnic group (access to mentors) | I have never felt a strong connection to any one culture. I identify with pieces of many cultures. My ethnicity is English, German, Scotch-Irish, French, and Canadian. In the primarily "white" population of Oregon I have easy access to mentors from the varying components of my ethnic group. |

## Deeper Discussion of Differences Among César, Rosa, and Jun

Each of the ELL students came to Ms. Casad with different levels of English development and specific cultural, linguistic, and behavioral needs. These differences required Ms. Casad to employ varied approaches to help students reach their full potential. Ms. Casad implemented CRP by: (1) connecting the pioneers' journey to ELLs' journeys as immigrants; (2) building positive relationships with students by developing empathy; (3) encouraging Rosa, César, and Jun to speak and read in their native languages; (4) utilizing kinesthetic learning styles to "walk" the Oregon Trail on a floor map; and (5) including

Chinese, American Indian, and African American perspectives in the Oregon Trail. It appeared that César produced the most progress.

## César

Through multiple strategies, Ms. Casad built personal relationships with César. In turn, he became confident to share his story, which increased his language development. César also met multiple learning objectives within the Oregon Trail unit. One example is that he stated one personal connection to the text by comparing his journey to the pioneers', which increased his reading comprehension skills. These successes contributed to César's movement from novice to expert in his classroom community (Lave & Wenger, 1991).

## Rosa

Ms. Casad built on Rosa's cultural assets by (1) bringing in maps to show trail locations and proximity to Mexico, (2) finding a private moment to give her praise, and (3) providing bilingual books that validated her native-language abilities. Some strategies worked for Rosa while others needed adjustments. Other than their unique cultures and languages (regional dialect), a major difference among Rosa, César, and Jun is their dispositions. Rosa's anger and explosive behavior is very different than César's and Jun's timid personalities. In the past, Ms. Casad has worked with students who demonstrated similar behaviors as Rosa; however, Rosa's behaviors seem to be motivated by ethnic, cultural, and gender contexts. Ms. Casad was uncomfortable with Rosa's strong dispositions, but attempted to view them as strengths by placing Rosa as a leader in group work, and empowering her to tell her story. She will continue these strategies, while seeking additional help from her Professional Learning Community (PLC).

## Jun

Ms. Casad attempted to connect Jun's cultural assets to the Oregon Trail by (1) showing him pictures of Chinese people active in establishing Oregon's businesses and (2) utilizing his kinesthetic learning style by walking the Oregon Trail on a floor map of the United States. Jun happily moved about the map, but when asked where the pioneers were going, he responded inappropriately by walking around in circles, which made his classmates laugh. Jun still appears unresponsive to many strategies. Even when worksheets were translated into his home language, he did not respond. Ms. Casad is unsure what to try next with him. He is different than any student she has ever had before. His culture, primary language, and behavior are new challenges for her. She is slowly learning how to build a foundation for his learning, but realizing there may be more going on with him than just "slow progress." Ms. Casad will collaborate with her PLC team to find more appropriate ways to reach Jun.

## Conclusion

Important cultural factors that affect teaching and learning need to be examined, for culture may be more influential than language in obtaining educational achievement. Culture enables or constrains us, by blinding us to those who are different than us (Hollins, 2008). A teacher's educational background, experiences, behavior management, personality, motivations, instructional paradigm, and commitment to social justice all have an impact on the ability to create inclusive environments of equity. Since teachers bring their own cultural lens into the classroom, they may unintentionally attempt to encourage students to conform to their values and beliefs (Hollins, 2008), which potentially can marginalize students who do not share the same cultural lens. Ms. Casad examined her beliefs and attitudes toward her ELL students by questioning her assumptions about their language and diverse cultural assets, showing reflexivity (Gay & Kirkland, 2003). Ms. Casad's commitment to social justice positively impacts her ability to create an inclusive environment of equity (Nieto, 2005). The critical dispositions of empathy and open-mindedness are helping her create an equitable classroom, sometimes referred to as the "third space" (Gutierrez, Baquedano-Lopez, & Tejada, 1999). Teachers seeking to explore intersections of knowledge that foster growth in students' voices know that transformation occurs when students' and teachers' cultural assets are combined in a community of learners. Teachers provide inclusive activities through a variety of organizing discussions, turn-taking, and participant structures (e.g., whole class, small group, one-on-one, fishbowl), and are rooted in individualism (independent tasks) and collectivism (e.g., buddy reading, choral reading, cooperative learning groups). In Chapter 4, Ms. Casad brings student data to her PLC in seeking new strategies for their success.

## Reflection Activities

### Reflection Activity #1: Comprehensive Pedagogies

Now that you have viewed Ms. Casad's growth in meeting students' diverse needs, it is time for you to reflect on your own teaching and learning philosophies. In looking at the Holistic Student Profile (see Table 3.7), think about your own philosophies that inform instruction (i.e., pedagogy). Based on the information in

**Table 3.7** Holistic Student Profile

| | Physical | Cultural-Linguistic | Social-Emotional | Cognitive |
|---|---|---|---|---|
| **Teaching and Learning Philosophies** | Universal Design for Learning (UDL), Maslow's hierarchy of needs | Culturally responsive pedagogy | Cooperative groups, Positive behavior supports Emotional Intelligence | Brain-based multiple intelligences |
| **Classroom Support** | Reduced stimuli: smells, sights, sounds. Plants, low lighting, private corner, wide walkways. | Know students and self, connect cultural assets to content, sentence frames, graphic organizers, visuals, word walls | Clear expectations, positive feedback, journaling and reflection, student choice and voice, empathy | Think-aloud, highlight text, partial outline, large print, manipulatives, daily agenda. |
| **Teacher** | | | | |

Chapter 3, write down your cultural-linguistic and socioemotional practices in Table 3.7. Now think about teaching practices that meet the areas of cognitive and physical domains, which is a pre-assessment for Chapter 4.

### Reflection Activity #2: Responding to Students' Trauma

Ms. Casad thought back to the time when Rosa shared her experience of coming to the U.S., in which she had to be in the water for a long time quietly. Her family was so motivated to come to the U.S., because "people don't get hurt here." Ms. Casad felt she had responded inadequately, and wondered how else she could have responded. Think of any possible connection to Rosa you may have. Has there been a time when you were forced to do something or go somewhere you either did not know about, or did not want to go? Has there been a time when you felt afraid of someone or felt their power in making decisions for you? Reflect and respond to these prompts, and then think of two ways you would have responded to Rosa.

### Reflection Activity #3: Vignette From Teacher in the Field, "How Can I Bring Cohesiveness to This Class?"

First read the vignette, then reflect and respond to prompts at the end of the vignette.

When I began teaching, I did not know very much about the cultures that were represented in my classroom. I was new to Hawaii and new to teaching. I realized that my course work that had prepared me to become a teacher had not prepared me with all the tools that I needed to address my students' multifaceted backgrounds, levels of English, and specific needs. Quickly though, I knew that I had to evaluate my own expectations of my students and compare them to my students' perspectives.

Initially, I thought students would want to hear what I had to say and display this by using eye contact, sitting up in their chairs, and facing forward as well as taking notes. I wanted my classes to be interactive: I expected students to participate in discussions either with their elbow partner or as a whole class—no matter what the topic. I expected them to raise their hands, propose ideas without hesitation, and remain engaged. What was I thinking?! That first year of teaching, Hawaii saw a massive surge of students from Micronesia. Our school had nearly 70 new students from this country! And how were we prepared? Not at all!!

Teachers were surprised that this new population of students tended to come to school late and arrive with no writing tool or paper—almost every single day. These behaviors were interpreted as unmotivated to learn and disrespectful. The following year, in response to the continual influx, the Department of Education provided several professional development opportunities to learn about their culture. Generally speaking, students from Micronesia do not have to attend school nor be on time, especially if they need to help their family. If your friend needed a pencil, you gave them yours as well as the other way around. Items were not necessarily "owned." Youth typically will avoid eye contact with adults as a sign of respect. If two students from Micronesia are in the same class but of opposite genders, the female will typically defer to the male. Additionally, there are many physical cues that could easily be missed; raising eyebrows means yes while using a single finger to point is rude. We had a lot to learn about our new students!

During my second year, I realized that my two major populations of students had a distinct dislike and disrespect for one another. I asked myself, "How could I bring cohesiveness to this class?" There is little learning when groups hold friction toward one another. With the information I learned through my professional development course about Micronesia's history and from my own research on the history of the Philippines, I created a "Project Comparison" Unit. Similar to Ms. Casad, we discussed and completed a K-W chart (what you know, what you want to learn), but I added an "H" or "How?" category. Students shared how they knew this information. This helped students to learn that their beliefs may not have been "factual" but learned by observation or what they have been told. Throughout that Unit, we explored how similar these two island nations were as well as acknowledged some of the differences. We kept the poster of our discoveries up with maps of their home countries for the entire year, visiting it to add more information when necessary. Although the two cultures rarely merged in the hallways outside of class, within the classroom, they were respectful and more at ease with each other. The atmosphere of learning was established.

As teachers, we have choices. We can choose not to learn about our students and possibly disrupt the environment of learning or we can rise to the challenge and create a classroom of respect and safety, one where learning can thrive. We can learn about our students' cultures in a variety of ways. We can learn through professional development opportunities where we share our ideas and learning with other professionals. We can research on the internet and ponder the information independently. Or we can merge all these learning opportunities by intentionally integrating our students' cultures into the curriculum. With the latter idea, we can learn about our students' ideas we often cannot find on the Internet nor in professional development opportunities.

With new students, even if they are not ELLs, ask yourself and try to find the answers to these questions: Are the students (and their families) in a survival mode? Are their parents looking for work? Struggling to make money? Hungry? Healthy? Why is the family here? Their choice or governmental? What's the history of our country and how is it linked to theirs?

Many families from Micronesia are in the U.S. as part of a compact or agreement. Many students' families are in Hawaii for medical treatment. Students' families, especially if newly arrived, are often in "survival mode" and are truly just trying to adapt to the high costs, healthcare system, and high expectations of our education system.

If any of your students and their families are still in "survival mode," understand that learning and behaving as "expected" may not be possible. Our responsibility as teachers is to teach all of our students. For this to occur, a student needs the best environment possible that enables them to learn. Learn about their situation; why are they in the U.S.? A framework, such as CRP, which delves into the students' cultural assets while also imploring us to reflect on our cultural selves, helps us to consciously build an environment and inclusive curriculum in which all types of learners can progress.

Now that you have read the vignette, suppose Rosa and César's cultural assets clashed as a result of unrest between Honduras and Mexico. What classroom activities could you implement to build cohesion among these subcultures in your class? What key lessons do you want students to learn about tolerance, acceptance, and value of diversity?

## Bibliography

2017 Common Core State Standards Initiative. *Preparing America's Students for College and Career*. Retrieved from: www.corestandards.org/ELA-Literacy/SL/6/1/d

Bair, M. A., Bair, D. E., Madera, C. E., Hipp, S., & Hakim, I. (2010). Faculty emotions: A self-study of teacher educators. *Studying Teacher Education*, 6(12), 95–111.

Banks, J. A., & Banks, C. A. M. (2010). *Multicultural Education: Issues and Perspectives* (7th ed.). Hoboken, NJ: Wiley.

Baron-Cohen, S. (2011). *Zero Degrees of Empathy: A New Theory of Human Cruelty*. London: Allen Lane.

Brown, J., & Doolittle, J. (2008). A cultural, linguistic, and ecological framework for Response to Intervention with English Language Learners. *Teaching Exceptional Children, 40*(5), 66–72.

Echevarria, J., Vogt, M. E., & Short, D. (2007). *Making Content Comprehensible for English Learners: The SIOP Model* (3rd ed.). Boston: Pearson Allyn & Bacon.

Freire, P. (1998). *Teachers as Cultural Workers: Letters to Those Who Dare Teach*. Boulder, CO: Westview Press.

Gay, G. (2010). Acting on beliefs in teacher education for cultural diversity. *Journal of Teacher Education, 61*(1–2), 143–152.

Gay, G., & Kirkland, K. (2003). Developing cultural critical consciousness and self-reflection in preservice teacher education. *Theory into Practice, 42*(3), 181–187.

Giroux, H. A. (1998). Education Incorporated?: Corporate Culture and the Challenge of Public Schooling. *Educational Leadership 56*(2), 12-17.

*Gutierrez*, K., Baquedano-Lopez, P., & Tejada, C. (1999). Rethinking diversity: Hybridity and hybrid language practices in the third space. *Mind, Culture, and Activity, 6*(4), 286–303.

Hawaii Content & Performance Standards III Database, & Hawaii Department of Education. (June 2007). *Department of Education*. Retrieved from: http://165.248.72.55/hcpsv3

Hollins, E. (2008). *Culture in School Learning*. London: Routledge.

Kent, L. (2015). *5 Facts about America's Students*. Cited in Pew Research Center (2015), FactTank News in Numbers. Editorial.

Kübler-Ross, E., & Kessler, D. (2005). *On Grief and Grieving*. New York, NY: Scribner

Lave, J., & Wenger, E. (1991). *Situated Learning: Legitimate Peripheral Participation*. Cambridge: Cambridge University Press.

Lee, C. D. (2007). *Culture, Literacy, & Learning: Taking Bloom in the Midst of the Whirlwind*. New York: Teachers College Press.

Mayer, J. D., & Salovey, P. (1997). *Emotional Development and Emotional Intelligence*. New York: Basic Books.

McLaren, P. (2015). *Life in Schools: An Introduction to Critical Pedagogy in the Foundations of Education* (6th ed.). Boulder, CO: Paradigm.

Nieto, S. (2005). *Why We Teach*. New York: Teachers College Press.

Sato, M., & Lensmire, T. J. (2009). Poverty and Payne: Supporting teachers to work with children of poverty. *Phi Delta Kappan, 90*(5), 365–370.

Van Leeuwen, J. (1994). *Bound For Oregon*. New York: Penguin Publishing.

Waxman, H., Tellez, K., & Walberg, H. J. (2004). Improving teacher quality for English Language Learners: Reports and next-step recommendations from a national invitational conference. In *The LSS Review: The Mid-Atlantic Regional Educational Laboratory*. Philadelphia, PA: Temple University.

# 4

# Collaboration for Resilient Socioemotional Identities

## Introduction

Chapter 4 focuses on ways the identities and language development of Culturally and Linguistically Diverse (CLD) students are affected by specific social/emotional factors. Social and emotional factors are particularly important for CLD and English Language Learner (ELL) students who have faced obstacles in coming to the U.S. from their native country. Similarities in behaviors of CLD/ELL students experiencing Acculturation and students experiencing Emotional Disturbance ED Attention Deficit Hyperactivity Disorder (ADHD) are discussed. The Professional Learning Community (PLC) and their role in identifying struggling students and creating interventions for student success provides Ms. Casad the support she needs when problem-solving for her CLD students' needs. Authors discuss the importance for collaboration with colleagues and parents for ELL students' healthy social and emotional development. Also, readers will see how the acculturation process for CLD/ELL students is necessary for creating resilient self-concepts, esteem, and identities. The Acculturation Quick Screen III (Collier, 2013) is introduced as a tool to help understand students' level of acculturation in a specific public school culture. Rosa and Jun are given the AQS III. The PLC gives intervention strategy suggestions to implement with Rosa and Jun based on their AQS III scores.

With a widespread of discriminatory and racist actions throughout Valley Elementary, the authors explain differences in these two constructs and how they are played out in school settings. Parent involvement and connections are discussed. Authors show how the potential of home visits and personal communication with parents when facilitated correctly can bring in a perspective of students that is often overlooked.

You are also introduced to activities that help with:

- Implementation of intentional social/emotional classroom approaches;
- Development of Emotional Intelligence; i.e., classroom agreements to create an inclusive welcoming community;
- Facilitation of understanding of "difference" i.e., student conversation starters;
- Creating lessons with strong family and community connections; i.e., ways role models overcame obstacles.

There are two activities at the end of the chapter: (1) reflection on issues about race, identity, discrimination, and the strength of understanding others and (2) reflection on ways you have been enculturated in specific forms of emotional expression.

> **Vignette:** During lunch, Ms. Casad received a telephone call from the office learning that Rosa was with the principal because she just got into a fight. During lunch recess Rosa was caught holding a boy down on the ground slapping him until he cried. Ms. Casad wanted to hear Rosa's reason for fighting so she went to the office. Rosa exclaimed, *"A boy was mean and he saying that I didn't speak very much English, and I was stupid because I was Mexican."* Rosa continued, explaining that a certain boy had been bothering her at recess and she didn't like him very much so, *"I wanted to show him that I don't like him saying lies about me! Soy pura Mexicana [I am pure Mexican]. See that is the way that I feel. That I have to be true to myself. I feel real bad when I was with the gringos or white people whatever they are, and that is why I never want to be with the gringos, but I wish at least they could treat us the same like them."*

Ms. Casad and the principal walked out of the room and discussed what action to take. The principal thought it best to warn Rosa that she could be expelled for fighting, therefore he would document this incident as a warning, and call her parents. Ms. Casad agreed, but suggested that she take on responsibility for calling Rosa's mother. She needed to find out more information about Rosa's home life, which may give insight into Rosa's anger. Ms. Casad and Rosa walked back to the classroom. Rosa said that she was sorry for getting in trouble but, *"if that boy teases me again I will slap him even harder next time and I am not afraid of being kicked out of school because I don't like being around those mean kids who are the 'stupid' ones."* This comment worried Ms. Casad, and the idea that Rosa was being singled out because of her Mexican identity. Why were those students teasing Rosa? It worried Ms. Casad that Rosa too was becoming angry toward "gringos" (i.e., white people). She wondered, what was causing all this anger?

## Sociocultural Challenges CLDs Face

The psychological impact of being uprooted, sometimes violently, from one's homeland certainly has an effect on children's academic learning, with peers at school, and interactions with educators (Lawrence-Brown & Sapon-Shevin, 2014). Most Culturally and Linguistically Diverse (CLD) students face many sociocultural challenges, which can be anxiety-provoking and promote culture shock (Collier, 1989, 2013). Herrera and Murry (2011) explain that CLD students must adjust to a new country, city, or neighborhood, adapt to a new education system, and cope with the nuances of school culture. Additionally, they can also experience psychosocial challenges such as ambiguity, anxiety, prejudice, discrimination, and sometimes racism (see Table 4.1).

One term that encompasses the process students experience when facing these obstacles is *acculturation.* In this chapter, you are introduced to a tool, Acculturation Quick Screen, which "measures" Rosa's and Jun's acculturation behaviors. Understanding behavioral responses indicating acculturation is imperative, as these behaviors can appear similar to those associated with Emotional Disturbance and/or Attention Deficit Hyperactivity Disorder. Readers will also view ways Ms. Casad collaborates with (1) her PLC,

**Table 4.1** Sociocultural Challenges ELLs Face

| External Factors | Internal Factors |
| --- | --- |
| ◆ Sociopolitical environment: immigration policies and residency demands<br>◆ Must adjust to a new country, city, or neighborhood<br>◆ Must adapt to a new education system and cope with the nuances of school culture<br>◆ Intergroup and intragroup tensions<br>◆ Economic and employment stability<br>◆ Access to healthcare<br>◆ Prejudice, discrimination, and xenophobia | ◆ Ambiguity and anxiety<br>◆ Homesickness<br>◆ Anger and depression<br>◆ Self-esteem and identity formation<br>◆ Forming positive interpersonal relationships<br>◆ Creating support network<br>◆ Finding motivation/agency |

Source: Adapted from Herrera & Murry (2011)

(2) the school psychologist, (3) the ELD teacher, and (4) CLD parents to help develop students' healthy social and emotional development, necessary for strong self-esteem and identities.

Stephen Krashen's (1982) second-language acquisition theory, *the affective filter hypothesis* explains how psychosocial challenges may inhibit or increase CLD students' classroom performance. He argues that CLDs with low anxiety, high motivation, strong self-confidence, and positive self-image are more resilient to acquire a new language. However, high anxiety, low motivation, and low self-esteem can raise students' affective filter, thus slowing language acquisition. We will see how Ms. Casad and her supportive community navigate ways to lower Rosa's *affective filter.*

## Supportive Communities

At the next Professional Learning Community (PLC) meeting, Ms. Casad brought the results from implementing Culturally Responsive Instruction (see Chapter 3) and news of the altercation with Rosa. The PLC team consisted of the other two fourth grade teachers, the Response to Intervention (RTI) interventionist, and the ELD teacher. Ms. Casad felt supported by her PLC team, who were a consistent network by meeting weekly to help support student success. They often discussed systemic structures to support all fourth graders, but the team's main focus was to analyze assessment data in order to identify struggling individuals and create interventions for success. Often, interventions were focused on ways to raise reading fluency scores or comprehension levels, but occasionally the team discussed and implemented socioemotional support.

The PLC members agreed that there was a school-wide problem of bullying. They agreed this problem of bullying was endemic to the school, a microcosm of the U.S., and reflected in many classrooms. Bullying is a phenomenon that acts as an umbrella for discrimination and racism. It is often easier for a "bully" to accept oneself as a bully than one who discriminates. Discrimination specifically refers to "behavior that denies equal treatment to people because of their membership in some group" (Herbst, 1997, p. 185). Discrimination involves behavior. Racism is a form of discrimination entirely based on race. Racism means supporting or being actively invested in the continuation of a racial hierarchy in which one's own group dominates. According to Cole (2017), racism refers to a variety of practices, beliefs, social relations, and phenomena that work to reproduce a racial hierarchy and social structure that yield superiority, power, and privilege for some, and discrimination and oppression for others. Racism exists when ideas and assumptions about racial categories are used to justify and reproduce a racial hierarchy and racially structured society that unjustly limits access to resources, rights, and privileges on the basis of race. Contrary to a dictionary definition, racism, as defined based on social science research and theory, is about much more than race-based prejudice; it exists when an imbalance in power and social status is generated by how we understand and act upon race.

The way that Rosa was being treated by the boy who was teasing her and calling her "stupid" because she was Mexican was a form of discriminatory and prejudice behavior, not necessarily racism. It could be considered an act of "racial prejudice," but in this case, it was not based solely on "race," but on ethnic difference. Therefore, it is accurate to say the school has more of a discriminatory or prejudice problem, than a racism problem. These discriminatory and prejudicial behaviors usually stem from a learned behavior or due to a misunderstanding of those who look, speak, dress, and act differently than ourselves. Cole (2017) suggested that prejudice

> is a pre-judgment that one makes of another that is not rooted in their own experience. Some prejudices are positive while others are negative. Some are racial in nature, and have racist outcomes, but not all forms of prejudice do, and this is why it's important to understand the difference between prejudice and racism.
>
> (p. 1)

For more on these constructs see www.thoughtco.com/sociology-to-counter-claims-of-reverse-racism-3026067.

Mrs. Tellez (ELD teacher) explained that one's own *enculturation process* contributed to discrimination against others. Through the *enculturation process*,

> we are gradually initiated into our home or native cultures, and almost without knowing it, we develop a sense of group identity that forms our set of values, guides our beliefs, patterns our actions, and channels our expectations. *Enculturation* gives us an ethnocentric view of the validity of our own social and cultural ways, leading us to believe our ways are better than others.
>
> (Herrera & Murry, 2011, p. 18)

Ms. Casad reflected on her own *enculturation process*, which included the ethnocentric view that people are supposed to behave in a calm, restrained manner. She was raised in a home in which emotions were not expressed. Now as an adult, she did not feel comfortable to express "negative" emotions,

**Table 4.2** Socioemotional Classroom Approaches

| | |
|---|---|
| ◆ Student check-in with Emotion list<br>◆ Reflection & journaling<br>◆ Student choice & voice<br>◆ Activities that facilitate understanding of "difference" & empathy (e.g., student conversation starters, Same & Different)<br>◆ Write classroom book, "About Us"<br>◆ Restorative Circles for social justice<br>◆ Classroom meetings w/ agreements for respect | ◆ Clear expectations<br>◆ Positive, direct feedback<br>◆ Kindness Week<br>◆ Ignore undesired behaviors<br>◆ Reward positive behavior with Kindness cards<br>◆ See classmates as "team members," working together to earn rewards<br>◆ Lessons with focus on resilience (e.g., ways role models overcome obstacles) |

but "happy" emotions were good. She uncovered her assumption that emotional suppression was superior to emotional expression, including negative outbursts of anger and frustration. Ms. Casad discovered her own bias that it was "bad" to act out, even in one's own defense, which may impact her relationship with Rosa, whose beliefs and behaviors are in contrast with her own (see Chapter 1 Reflection Activity #2 for follow-up reflection).

The PLC team acknowledged that the Valley Elementary School culture needed systemic intensive support; thus they would implement intentional socioemotional classroom approaches seeking to develop students' Emotional Intelligence, including: (1) classroom agreements to create an inclusive welcoming community, (2) activities that facilitate understanding of "difference" (e.g., student conversation starters, Same and Different Game), (3) writing individual stories that will result in classroom book "About Us," (4) lessons with strong family and community connections (e.g., ways role models overcame obstacles), (5) assigning peer mentors, and (6) Positive Behavior Support (PBIS) with awarding Kindness cards (see Table 4.2).

## Create an Inclusive Welcoming Environment

Lawrence-Brown and Sapon-Shevin (2014, p. 8) offered two principles for inclusive classroom communities:

1. Principle #1 All children are valuable members of classroom and school communities, with differing voices, strengths, abilities, and contributions. Inclusive communities embrace and expand children's sociocultural repertoires while also dealing with controversy and conflict in creative and constructive ways.
2. Principle #2 Students learn in many different ways. In order for students to be successful, educators must be flexible in their

approaches, drawing from a repertoire of methodologies that value differentiation and support individualization.

Students in Ms. Casad's class created an inclusive class motto, classroom agreements, and then signed a pledge to follow them. They brainstormed, discussed, and agreed on the motto, "We are all the same, we are all different." Some agreements included (1) show kindness in words and actions; (2) respect others' space, bodies, and property; and (3) ask someone to explain more if you do not understand. These agreements were signed and posted on the wall. Fourth grade teachers kicked off the week with "Kindness Week." All week, students were encouraged to be extra kind to those around them, write their actions on a note card, and place them in the "Kindness box." Ms. Casad recorded the events that Rosa wrote on the Kindness cards (see Table 4.3).

Note cards were selected from the box, and students had chances to win a T-shirt in school colors with the motto, "Kind is the new Cool." Staff members also wore the shirts all week as reminders for positive actions. In art class, students submitted designs to go on a school wall as a mural. "Positive school behaviors are a side effect of improved quality of life" (Lawrence-Brown & Sapon-Shevin, 2014, p. 161). The week appeared successful, as school culture is the foundation for students' safety. The base of Maslow's hierarchy of needs is safety, which is a prerequisite for academic learning (McLeod, 2007, 2016). As an educator attempting to be as holistic as possible, Ms. Casad believed that education is about creating outstanding citizens and improving their quality of life.

**Table 4.3** Rosa's Kindness Cards

| EVENT | Date | Time/context |
|---|---|---|
| Rosa got off the bus quietly and walked to class respectfully. | 10/20 | Before school |
| When asked by teacher, Rosa agreed immediately and showed a new student where the bathroom was. | 10/21 | Lunch recess |
| When asked if Rosa could help student read a sentence aloud, she happily agreed and began helping her. Became leader in asking if student wanted to take turns reading. | 10/27 | Book Circle |
| Rosa showed patience while waiting in line to play tether ball. | 11/2 | Morning recess |

She also believed that she "owed students a duty to take reasonable care to protect them from foreseeable risk of injury" (Rowling, 2003, p. 33). She then realized she did not have training to deal with students' physical aggression, and needed to collaborate with experts who could help facilitate conflict-resolution strategies.

## Conflict-Resolution Strategies

The PLC team agreed that the issue of discrimination and prejudice were part of the bullying that had taken place and students' needed more intensive interventions from a specialist. One teacher suggested implementing *Restorative Circles*, a process in which those affected by an injustice have an opportunity to discuss how they have been harmed by the injustice, and to decide what should be done to repair the harm (Stinchcomb, Bazemore, & Riestenberg, 2007). This process follows the premise that conversations with those who have been hurt, and with those who have inflicted the harm, are central in creating the outcome. They agreed this would be productive, and would look into ways other schools had implemented Restorative Circles. The school psychologist, Mrs. Mola, agreed to lead fourth grade students in five activities on ways to resolve conflicts based on Denborough's (2014) work: (1) collective conversations; (2) listening as a witness; (3) writing a letter to the problem; (4) drawing a picture of your favorite safe place, and a picture of people who support you, and then writing a message to them; and (5) writing a letter to someone who is facing a similar problem as you.

### Collective Conversations

Denborough (2014) describes the process of *collective conversations* as (1) naming the problem, (2) externalizing the problem, (3) interviewing the problem, and (4) writing a letter to the problem. After the three classes of fourth grade students sat down in the cafeteria, Mrs. Mola began facilitating activities. She told a story about herself as a young girl and a situation when she teased a friend for not knowing an answer, and the resulting emotions of guilt and sadness. She asked the children to tell their neighbor why they thought Mrs. Mola had done this. Students responded with, "You wanted to stand out as being smart!"

"Exactly!!" she exclaimed. "The main reason people put others down is that they want to look better than someone else, often because they have low self-esteem and need to feel power over others. This is how a person discriminates against someone." She then told students to see the problem "outside" of individuals (i.e., externalize), as the problem does not belong to the person who is being discriminated against; it is a product of society's thoughts of fear of someone else, and lack of trust. Discrimination is what this fear is based on. Acts of "discrimination" are when someone feels threatened by others who do not look or act the same as them, so they enact a behavior that shows their power over them, which puts that person down. She then led an activity to "interview discrimination," in an effort to understand why people feel threatened by someone else and say mean things to them. Half of the students created questions to ask the personified act of discrimination, and the other half thought up answers. The students then were assigned to "write a letter to the problem" (Denborough, 2014, p. 43).

### Listening as a Witness

Mrs. Mola then handed out lists of emotions (see Appendix B), and asked students to find a partner. The directions were for one person to think of an event when someone was mean to her/him. That person then chose two–three emotions (on list) that expressed how s/he felt, and shared with the partner. The student must use "I statements," so blaming does not occur. The other partner "listened as a witness" (Denborough, 2014, p. 70), listening to define the problem, and describe how the person reacted. When s/he was finished, the listener reflected back the person's strengths in the event (Denborough, 2014). These resiliency factors would become part of student stories, and compiled into a class book, "About Us." Ms. Casad had also used the list of emotions in the Oregon Trail lesson when seeking to connect the pioneers' feeling of leaving home to students' feelings of loss (see Chapter 3).

### Resilience

The next activity was for students to draw a picture of their favorite place where they felt safe, and a picture of people who supported them (Denborough, 2014, p. 123). Next, Mrs. Mola asked students to write a message to them (Denborough, 2014, p. 137). Rosa drew a picture of her church where her mother, father, brothers, sisters, and grandfather stood. She wrote, "thank you for loving me. I want to be like you!" César drew a picture of his mother, father, sisters, dog, and grandmother in their house in Honduras, and wrote "Mis yuu." Trent drew a soccer field with him and his family watching him play, and wrote "I just want us all to stay together." Jun drew a picture of many people in a tall building. When asked who they were, Jun smiled and nodded. He wrote, "Hello!" many places on the picture. The last activity was for students to write a letter to someone who was facing a similar problem (Denborough, 2014, p. 43). Rosa wrote a letter to her brother, encouraging him to "be strong and nice."

## Activities That Facilitate Understanding of "Difference"

Ms. Casad walked around the gymnasium listening to student conversations during the conflict-resolution activities, thereby witnessing peer relationships strengthen. One skill in relationship-building is possessing Emotional Intelligence, defined as the ability to perceive and express emotions, to understand and use them, and to manage emotions to foster personal growth (Mayer & Salovey, 1997). She continued giving out Kindness cards, and implemented three additional activities to strengthen her classroom community and Emotional Intelligence: (1) conversation starters, (2) "About Us" class book, and (3) Same and Different Game. Ms. Casad located the "conversation starters" prompts in her culturally responsive pedagogy (CRP) training manual (see Table 4.4), made copies, and cut the prompts into strips.

She placed the strips into an empty coffee can and situated the cans in the center of each table group cluster. She explained that throughout the day students would pull one strip out to start a conversation. The strips were similar to questions on the About Me survey (see Chapter 2 Table 2.5), but now students were able to talk and ask questions about each other. She made copies of students' About Me surveys, and created a class book titled "About Us." Students were chosen each day to be "star of the day," and presented her/his cultural assets to the class. While listening, the other students filled out the "Same and Different Game" (see Table 4.5), noting similarities and differences with peers, and additional questions to ask them later.

**Table 4.4** Conversation Starters

| |
|---|
| What is a favorite tradition in your family? |
| What object best describes your family? |
| Why do you have the name you have? What is the meaning? |
| What kind of art or music do you like? Why? |
| How would you describe your culture to those who do not know you? |
| Name a family member you admire and describe why. |
| Discuss ways your people in your cultural group need to be better understood. |
| What languages do you speak? What is the advantage of knowing another language? |

Source: Adapted from Saifer, Edwards, Ellis, Ko, & Stuczynski (2005)

**Table 4.5** Same and Different

| _____ Is the SAME as me in that we both _____ _____ | _____ Is different than me in that _____ _____ and I _____ _____ | I want to ask _____ more about _____ _____ _____ |
|---|---|---|

## Effects of Acculturation

At the next PLC meeting, Ms. Casad reported that the socioemotional activities seemed to be going well, but it was too soon to measure the effectiveness of reducing Rosa's physical outbursts. Rosa did not seem to have any friends. Mrs. Tellez wondered if Rosa's behaviors were a result of the acculturation process (for factors to consider in assessing acculturation needs, see Table 4.6). She explained that when a student moves away from his/her home to a new country, s/he faces a period of adjustment, which may manifest in a variety of ways including integration, assimilation, rejection, or deculturation (Padilla, 1980; Collier, 1989; Collier, 2013). Rosa's family fled Mexico to escape political violence, and is facing obstacles of acculturative stress, anxiety, homesickness, and separation from support networks that are now affecting the development of positive interpersonal relationships. After leaving Mexico and entering the United States, Rosa attends a U.S. school in an English-only classroom (i.e., without formal native-language support), thus experiencing *assimilation* into American beliefs and practices. She is also experiencing *integration* by attempting to "fit in" with peers by speaking English and adopting some U.S. values and behaviors, while at the same time, retaining her native language. Collier (2013) describes *rejection* as an intentional choice and action by a person to adhere to only one pattern of behavior and language. Rosa may reject the new culture and language, while still using only her home language, practicing only her traditional way of life with absolutely no attempt at integration. In contrast, a person may intentionally cut themselves off from all contact with their heritage and reject all use of the language and culture, trying to assimilate to the new environment by rejecting anything that is not part of the new situation or language. One example of Rosa rejecting some of the U.S. culture is her stating, "*Soy pura Mexicana [I am pure Mexican]. See that is the way that I feel. That I have to be true to myself. I feel real bad when I was with the gringos or white people whatever they*

**Table 4.6** Assessing Acculturation

| **Questions to Consider in Assessing Acculturation Needs** |
| --- |
| Previous experience with other cultures |
| Involvement with people from other cultures |
| Compatibility of culture 1 and 2 |
| Attitude towards 1 and 2 |
| Relationships with members of culture 1 and 2 |
| Level of cultural values support within native culture |
| Preference to maintain native culture |

*are, and that is why I never want to be with the gringos, but I wish at least they could treat us the same like them."*

According to Berry (1980), *deculturation* results when members of nondominant cultures (i.e., minority) become alienated from the dominant culture (U.S. norms), and from their own minority group. A consequence of deculturation is increased stress and psychopathology for the individuals involved. We do not know if Rosa is experiencing deculturation or not, because we do not know how the members of her ethnic minority group believe or act towards her or her family (e.g., accept or reject). If Rosa's brother was cut off from supportive community interactions within his home community, and not given assistance to transition into effective participation (in new language and culture), his choice of gang affiliation could be the result of deculturation (Collier, 1987, 2013).

Although Rosa has been in the U.S. three years, she can still experience acculturative stress that may manifest by deviant behavior, psychosomatic symptoms, and feelings of marginality (Berry, 1980, as cited in Collier, 1987). Symptoms of acculturative stress include (1) distractibility, (2) response fatigue, (3) withdrawal, (4) silence or not responding, (5) code-switching, and (6) confusion in locus of control. This type of stress is complex, in that the side effects look similar to Emotional Behavioral Disabilities, and sometimes are used to place children in special education classes (Hoover, 2004; Collier, 1987). (See Table 4.7.) Youth with emotional/behavioral disorders may (1) be socially withdrawn; (2) be aggressive towards others; (3) be failing academically; (4) not be socially popular; (5) not have friends, but if they do, their friends may be deviant, antisocial, or misfits; (6) arouse negative feelings and induce

**Table 4.7** Characteristics of Acculturation and Emotional Disturbance

| Acculturation | Emotional Disturbance |
|---|---|
| Heightened anxiety;<br>Confusion in locus of control;<br>Withdrawal;<br>Silence, unresponsiveness;<br>Response fatigue;<br>Code-switching;<br>Distractibility;<br>Resistance to change;<br>Disorientation;<br>Stress-related behaviors;<br>Post-traumatic responses;<br>Survival guilt. | Socially withdrawn;<br>Aggressive towards others;<br>Failing academically;<br>Not socially popular or leaders;<br>Not have friends, but if they do, their friends may be deviant, antisocial, or misfits;<br>Arouse negative feelings and induce negative behavior in others (including teachers);<br>Have problems measuring emotions and behavior. |
| Collier (1989), 1987, 2013) | IDEA (2004); DSMV |

negative behavior in others (including teachers); and (7) have problems measuring emotions and behavior.

## Rosa's AQS

Mrs. Tellez introduced the Acculturation Quick Screen (AQS III, Collier, 2013), a tool to help understand students' level of acculturation in a specific public school culture. This tool may help predict students' levels of integration within the school, and provide suggested interventions to address levels of acculturation (Collier, 2013). With Ms. Casad, they began filling out the form together. On Rosa's Native Language Proficiency Exam (Woodcock-Muñoz Spanish Language Assessment), she scored all 3s, (Intermediate level—see Table 2.3, Chapter 2), which indicates she is fairly proficient in speaking and understanding Spanish. On the ELPA (English Language Proficiency exam) given in second grade, Rosa scored level 2, in third grade she received a score of 3, and in fourth grade she scored 3.5 (Intermediate level). She had similar scores in both languages, a true balanced bilingual! (See Table 4.8.)

Ms. Casad scanned Rosa's report cards and noticed her grades were average. A second grade teacher, wrote that Rosa was *impulsive and aggressive towards other students*. Rosa's behavior had been a challenge since she arrived in the U.S.! Rosa's AQS III overall score of 24 (see Appendix C) is in the lower score range (23–29) for being *in transition*. Collier (2013, pp. 20–21) explains that students in transition are in:

> the midst of cross-cultural adaptation and second language acquisition. They are still experiencing some culture shock and acculturative stress. Assistance with the acculturative process in the form of conventional bilingual and cross-cultural instructional techniques and assessment procedures should work well with her.
>
> Interventions appropriate for students in transition include: sheltered instruction with cross-cultural content, peer tutors and cooperative

**Table 4.8** Language Proficiency Scores

|  | Grade 2 | Grade 3 | Grade 4 |
| --- | --- | --- | --- |
| Rosa—English | 2 | 3 | 3.5 |
| Rosa—Spanish | 3 |  |  |
| Jun—English | N/A | 2.5 | 3 |
| Jun—Mandarin | N/A | 1 |  |

learning strategies, access to translation in content areas, cross-cultural communication and instructional strategies, cognitive learning strategies, and authentic assessment. She will benefit from continuing to participate in diverse community activities and school activities that strengthen her connection to her ethnic and linguistic heritage.

The AQS results show that Rosa was adapting to her surroundings as expected, and her language development was on track. Ms. Casad was also confident in providing some of the suggested strategies (1) sheltered instruction with cross-cultural content, (2) access to translation in content areas, and (3) school activities that strengthen her connection to her ethnic and linguistic heritage. She would talk to Rosa's mother to investigate factors contributing to Rosa's aggressive behavior.

## Parents as Partners

It is critical for educators to "do what is best for students," regardless what the challenges might be. We must not forget why we are doing what we do, and that listening to other perspectives and finding new resources is often needed to do what is best for our students. Teachers are often too busy or reluctant to seek out new resources concerning their immediate classroom concerns, and tend to tackle them on their own. One major resource that is often overlooked is the parents or the family of our students. We should not forget that most parents want what is "best" for their child too. Some parents may not have a full command of English or a complete understanding of how the education system works in the United States, but are typically very supportive of what is best for their children. They may also be a viable resource and a wealth of information for many issues in your classroom. Even if you do not agree with parents' expectations for their child, as a teacher you are obligated to listen to them, and may learn so much! Regardless of the education level of parents, communication and collaboration are key for the child's success in school. We also hope to avoid power struggles over what is *believed* to be best for the child without evidence or research. Lee (n.d.) from the Parent Services Project suggests:

When language barriers exist, it is common to feel frustrated, powerless or alienated. Some parents equate lack of recognition for their language as a lack of respect for their culture. Although unintended, parents may feel rejected and may isolate themselves. Parents who do not speak English often feel they cannot help their child because they cannot understand. Out of respect for the teacher, they may nod affirmatively to comments without true understanding. Others may apologize that their English is "not good" and decline to participate in school functions or to take leadership roles.

(p. 1)

## Parents and Culture

Students and families from culturally diverse groups may hold different beliefs about the role of parents in education. Artiles and Ortiz (2002) describe parents whose worldviews differ from American mainstream views may experience cultural discomfort when participating in their children's education. Traditional definitions of "parent" need to be broadened to include extended family to reflect the family's kinship system. For some students, an individual other than the parent (who has primary child-rearing responsibilities) may be able to provide more detailed information about the child than the parent. Roles for decision-making may be defined by cultural norms based on gender, age, or kinship. Thus, the individual attending a school meeting may be reluctant to make any decisions without first consulting other family members. The expectation that parents have the right to disagree with school personnel may conflict with the cultural belief that group harmony (i.e., collectivism) takes priority over individualized rights (see Chapter 1, Table 1.2). This belief may lead some parents to be silent during meetings or even give consent despite their concerns.

## Families as Resources

Ms. Casad wanted to find out more about Jun and Rosa from their parents. Maybe they also had concerns. Earlier in the school year, Ms. Casad called Rosa and Jun's home (with an interpreter) and learned that Rosa's mother, Mrs. Ramirez, spoke some English and that Jun's parents both spoke Mandarin. Although the first contact home was to welcome Rosa and Jun into her classroom and to introduce herself, she now wanted to delve deeper into each of their lives within the family.

## Contacting Rosa's Mother

Ms. Casad said she felt more comfortable if Mrs. Tellez accompanied her to talk to Rosa's mother (Mrs. Ramirez) for support and to translate if needed. Mrs. Tellez called Mrs. Ramirez during her work break and arranged a time when they could all meet in person to discuss Rosa. They decided to meet at the nearest city park after her work day. Sometimes CLD parents can be apprehensive to go into a school building, depending on their own schooling experiences, or those with government (i.e., official) associations, depending on their residency status.

Ms. Casad began telling Mrs. Ramirez about how smart Rosa is, how well she is doing academically, her English is getting stronger every day, she is eager to learn, and bright and full of energy. Mrs. Ramirez thanked Ms. Casad for her comments, and expressed her gratitude for being in the U.S. She then described challenges her family had faced in coming to the U.S., and Rosa's resulting anger. Ms. Casad told her about Rosa's angry outbursts in class, especially when she does not get her way. She then broached the subject of the fight Rosa was in at lunch recess. Mrs. Ramirez did not seem shocked, but showed concern, and expressed interest in finding ways to help Rosa be successful.

*Ms. Casad:*     Does Rosa ever ignore you when you are talking to her or trying to help her? If she does, what do you usually do about that?

*Mrs. Ramirez:*     We argue about how she needs to listen to me because I am her mother, but it usually ends up that we just walk away and stay angry with each other for a while, and I ask God for help. I usually give up arguing with her. It takes a lot of energy to fight with her.

*Ms. Casad:*     We have had Rosa take on some responsibility that showed us we could rely on her with tasks like taking notes to the office, or helping other students with their work. She shows an eagerness to help, but gets frustrated easily. Do you give her "important" tasks to do by herself? How does she react?

*Mrs. Ramirez:*     It depends on her mood that day, sometimes she is great about doing things by herself or making sure her brothers are doing their fair share. She likes taking charge and is good at it, but sometimes if she is in a bad mood, you can't get her to do anything.

*Ms. Casad:*     Does Rosa get along well with her siblings?

*Mrs. Ramirez:*     Rosa is the youngest of three children, she has two brothers. Rosa's father and I are separated, and she has only seen him once since we arrived here. Rosa lives with me and her two brothers. One brother is doing well, and one is not. She fights a lot with them. I just think that is because she is still young. I am not concerned about that at all. I was like that with my brothers.

| | |
|---|---|
| *Ms. Casad:* | Do you have any suggestions that we might try with Rosa so she can keep doing well with her schoolwork and behavior? |
| *Mrs. Ramirez:* | Just do what you think is best. She is smart enough to figure it out. She is a good kid. I also think it is the school's job to educate Rosa, not mine, I can't do that, but will take care of her at home. |

After the meeting Mrs. Tellez and Ms. Casad discussed how they thought the visit went well overall. Ms. Casad thought Mrs. Ramirez was doing the best she could raising her kids and working full time, but thought she was not helping Rosa with her anger or schooling. Ms. Casad felt like it was up to her to "fix" Rosa's behavior, but at least Mrs. Ramirez seemed to understand and share her concerns. Mrs. Tellez thought Rosa's mother was very "open" about sharing information with them. She got the impression that Mrs. Ramirez was happy to talk with them, and had given them important information. For starters, knowing that Rosa acts similarly at home when taking on responsibilities could empower her to take on leadership roles, which may help her feel needed, and give her a sense of belonging. It may also help her stay on task and forget about her anger. She told Ms. Casad, "Remember how happy Rosa is when you give her specific duties?" Once Mrs. Tellez explained what she took from the meeting, Ms. Casad realized that now she had a better idea of what Rosa might need in the classroom.

Home visits can be very productive when critically looking at the outcome of the visit. If we only focus on one or two things in a discussion with parents, then we often miss more than we realize. It is always good to have a colleague with you during a home visit for several reasons: (1) Mrs. Tellez provided needed translation, and by speaking Spanish, put Mrs. Ramirez at ease showing culturally appropriate respect. Due to lack of exposure with people from Mexican cultures, Ms. Casad may not be familiar with culturally appropriate ways of creating relationships and expressing care for Rosa; (2) For reasons of safety, it is a good idea to have another adult with you when making a home visit or meeting with a student's family member; (3) Another person can serve as a witness to what takes place. Mrs. Tellez served as a witness, and because she is also CLD; and (4) she provided another perspective about the meeting. Home visits can:

◆ Put parents at ease by staying in the comfort of their own home.
◆ Help build a working relationship with the parent and school.
◆ Help teachers learn more about their students to provide effective support structures.
◆ Encourage parents to become more involved in their child's education.

Home visits may not be the best method of gathering information about the child's home life, and can also turn out detrimental. Remember that you are a "professional" and you are the "educator" who is expected to know what is best for their child when it comes to academics. Some general suggestions for home visits and family meetings are as follows: (1) show respect and stay professional at all times regardless of how the discussion goes, (2) remember why you are there, for the child's best interest, and (3) try not to talk "above" the family members or use vocabulary that is beyond their grasp, which can alienate them and create feelings of inadequacy or ignorance about their child's schooling. When needing to get a better understanding of your student's home life, and a sense of what role parents play in their education, home visits are often very helpful (if parents feel comfortable with educators coming into their home). Often, parents and students may feel embarrassed of their home, and feel they may be judged negatively, depending on their own educational experiences (Gay, personal communication, May 12, 2016). Other options include: telephone calls, home surveys, or meeting at a neutral place; such as a park, sporting event, local community event, or public library.

## Contacting Jun's Parents

The PLC team suggested to continue gathering data on Jun to see if his classroom performance showed patterns of behaviors, or academic concerns, other than language. They scanned his report card from third grade and saw that Jun had poor grades due to completing little work. This made sense because it was his first year in the U.S. and his language acquisition level was low. Ms. Casad now wondered if Jun had received academic work at his language and ability level (i.e., comprehensible input, Krashen, 1982), which would influence his ability to stay on task and complete work.

Ms. Casad decided to call Jun's parents (Mr. and Mrs. He) instead of making a home visit. Mrs. Tellez and the district-appointed Mandarin interpreter (Mrs. Zhang) would all be in the conversation via telephone speaker. Ms. Casad began the phone conversation by explaining that Jun enjoys making the class laugh, is well liked in school, writes his letters neatly, and has many math skills.

*Mr. He:* Jun has always loved numbers. My son is very good about cleaning up his room and helping his mom with chores in the kitchen, but not strong in academics. Jun had poor grades in China and his teachers there also noted Jun's inattention.

Ms. Casad mentioned that Jun leaves his seat when expected to sit, doesn't follow through on instructions and often fails to finish work.

| | |
|---|---|
| *Mrs. He:* | Do you think Jun should have repeated third grade? |
| *Ms. Casad:* | I do not support students repeating grades or holding them back. It is more important for teachers to find out how each student learns best. Jun has unique needs that we want to meet before too much time passes by. |
| *Mr. He:* | We are hoping that Jun gets what he needs in the U.S., more than he received in China. |
| *Ms. Casad:* | Can you expand more on how Jun acted in school in China? |
| *Mr. He:* | We had to keep up with the school's expectations and authorities, so we did not learn much about Jun's social skills. We knew he has some odd behaviors but there weren't many options there as I understand there might be here. What do you think is going to work for Jun this year in your classroom, Ms. Casad? |
| *Ms. Casad:* | We are still trying to find out Jun's strengths and interests are, then we can help him succeed. Can you tell me more about his home life? |
| *Mrs. He:* | Jun has one older sister and one older brother. They have many friends. They call and text each other constantly. Does Jun have any friends at your school? |
| *Ms. Casad:* | Jun seems to have one friend in my class. They do not speak often, but they like to follow each other around and sit next to each other. Did Jun have friends in China? |
| *Mr. He:* | Not really, Jun has almost always preferred to be on his own. Another thing I am concerned about is it seems that Jun is doing worse the older he gets. |
| *Ms. Casad:* | The first year a student comes to the U.S., the teacher often grades him based on effort. Since Jun did not speak for several months in third grade, his marks were low. However, he did very well in spelling. I believe what we are seeing is that the older Jun gets, the more rigorous the work is becoming, so his challenges get bigger. |
| *Mrs. He:* | I should have kept him back in school. If his English is better, he would have higher grades. |
| *Ms. Casad:* | I'm not sure if keeping Jun in the same class would change anything. I think eventually, he would continue struggling. We believe that Jun's academic struggle may be more than just his language development. |

After a long pause, Mrs. He responded.

| | |
|---|---|
| *Mrs. He:* | I often ask Jun to help me understand letters we get in the mail. He reads aloud to me better than his sister sometimes, but when I ask him to translate, he can't tell me what he just read. So, I rely on his sister to read and translate for me. |

Ms. Casad asked why Jun did not attend the Chinese school his sister did and why they think he never really learned Mandarin.

*Mr. He:* Jun is a happy boy and we felt putting more pressure on him to study Chinese was not helping. We thought if he learned English while he is still young it will be more useful for him than Mandarin.

Ms. Casad explained that although learning English is very important, keeping his native language up is just as important. She then explained how she was helping him in class with English (word banks, picture clues, graphic organizers), but he did not seem to use them. Mrs. Tellez also explained to them about the language acquisition stages and ways she helped him in ELD class. Mrs. Tellez and Ms. Casad both agreed that Jun showed attention to his classmates in small groups. But in whole-class instruction, he often stood up and walked around.

*Mr. He:* When he was a young boy, maybe 5 years old, we did not know what to do with Jun's short attention and energy. So, we gave him a karate video game. He loved it. He could play for hours. After we made him stop the playing the game, he began punching and kicking the air, moves we believe he had learned from the game. Now we do not know how to make him stop.

Ms. Casad thanked them for sharing so much with her, and asked if they had any more to share. Jun's parents said no, but they were very grateful for Ms. Casad's time and her concerns about their son. They expressed her call was a great honor for them.

Ms. Casad thought the telephone conversation went well with Jun's parents. She could tell that the parents knew about and accepted Jun's peculiar behaviors. It seemed they were concerned and wanted the best for Jun. They expected the U.S. school system to provide better opportunities for their son than in China, and Ms. Casad felt confident she could do that. She knew Jun was a challenge, but felt up to the challenge. She also felt that his parents were grateful for her reaching out to them. Ms. Casad now saw a bigger picture in getting Jun what he needed. She would now team up with Mrs. Tellez and gather more information by revisiting his cumulative file data and completing the AQS III to help design more appropriate instruction for Jun.

## Jun's AQS

Ms. Casad and Mrs. Tellez filled out the AQS III for Jun, and located his native-language proficiency (NLP) assessment results (given in his home language, Mandarin), in which all scores were 1s (see Appendix D). Mrs. Tellez said, "Typically, a student scores 3s if he can respond to simple prompts such as, "Tell me how to get from here to the library, or describe a member of your family." Comments on the assessments indicated that Jun did not answer in complete sentences. So, he can listen and understand Mandarin (i.e., receptive language), but similar to his English skills, he is challenged at responding (i.e., expressive language). If a child does not have a foundation or background of their home language, that can often affect their learning a new language (Genesee, Paradis, & Crago, 2010; see Table 4.8).

Jun's native-language development is much different than Rosa's native-language development. Research in language development for second-language learners shows that it is best to use the child's native language as a foundation to develop the target language (Krashen, 1982; Crawford, 1995; Cummins, 1984, 1991, 1994). When non-English speaking students are not proficient (i.e., thinking, listening, speaking, reading, writing) in their native language, English language acquisition is often slower to develop than for ELLs who are proficient in their native language. Therefore, this slow progress can often indicate more going on than just language development (i.e., language disorder). Could this be the case for Jun?

## AQS Results and Interventions

Mrs. Tellez explained Jun's score of 20, reading from the AQS Manual: the 15–22 score range is titled *less acculturated* (see Appendix E). This category means that Jun may exhibit high levels of anxiety, and possibly depression due to the intensity of the adjustment he is facing. Care should be used at this stage since it can be accompanied by a variety of unexpected emotional reactions (see Table 4.7). Ms. Casad sat back and remarked, "Poor Jun! This sounds so much like him; easily distracted and not speaking much. I would have thought this was behavioral for sure, not acculturation! He should be receiving assistance not only with the acculturation process, but also with stress reduction and positive coping methods. Maybe he is behaving this way and struggling academically because of 'culture shock.' What have previous teachers done to help him acculturate or adapt to the U.S.? Maybe he is walking around punching and kicking the air because he's stressed out? Maybe he cannot learn because he still does not feel safe!"

Ms. Tellez nodded and said, "Your strategy of providing pictures and graphic organizers is great, and I agree that using a dictionary or translator tool may only frustrate him since he does not know how to read Mandarin characters. You have done a great job ruling out translations and bilingual materials since we know you tried to translate documents. When you tried rewarding Jun for positive behavior (i.e., Kindness card), he did not respond as most students needing behavioral support do." They also noted in his cumulative file a copy of his passport. They discovered that his family was in the U.S. due to political asylum. With curiosity, they researched online some reasons families from China were granted asylum. Mr. He said there was an older brother, making Jun the third child. Therefore, Jun could have been denied social services (e.g., insurance and education) and making the case for asylum.

They looked at the interventions listed in the ASQ III guide: translation, interpretation, and modification of normed instruments, assistance with acculturation process, bilingual assistance and bilingual materials, cross-cultural communication strategies and first language instruction in content areas, school survival and adaptation assistance, and sheltered instruction (Collier, 2013). They agreed that *school survival and adaptation assistance* might decrease Jun's anxiety, so they would design and implement an intervention that may help him with survival tools (see Chapter 5).

## Conclusion

The PLC offered Ms. Casad much needed support (i.e., information, suggestions, and collaboration). Mrs. Mola helped her see Rosa from a different perspective as well as to look deeper into herself. Help from Mrs. Tellez with the interpretation of language assessment scores, AQS scores, and parent conversations provided Ms. Casad with insightful ideas for understanding ways culture and language affect students' academic abilities. Talking with Jun's and Rosa's parents encouraged Ms. Casad to think she was on the right track in assessing students' needs, regardless of how "different" they may be. Hearing parents' perspectives provided a better picture of their children, but she sensed there was still so much to learn. The main point she took away from the conversations was that parents were depending on her as the teacher to do what was best for their children and that she was preparing to do just that.

In the next chapter, readers will look closer into (1) parent suggestions that provide direction in developing specific instructional strategies and interventions, (2) ways to collect and analyze data for academic and behavior patterns that need attention, and (3) characteristics of exceptionalities that appear similar to Rosa and Jun, all which are needed to create a comprehensive, holistic profile of CLD students.

### Notes From the Field: A Classroom Teacher's Voice
When I began teaching at high school level, my English Learner (EL) students were typically from the Philippines and Micronesia. Since I had traveled in the Philippines for several months, I felt familiar with

the culture and was comfortable reaching out to the parents or guardians of my students. Additionally, there were many staff members available who could call and translate for me. On the other hand, I had to learn from my students and various sources about Micronesia before understanding how to communicate successfully with guardians. Most guardians from both cultures families spoke enough English to not need a translator.

What surprised me most was when I transferred to a nearby middle school. Little did I know the EL population's culture would completely shift; my students at this school came mostly from China. I hadn't a clue about their culture nor how to reach out to parents. But, since this was a common challenge in this district, they had organized a system of BSHAs or Bilingual School Home Assistants. These persons were hired to translate documents and make parent contact for our schools.

Initially, the protocol was to email the person directly. But, as the years progressed and more people accessed them, the protocol became more cumbersome; oftentimes requiring a two-week turnaround and numerous follow-up emails to complete one conversation.

For example, I had completed a template asking a person to contact a family about a student that kept falling asleep in her classes. I had tried to ask the student, but they resisted answering. This situation was not new since our school had experienced students working after school to help support their family's income. But, what was new was that these parents explained she shared her room with her younger brother and he enjoyed playing video games late into the night. I completed another template asking the BSHA to ask the parents if there was a bedtime hour and encouraged the BSHA to investigate further into the problem for me. The return email said that there was a bedtime, but also the room got hot. In an additional email, I suggested possibly restricting the hours of gameplay, getting a headset for the younger brother, and installing an air conditioner or fan to help the sister cool down so that she could sleep. This inquiry ended as I was informed the BSHA felt uncomfortable "advising" the parents who would most likely not listen since they did not know her.

Upon reflection, instead of the numerous emails and sporadic phone calls from myself to the BSHA to the parents, I could have organized a meeting including the parents and the student with a BSHA present to translate. This would have removed the BSHA from his uncomfortable position while involving the student and parents in the understanding of the situation and finding a solution in a timely, collaborative manner.

# Reflection Activities

## Reflection Activity #1: Understand Yourself First

Look back to the vignette in the beginning of the chapter. Rosa was being bullied by a boy who insulted her with a racial slur. Has this situation ever happened to you as a child or an adult? How was it handled? What do you think the educators at Valley Elementary should do about the specific event? Reflect and respond.

Lesson/activity: *Teaching Tolerance* is a wonderful resource for informing yourself and your students on issues about race, identity, discrimination, and the strength of understanding others. See: www.tolerance.org/classroom-resources/tolerance-lessons/looking-closely-at-ourselves for a lesson provided by *Teaching Tolerance* that provides you and your students opportunities to gain a better understanding of each other while looking closely at yourself. These kinds of lessons are crucial for all of us to examine ourselves and our biases.

## Reflection Activity #2: Emotional enculturation

Ms. Casad was raised in a home in which emotions were not expressed (e.g., Funds of Knowledge). Now as an adult, she did not feel comfortable to express "negative" emotions, but "happy" emotions were good (e.g., Funds of Identities). She uncovered her assumption that emotional suppression was superior to emotional expression, including negative outbursts of anger and frustration. Ms. Casad discovered her own bias that it was "bad" to act out, even in one's own defense, which may impact her relationship with Rosa, whose beliefs and behaviors are in contrast with her own. Reflect on ways you were enculturated regarding emotional expression. Were you encouraged to express yourself? Were all emotions seen as equally important ("good" and "bad")? Now reflect on your views on emotional expression as an adult. Have they changed? Do you feel it is okay to express your anger? Sadness? Etc. See Emotions List Appendix B. How might your beliefs affect those who show contrasting beliefs? How do you manage behaviors in the classroom? What rules and behaviors are easier to enforce than others? Reflect and respond.

# Bibliography

Artiles, A. J., & Ortiz, A. (2002). *English Language Learners with Special Education Needs*. Washington, D.C.: Center for Applied Linguistics.

Berry, J. W. (1980). Acculturation as varieties of adaptation. In A. Padilla (Ed.), *Acculturation: Theory, Models, and Some New Findings*. Boulder, CO: Westview Press.

Cole, N. L. (2017). *What's the Difference between Prejudice and Racism? How Sociology Explains the Two and Their Differences*. Retrieved from: www.thoughtco.com/sociology-to-counter-claims-of-reverse-racism-3026067 and www.thoughtco.com/racism-vs-prejudice-3026086

Collier, C. (1987). Comparison of acculturation and education characteristics of referred and nonreferred culturally and linguistically different children. In L. M. Malare (Ed.), *NABE Theory, Research and Application: Selected Papers, 1987* (pp. 183–195). Buffalo, NY: State University of New York at Buffalo.

Collier, C. (1989). Mainstreaming the bilingual exceptional child. In L. Baca & H. Cervantes (Eds.), *The Bilingual Special Education Interface* (2nd ed., pp. 280–294). Columbus, OH: Merrill.

Collier, C. (2013). *Acculturation Quick Screen AQS III* (pp. 1–103). Ferndale, WA: CrossCultural Developmental Education Services.

Crawford, J. (1995). *Bilingual Education: History, Politics, Theory, and Practice* (3rd ed.). Los Angeles, CA: Bilingual Educational Services.

Cummins, J. (1984). *Bilingual Education and Special Education: Issues in Assessment and Pedagogy*. San Diego: College Hill.

Cummins, J. (1991). Language development and academic learning. *Language, Culture and Cognition, 161*, 75.

Cummins, J. (1994). The acquisition of English as a second language. In K. Spangenberg-Urbschat & R. Pritchard (Eds.), *Reading Instruction for ESL Students*. Newark, DE: International Reading Association.

Denborough, D. (2014). *Retelling the Stories of Our Lives*. London: W.W. Norton & Company.

Genesee, F., Paradis, J., & Crago, M. (Eds.). (2010). *Dual Language Development and Disorders: A Handbook on Bilingualism and Second Language Learning* (2nd ed.). Baltimore, MD: Brookes Publishing.

Herbst, P. H. (1997). *The Color of Words: An Encyclopedic Dictionary of Ethnic Bias in the United States*. Yarmouth, ME: Intercultural Press.

Herrera, S. G., & Murry, K. G. (2011). *Mastering ESL and Bilingual Methods: Differentiated Instruction for Culturally and Linguistically Diverse (CLD) Students* (2nd ed.). Boston: Pearson.

Hoover, J. J. (2004). Differentiating standards-based education for students with diverse needs. *Remedial and Special Education, 25*(2), 74–48.

Hoover, J. J. (2009). *Differentiating Learning Differences from Disabilities: Meeting Diverse Needs through Multi-Tiered Response to Intervention*. Prentice Hall. Upper Saddle River, New Jersey.

IDEA (2004) https://sites.ed.gov/idea/

Krashen, S. (1982). *Principles and Practice in Second Language Acquisition.* Oxford, UK: Pergamon Press.

Lawrence-Brown, D., & Sapon-Shevin, M. (2014). *Condition Critical.* New York: Teachers College Press.

Lee, L. (n.d.). *Working with Non-English Speaking Families.* Retrieved from: www.teachingforchange.org/wp-content/uploads/2012/08/ec_nonenglishspeakingfamilies_english.pdf

Mayer, J. D., & Salovey, P. (1997). *What is emotional intelligence?* In P. Salovey & D. J. Sluyter (Eds.), Emotional development and emotional intelligence: Educational implications (pp. 3–34). New York: Harper Collins.

McLeod, S. (2007, 2016). *Maslow's Hierarchy of Needs.* Retrieved from: www.simplypsychology.org/maslow.html

Padilla, A. M. (1980). The role of cultural awareness and ethnic loyalty in acculturation. In A. M. Padilla (Ed.), *Acculturation: Theory, Models and Some New Findings* (pp. 47–84). Boulder, CO: Westview Press.

Rowling, L. (2003). *Grief in Classroom Communities: Effective Support Strategies.* Philadelphia: Open University Press.

Saifer, S., Edwards, K., Ellis, D., Ko, L., & Stuczynski, A. (2005). *Classroom to Community and Back: Using Culturally Responsive, Standards-Based Teaching to Strengthen Family and Community Partnerships and Increase Student Achievement.* Portland, OR: Northwest Regional Laboratory.

Stinchcomb, J. B., Bazemore, G., & Riestenberg, N. (2007). *Beyond Zero Tolerance: Restoring Justice in Secondary Schools.* Retrieved from: www.ncjrs.gov/App/Publications/abstract.aspx?ID=234985

# 5

# Moving Beyond Behavior Management to Student Empowerment

## Introduction

Chapter 5 begins with a discussion about factors that contribute to overrepresentation of English Language Learners (ELLs) qualifying for special education services, including teachers' lack of understanding why ELLs are not making adequate progress, and poorly designed and implemented referral processes. Response to Intervention (RTI) is discussed as one process to help education teams determine appropriate referrals and recognize the complexities for ELLs related to literacy and behavior.

Examples of viewing behavior from a culturally responsive perspective are provided to provide a better understanding of behaviors rather than only managing them.

Behavior data is collected on Rosa and Jun using Functional Behavior Assessments and Behavior Rating Scales in order to gain a more comprehensive picture of their behaviors. That collected behavior data is then analyzed through a culturally responsive lens, which moves beyond behavior management (extrinsic motivation) to student empowerment (intrinsic motivation). Ms. Casad also listens to Rosa's perspective on her experiences which validates the student's voice.

Holistic profiles are completed for each student and their families to begin connecting family cultural assets to school activities. The PLC presents baseline data on Rosa and Jun and suggests classroom supports and specific interventions to support their needs. Similar characteristics of Attention Deficit Hyperactivity Disorder (ADHD) and acculturation are also discussed.

You are also introduced to interventions and accommodations such as:

◆ Daily self-monitoring plan,
◆ Thermometer 1–5 scale,
◆ Portfolio,
◆ Peer models,
◆ Strategies for students who are less acculturated,
◆ Guided practice in classroom behavior expectations.

The chapter concludes with Ms. Casad reflecting on her own beliefs and practices of behavior management, and mis-management, often resulting in power struggles.

There are two reflective activities:

Reflection Activity #1: Parent Involvement Plan.

Reflective Activity #2: Valuing Behavior from a Culturally Responsive Perspective.

## Complex Issues: Overrepresentation, Response to Intervention, and Behavior Management

Overrepresentation of Culturally and Linguistically Diverse (CLD) students in special education remains a problem even after 40 years of inquiry (Artiles, Kozleski, Trent, Osher, & Ortiz, 2010). One factor contributing to the overrepresentation of CLD students qualifying for special education services is that most general and special education teachers do not have adequate training for working with CLD learners, nor understanding of the specific needs of ELLs (Kushner & Ortiz, 2000). More specifically, factors that lead to inconsistent identification of ELLs who may experience learning disabilities include (1) teachers' lack of understanding about why ELL students are not making adequate progress, and (2) poorly designed and implemented referral processes (Burr, Haas, & Ferriere, 2015). Factors that lead to determining eligibility for high-incidence exceptionalities (i.e., Attention Deficit Hyperactive Disorder [ADHD], Emotional Disturbance [ED], and Specific Learning Disability [SLD]) require subjective judgment because these categories do not have clear biological causes (Artiles & Ortiz, 2002). The process of determining high-incidence exceptionalities is complex and subjective, with identification criteria that vary across districts and states (Artiles & Ortiz, 2002; Artiles et al., 2010).

## Response to Intervention

The use of Response to Intervention (RTI) as an alternative means of identifying students with high-incidence exceptionalities for special education was added to the reauthorization of Individuals with Disabilities Education Act (IDEA) in 2004. With the three-tier RTI approach, students' skills are monitored at each tier level to determine if they are demonstrating appropriate growth and development. Although RTI is not mandated, states are authorized to choose a more effective way to identify specific learning and behavior disabilities than the antiquated culturally biased discrepancy model and checklist screening (Bradley, Danielson, & Doolittle, 2005).

In Tier 1 (in a three-tier RTI approach), classroom teachers provide high quality instruction including appropriate curriculum (i.e., Culturally Responsive Instruction), as well as *differentiated instruction* to meet individual's needs. Educators differentiate instruction for students in terms of assessment techniques, general education curriculum accessibility, technology, universal and physical design accommodations, classroom management techniques, and a wide array of resources and related services based on student needs (Ford, Davern, & Schnorr, 2001). An initial step in differentiating instruction is individualizing curriculum by identifying the most important concepts and skills. Two examples include (1) chunk course content written on note cards and then play BINGO with them, and (2) write tasks or questions following Bloom's Taxonomy on note cards, place in coffee can, and then have students pick one and respond (see Chapter 3 for more examples).

When a school team (membership varies) determines that individual students are not responding to Tier 1 instruction, s/he is moved to Tier 2. In Tier 2, student progress is evaluated to determine an appropriate *intervention*, which most often involves small-group strategies, with frequent progress monitoring. Collier (2011, 2015) informs us that there is nothing "magic" about instructional and intervention strategies; they all take extra effort and focus on the part of instructional personnel. A major difference among school districts at Tier 2 is the way in which interventions are developed. Some districts determine interventions at Tier 2 through problem-solving teams that develop specific interventions based on individual student needs. Other districts predetermine a list of research-based interventions that target specific skill deficits and try to maximize efficiency of resources by grouping students who have similar academic needs (Collier, 2011, 2015).

There are also differences in Tier 2 regarding who is involved in the problem-solving and implementation process. In some districts, Tier 2 interventions are the responsibility of the classroom teacher, special education teacher, English Language Development (ELD) teacher, speech language pathologist, or other specialists. In other districts, any trained staff member under the supervision of a specialist can provide Tier 2 interventions with expertise in the intervention. Collaborative problem-solving among team members and parents should occur within a data-based decision-making framework. Team members need to share the responsibility for determining students' skill levels, identifying instructional environment variables, targeting appropriate interventions, monitoring student progress as a function of interventions, and evaluating outcomes (Collier, 2011, 2015). For more information on detailed RTI processes, see IRIS (n.d.) website through Vanderbilt University (https://iris.peabody.vanderbilt.edu/module/rti01-overview/).

## RTI With ELLs

There is a growing body of research on effective reading instruction for ELLs with and without disabilities (Artiles & Klingner, 2006) that suggests that ELLs are not receiving appropriate literacy instruction (Saenz, Fuchs, & Fuchs, 2005). Often, RTI service delivery models focus Tier 2 interventions on students' literacy skills, using a vast array of screeners and diagnostic tools that create a maze of complexity. There is also ambiguity and inconsistency in the way school personnel implement the RTI process. Due to the complexities of RTI for ELLs, the authors chose not to align this book around an RTI model; instead, we focus on appropriate instruction and interventions. If schools implement models with culturally and linguistically appropriate foundations aligned with this book, we do believe RTI models show great promise in reducing inappropriate referral of ELLs for special education (SPED) assessment. However, the use of RTI without a foundation in culturally and linguistically appropriate instruction may lead to greater disproportionality (both under and overrepresentation) of ELLs in special education (Brown & Doolittle, 2008).

If Valley Elementary was implementing the RTI process, Ms. Casad's instructional strategies demonstrated in Chapters 2, 3, and 4 would be considered Tier 1 differentiation in the general education classroom. In this chapter, the fourth grade PLC team would determine that both Rosa and Jun are not responding to these Tier 1 differentiated instructional strategies (with suggestions for more data), and recommend that both students be moved to Tier 2 and receive appropriate Tier 2 interventions. Collier (2015) has developed a list of interventions appropriate for ELLs, with research bases, and descriptions of ways to implement in Tier 1, Tier 2, and Tier 3 (a few included here in Chapter 5). They are designed to work with ELL students who are in integrated classrooms with fluent English-speaking students of mixed ability level but are also beneficial in English Language Development (ELD) and special education pull-out settings.

## Differing Behavior Perspectives

Differing perspectives on effective ways to work with behavior concerns do exist, but teacher education licensure programs across the U.S. continue to train pre-service teachers from a traditional behavioristic perspective that influences the way they think, teach, assess, facilitate, observe, collect data, and analyze behaviors. The goal in traditional behavior management is to reduce the number of undesired behaviors students exhibit, and increase positive behaviors, which often rely on extrinsic consequences to accomplish this goal. This perspective often leads to inappropriate referral of CLD students for SPED services under the high-incidence categories (ED, SLD, and ADHD), because the effort to understand why these behaviors are occurring or the causes of these behaviors are often absent. The authors purport that a "traditional behaviorist" practice when working with CLD students does not only add to disproportionate referral of students for school expulsion or suspension, but also limits teachers and CLD students from understanding the underlying conditions that may be causing the very behaviors that behaviorists are trying to control. According to Vincent, Sprague, and Tobin (2012),

> Students from traditional minority backgrounds, especially students from African-American, Hispanic and American Indian /Alaska Native backgrounds, were disproportionately over-represented in exclusionary discipline actions and lost the greatest number of days to those discipline actions. These patterns were constant across students with and without disability and appear to reflect the persistent national trends documenting poorer school outcomes for non-White students compared to White students.
> (Aud, Fox, & KewalRamani, 2010, cited in Vincent et al., 2012)

Once disproportionate referrals are made, African American and Hispanic students are more likely to be suspended or expelled from infractions that White students are not expelled from (Skiba, 2013). Additionally, once suspended or expelled, African American and Hispanic students are at a higher risk for long term negative outcomes, including decreased school engagement, and increased chance for drop-out and involvement with the juvenile justice system (Skiba, 2013). The authors suggest moving from a traditional behavior perspective to a culturally responsive perspective that views behaviors through cultural lenses (e.g., students' cultures, teachers' cultures, institutional cultures, sociopolitical contexts). This lens offers a deeper look into "why" behaviors may be taking place, instead of attempting to control them.

Both Rosa and Jun have been consistently displaying behaviors that are challenging for Ms. Casad, and resemble those associated with Emotional Disturbance (ED), Attention Deficit Hyperactivity Disorder (ADHD), and acculturation (see Tables 4.7 and 5.12). Let's now look at how the Professional Learning Community (PLC) team adopts a culturally responsive perspective when viewing Rosa and Jun's behaviors. Ms. Casad begins with reflecting on her interaction with Mrs. Ramirez (Rosa's mother), and seeking to understand the home context in which Rosa's behaviors were co-created.

## Mrs. Ramirez's (Rosa's Mother) Cultural Assets

Ms. Casad reflected on her conversation with Rosa's mother, which added some additional puzzle pieces of Rosa's identity. As a culturally responsive practitioner, she now saw Mrs. Ramirez's strengths and *Funds of Identities* (see Table 5.1). She holds (1) strong confidence in her role as mother,

Table 5.1 Mrs. Ramirez's Cultural Assets

| | | |
|---|---|---|
| "She likes taking charge and is good at it. She is smart enough to figure it out. She is a good kid." **Positive view of daughter** | Mother tells Rosa stories of Mexico, both fiction and nonfiction. **Strong belief in storytelling and oral tradition** | "I ask God for help." **Humble, collaborative, accesses available resources** |
| "It is the school's job to educate Rosa, not mine, I can't do that." **Lack of confidence in academic abilities** | A few bilingual books in the home, TV shows watched in Spanish. The mother speaks to Rosa in Spanish. **Supporting native-language development** | "We just walk away and stay angry with each other for a while. I usually give up arguing with her. It takes a lot of energy to fight with her." **Enacts strategies of ignoring, de-escalating behavior, and avoiding power struggles** |
| "We argue about how she needs to listen to me because I am her mother . . . I will take care of her at home." **Strong confidence in her role as mother** | "Do what you think is best." **Trust in school** | "If she is in a bad mood, you can't get her to do anything." **Acknowledges Rosa's fierce independence and strong will** |

(2) positive view of her daughter, and (3) strong belief in storytelling and oral tradition. She (4) supports Rosa's native-language development, (5) accesses available resources, and (6) enacts behavior management strategies of ignoring Rosa's undesired behavior, using de-escalating techniques, and avoiding power struggles. She also (7) acknowledges Rosa's fierce independence and strong will, (8) is willing to collaborate, and (9) trusts Ms. Casad and the school!

Ms. Casad wanted to affirm students' and families' cultural assets by asking them to bring artifacts (i.e., physical representations) into the classroom. She remembered an activity in her teacher preparation program in which students brought artifacts associated with their cultural values and beliefs. She had brought a basket with items representing her own cultural assets including a special food her mother often made (scones), a tablecloth from her grandmother, a sports jersey from her college soccer days, and a photo of a family vacation. She decided to implement this activity to involve parents in their children's education (e.g., Parent Involvement Plan), and was curious if Rosa and Mrs. Ramirez would participate. The message of the project is that all families are special and unique, and no two are the same or have the same story. She created a letter home to describe the *Sharing Basket,* and asked Mrs. Tellez to translate it into Spanish (see Appendix F. Readers can create their own Parent Involvement Plan in the end-of-chapter Reflective Activity #1).

Ms. Casad then reflected on Mrs. Ramirez's belief that it was the school's job to educate Rosa, not the parent's job. Ms. Casad had heard this belief from a parent last year, who explained that in Mexico, the parent's job is to teach the child self-discipline, respectful behavior, and contribution to the family; and the school's job is to teach academic skills (Mackenzie, 2010). Ms. Casad reflected on her own belief about parent involvement in schools. She held the assumption that parents had to show their involvement in their children's education by coming into the school building. Where did that belief stem from? She thought back to her own schooling experiences and heard voices of her previous teachers from dominant cultures (e.g., white, middle class, monolingual) reproducing this static, narrow definition of parent participation. Ms. Casad questioned her role in reproducing this pattern of hegemony (i.e., dominant cultural reproduction of practices, based on a set of exclusive dominant values) and wondered if she could create a culturally appropriate plan to invite Mrs. Ramirez to participate in Rosa's educational experiences, that did not involve walking into her classroom. Ms. Casad could help lower Mrs. Ramirez's *affective filter* (Krashen, 1982; see Chapter 4) by providing ways to help Rosa develop critical thinking skills in their home environment. Therefore, Ms. Casad found a list of activities and discussions that could take place at home or at the store, and would send the list home to all students (see Table 5.2). After reflecting

**Table 5.2** Literacy and Numeracy at Home . . . Ask Your Child To . . .

| | |
|---|---|
| Sort laundry by color | Sort boxes in order from smallest to largest |
| Locate items that match (e.g., socks) | Identify items that belong in the same group (fruits, desserts, etc.) |
| Tell you which shirt is larger | Describe foods with particular characteristics (smooth, sweet, hard, etc.) |
| Sort boxes or cans in the kitchen | Tell you which bowl has more or less |
| Tell you where items go | Select the correct number of spoons to set the table |
| Describe temperature of items (e.g., ice cream is cold, hot chocolate is hot) | Estimate the time it may take to . . . make a cake, eat a meal, walk to the store, etc.) |
| Estimate distance between two points (e.g., car and front door) | Estimate number of beans in a can |

Source: Adapted from Herrera, Cabral, and Murry (2013)

on ways Rosa and her family had overcome many challenges, Ms. Casad uncovered a deep respect for their perseverance, courage, and resilience. This lens would deepen her relationship with Rosa and her family, laying the foundation for trust and equal power relationships. She now regularly practiced placing herself in her students/families' shoes, and was getting better at viewing different ways to approach challenges.

Ms. Casad knew that Rosa was dealing with some very stressful family issues: her parents being separated, her brother being in a gang and in and out of jail, learning English, experiencing grief and trauma, leaving her home and starting over, and losing confidence in herself. Ms. Casad felt that no child should have to deal with that level of stress and then come to school and face ridicule for being different. Following is an excerpt from Rosa's story.

> When I came to the U.S., the secretary put me in first grade when I was supposed to go to second. Really the whole school messed up, I think. I didn't want to go to school because I didn't know nothing, but then when I started to learn English I want[ed] to go. I was thinking that I needed to learn more English to be more like a white person. . . . It was all in English so I just felt stupid in there. In Mexico they knew there was nothing wrong with me, but here everyone thinks I am just stupid. . . . I know that I am smart at reading and math too, I don't like math as much as reading so I don't do the math work very good. Some teachers don't understand that they treat you mean. I have tried to be nice to the other students in my classes, especially the white students but they only laugh at my bad English. I am

nice to them and they are mean to me so I am mean back now and have to let them know I am as smart as they are, so I fight them to make them understand. I wanted to quit [school]. . . . My mom says to speak English and to get a good job because she doesn't want me to be cleaning houses and the bathrooms. That is why she brought me over here, to learn English and to graduate and get a good job.

(see Rosa's complete story in Appendix G)

Ms. Casad recalled her conversation with Rosa when she was sent to the principal's office for fighting with another student. She wanted to know more about Rosa's anger and wanted to hear it from Rosa. She inquired about the recent fight Rosa was in and hoped it would give her a better idea of "why" Rosa was allowing her anger to get in the way of her education. Rosa was very clear about how she felt toward several of the students who teased her. Ms. Casad tried to talk with Rosa about this on several occasions but did not get much from her except that she is frustrated and expects more help from her teachers and the school. Ms. Casad began to see that Rosa knows that she is intelligent and feels like she could do better if given the opportunities.

## Rosa's Voice

*Ms. Casad:*   Rosa, do you realize that when you get angry and fight with other students that you are actually being dragged down to their level and that you are better than that?

*Rosa:*   No, I don't see it that way. I want them to leave me alone but they always find a way to make me mad. Really I just wish they would like me for who I am, and I am Mexican so they will never like me.

*Ms. Casad:*   Have you ever thought that they might be jealous of you? Maybe they are jealous because you are able to speak two languages, your English is coming along great, and they know you can do the work in class as well as they do.

*Rosa:*   I get so angry! But what else can I do to show them I am better than them?

*Ms. Casad:*   Well, it isn't about anyone being better than anyone else. It is about you learning how to control your anger when they make you mad. I think one way is to ignore them and put that energy toward learning. You have a lot to offer and are very bright, can you try to put more energy in your schooling than in fighting? I am here to help you! If we work together on the same thing, you

|        | avoid and ignore what they say, and put your energy into school, then I think you will do better in school and that will make you and your mother happy too. What do you think? |
| Rosa: | I know I can do better if they leave me alone. I like you for my teacher and want to do better, because I know I can. It may be easier if you help me to not get so mad, okay? |

## Rosa Baseline Data

The PLC team invited Mr. Hill, the Special Education teacher, to the PLC meeting to discuss Rosa and Jun. Both students had been puzzling, and the team felt they needed additional expertise to help with problem-solving students' behaviors. The meeting began by team members discussing the need to (1) continue school psychologist Mrs. Mola's work with all fourth graders (see Chapter 4) and (2) teach additional lessons on understanding difference and teaching tolerance (see www.tolerance.org/classroom-resources for class-room resources to teach social justice). Developmentally, all students needed these skills; therefore, they would continue implementing socioemotional classroom approaches (see Table 4.2), intended to address power inequalities (i.e., discrimination and bullying).

Ms. Casad had organized multiple data sources on Rosa (e.g., phone call with mother, AQS results, file review) in a three-column layout, which aligned with her visual learning style and philosophy of holistic teaching and learning. Ms. Casad presented Rosa's holistic profile to the team, which included (1) information from file review: cultural, linguistic, and socioemotional profiles and (2) instructional supports provided (see Table 5.3).

Ms. Casad presented Rosa's strengths: highly verbal, independent, strong leader, at grade-level reader, hard worker, and a balanced bilingual speaker (English and Spanish). Ms. Casad has been supporting Rosa's (1) academic and linguistic strengths with access to bilingual materials, and Sheltered English strategies and (2) cultural and socioemotional support (see Tables 4.2 and 5.3). Rosa's mother also supported Rosa's native-language skills by providing bilingual books at home, holding a positive view of her daughter, enacting behavior management by avoiding power struggles, acknowledging Rosa's fierce independence, and trusting the school to make appropriate decisions (see Table 5.1). Believing in strength-based education, the team agreed that Rosa's strengths were being supported at home and at school, providing foundations for resilience and success.

Ms. Casad then presented Rosa's challenges. Academically, she was below grade level in math; and socially, she showed physical aggression, and has

**Table 5.3** Holistic Profile: Rosa

| FILE REVIEW Cultural | Linguistic | Social-emotional |
|---|---|---|
| Moved here from Mexico. Left family and friends there.<br><br>Lives w/ mother and brothers (may be in gangs).<br><br>Attends catechism classes.<br><br>Crossed US-Mexico border on inner tube.<br><br>Suffering from prejudice and discrimination from students.<br><br>Strong self-esteem and identity. | **Home Language Survey:** English and Spanish<br><br>**ELD previous services:** Grades 2 and 3<br><br>**LAS score English:** Level 3.5–4 Spanish 3.0<br><br>**Parent English level:** Basic English and Spanish<br><br>**Length of time in U.S. schools:** 3 years<br><br>**AQS score:** 25 *in transition* | Highly verbal and independent.<br><br>Strong leader. Hard worker.<br><br>Shows physical aggression.<br><br>Loud voice and angry outbursts.<br><br>Lacks social skills due to independence.<br><br>Difficulty in forming positive interpersonal relationships. |
| **CLASSROOM SUPPORTS Cultural** | **Linguistic** | **Social-emotional** |
| Made connections from Rosa's cultural assets to content: connected pioneers' journey to immigrants' journey.<br><br>Wrote classroom book, "About Us."<br><br>Activities that facilitate understanding of "difference" and empathy. | Post vocabulary words, sentence frames and objectives.<br><br>Oral language development, "tell a friend."<br><br>Encouraged native-language use, provided bilingual books.<br><br>Realia, manipulatives, graphic organizers. | Student check-in with emotion list.<br><br>Reflection and journaling.<br><br>Giving student choice and voice.<br><br>Clear expectations and positive, direct feedback.<br><br>Classroom meetings w/ agreements for respect.<br><br>Ignore undesired behaviors.<br><br>Reward positive behavior with Kindness cards. |

difficulty in forming positive interpersonal relationships. The team asked Ms. Casad if she had collected data on Rosa's progress to the academic and social classroom supports, and she paused. The only data Ms. Casad had collected was the number of Kindness cards Rosa earned for positive behavior during Kindness Week. Rosa had earned 18 cards, which seemed like a lot of cards; but there was no baseline data to compare with. The team decided the best way to illustrate Rosa's classroom performance was with a "Portfolio," which would paint a comprehensive (i.e., holistic) picture of her strengths and challenges. A Portfolio is an alternative, authentic assessment that emphasizes the instructional environment and student performance. It is considered a performance-based assessment illustrating real-world tasks, which are relevant and culturally responsive (Gargiulo & Metcalf, 2010). Students and teachers can choose work samples, organized in a folder with a Portfolio cover page (see Table 5.4). Students can then present their progress to parents/caregivers during conferences by describing (1) assignments, (2) how they performed,

**Table 5.4** Portfolio Work Samples

NAME_____          **Term: FALL WINTER SPRING**

| Cultural-Linguistic Content areas | Progress | Reading | Progress | Math | Progress | Social Emotion Behavior | Progress |
|---|---|---|---|---|---|---|---|
| *Oregon Trail* vocabulary dictionary | | Reading Log | | Perimeter dictionary | | Kindness Cards | |
| States of Matter CLOZE paragraph | | Dialogue Journal | | Perimeter word problems | | Self-Assessment Daily Summary | |
| Vapor? Liquid? Solid? Reflection | | Self-Assessment and Peer Assessment | | Angles and measurement end of chapter quiz | | Emotions List | |
| *Oregon Trail* Dinner Party Journal entry | | *Oregon Trail* Comprehension questions | | Angles word problems | | Classroom meetings *Respect Agreements* reflection | |
| Student Choice | | Student Choice | | Student Choice | | Student Choice | |

and (3) what they found meaningful, which can help them take responsibility for their own learning.

## Collecting Behavior Data

Rosa was near grade level in Language Arts, but struggled with math. The PLC wondered if Rosa's behavioral outbursts were due to frustration because math instruction was not taught at her instructional level, thus outside of her Zone of Proximal Development (ZPD, Vygotsky, 1987). Ms. Casad shared with the team what she had taken from her conversations with Rosa about her behavior and frustration with school (see "Rosa's Voice" section). She told them that Rosa said, *"In Mexico they knew there was nothing wrong with me, but here everyone thinks I am just stupid."* She also shared that Rosa said that all she needed to do was learn English and get a good job because that was what her mother wanted for her. Ms. Casad believed that Rosa was intelligent and liked learning; therefore, believed Rosa was feeling frustrated from what her mother wanted for her and what her peers thought about her (i.e., external expectations), which contributed to her anger. She told the team that Rosa might be feeling that she was not being academically challenged so becomes easily frustrated, which interferes with her learning. The team wondered about the context (i.e., when, where, how, why) and duration (i.e., length of time) of Rosa's outbursts, and if they might occur more often in math class than other times of the day. They agreed Rosa should be observed both in and outside of the classroom to develop a baseline description (type and frequency) of behaviors occurring. Mr. Hill agreed to perform a Functional Behavior Assessment (FBA) on Rosa during math instruction the following day while he was checking in on Trent. The students in Ms. Casad's class knew Mr. Hill and were familiar with his presence, as he offered push-in support for Trent, a student who was on his caseload (with IEP) receiving service for Specific Learning Disability.

Baseline data of behaviors are needed that provide descriptions (e.g., type and frequency) of behaviors, which help teams to interpret the causes and/or functions the behaviors serve, and are needed to match with an appropriate behavioral intervention. Mr. Hill explained that an FBA is a process used to help evaluate a student's behavior by (1) identifying factors regarding behaviors that may not be obvious; (2) finding behavior patterns or trends, which lead to (3) identifying the root causes, functions, and reinforcers of behaviors; and (4) providing data for developing an appropriate theory as to the function of the behavior (PBISWorld.com). An *Antecedent, Behavior, and Consequence* (or ABC chart), or similar tool, is used to collect data on moment-to-moment student behavior. Typically, ABC charts are created to record what happened before and after specific behaviors and may also include frequency, duration, or interval recording (for more information, see *Functional Behavior Assessments*, www.pbisworld.com/tier-2/functional-behavior-assessment-fba/).

Until the FBA results were reported, Mrs. Tellez explained the possibility of understanding Rosa's behavior challenges by looking at her acculturation measure (i.e., adjustment to U.S. schools and society). Rosa's Acculturation Quick Screen (AQS) score showed *in transition*, which means she was adapting to her surroundings as expected (Collier, 2013), but Rosa still required support for being *in transition*. Although Ms. Casad was supporting Rosa's strengths through classroom support with extrinsic motivation, Rosa needed behavioral support increasing intrinsic motivation to learn alternative and effective ways to meet her own needs, leading to *self-empowerment and self-advocacy.*

Two of Rosa's physical outbursts occurred in social interactions with peers, in which she was expressing disagreement. One fourth grade teacher offered to share with Ms. Casad a model of effective communication using sentence frames to express an opinion, agree and disagree with peers: (1) I believe _____ because____. (2) I agree with _____ because____. (3) I respectfully disagree with _____ because_____. The teacher also suggested to post a message on the classroom wall reading, "You are free to make any choice you want; however, you are not free from the consequences of those choices." Ms. Casad decided to also lead classroom meetings to discuss this message and need for effective communication, and ask students to reflect on possible consequences for specific personal choices.

Because Rosa was not responding to classroom (i.e., Tier 1) behavior supports (e.g., school and classroom rules and expectations) as her peers were (see Chapter 6 for more information), the team determined Rosa needed additional intensive behavioral supports designed for both intrinsic and extrinsic motivation. These supports would now be called "interventions," with individualized, intensified targeted efforts in (1) socialization with peers and (2) self-management of behavior.

## Behavior Intervention: Peer Mentor

The team looked at the AQS suggestions, and chose "Peer Mentor," in which they theorized that a mature model may help Rosa choose healthy outlets for her energy and anger. Cognitive development occurs as people learn from more experienced others. One concept of participation is that students participate in later situations according to how they relate to previous ones (Rogoff, Paradise, Arauz, Correa-Cavez, & Angelillo, 2003). Seeing the connection between the old and new situations involves support from a more skilled participant, who can help the child see the applicability to classroom activities. For students to generalize appropriately across experiences, apprenticeship helps in deciding which strategies relate to each other, and which approaches fit different circumstances. Assigning an older mentor can help scaffold opportunities to help students become responsible for their own learning and solving problems both in and out of the classroom.

Ms. Casad spoke with the sixth grade teacher about choosing an appropriate female mentor for Rosa. One student Maria was chosen for several reasons: She was also of Mexican ethnicity, socially popular, a soccer player, earned high grades, and appeared successful at navigating multiple worlds. Maria was shy, appeared to be a leader in the school community, and balanced academics and family commitments. Ms. Casad learned later that Rosa and Maria attended catechism classes together, and their moms were friends. The two teachers decided that the sixth graders would teach the fourth graders the rules of soccer by participating in a six-week unit in Physical Education. The goals of the unit were for sixth graders to learn the official rules of the game so they could apply to be paid referees in a local soccer league, and the fourth graders could learn basic rules, and practice to play in the soccer league.

**Table 5.5** What I Learned From My Peer Mentor

| Name and Date | |
| --- | --- |
| What I learned about soccer … | |
| To be a successful sixth grader I need to … | |

**Table 5.6** Thermometer

| 5 | I need to leave! |
| --- | --- |
| 4 | I need some space |
| 3 | Please don't talk |
| 2 | I am a little nervous |
| 1 | I can handle this! |

Ms. Casad developed a written form for fourth graders to reflect and record their learning from the PE unit, and from their mentor (see Table 5.5). The PLC next focused on interventions to help Rosa manage her own behaviors, and build intrinsic motivation.

## Intervention: Behavior Self-Assessment

To help Rosa manage her own behaviors, Mr. Hill suggested two interventions: (1) Thermometer self-monitoring scale and (2) Daily Self-Assessment report. Ms. Casad would explicitly teach and model ways to assess and monitor the intensity of emotions on five different levels using a 5-point scale, which resembled a thermometer (see Table 5.6). Ms. Casad would model to all students how to use the scale, which may empower them to feel they had some control over their behaviors (i.e., manage). She would also perform whole-class read-alouds that focused on positive ways to express and manage anger (see Appendix H).

Ms. Casad would also collaborate with Rosa and Mrs. Ramirez to create a Daily Self-Assessment report, which would be used to monitor Rosa's choices of behaviors (see Table 5.7). She would call Mrs. Ramirez to gather realistic expectations and familiar language used at home to connect school and home by holding similar expectations.

Mr. Hill gave Ms. Casad the district's *Intervention Tracking Sheet* to describe and track the three interventions for Rosa: (1) Portfolio progress monitoring, (2) Daily Self-Assessment (and Thermometer), and (3) Peer modeling reports (see Table 5.8). All interventions are intended to increase Rosa's intrinsic

**Table 5.7** Daily Self-Assessment of Behavior

| **Name:** | | Date: _____ | | | | | | |
|---|---|---|---|---|---|---|---|---|
| **BEHAVIOR TARGETS** | **1st Period** | | **2nd Period** | | **3rd Period** | | **Lunch** | |
| | S | T | S | T | S | T | S | T |
| I showed respect to myself, others, and property | | | | | | | | |
| I handled my anger in an appropriate manner (e.g., used Thermometer Scale) | | | | | | | | |
| I stopped unkind behavior or inappropriate comments the first time staff member or student asked | | | | | | | | |
| TOTAL | | | | | | | | |

DAILY TOTAL: _____

RATING SCALE:  3—Yes, all of the time
2—I had some minor problems in choosing appropriate behaviors
1—I had some major problems
0—I had severe challenges

Student Reflection:

Teacher Comments:

**Table 5.8** Intervention Tracking Sheet

STUDENT NAME_____DATE OF BIRTH_____
TEACHER NAME_____GRADE_____
Student's dominant language_____ LAS LEVEL_____
Parent's dominant language_____ Translation/interpreter needed?_____

Circle each grade completed and write if outside U.S. On lines below numbers, write number of days absent

PreK   1    2    3    4    5    6    7    8    9    10

___  ___  ___  ___  ___  ___  ___  ___  ___  ___  ___

Previous concerns indicated in student file or by parents:

Health/Developmental factors:
Strengths:
Most recent assessment data:
Classroom data

| Differentiation attempted | Frequency | Progress |
|---|---|---|
| | | |
| | | |
| | | |
| | | |

**Table 5.8** (Continued)

Top concerns and baseline data related to concerns:

*Intervention Goal #1: Describe*_____

Begin date: _____ End date_____
Time (amount per day): _____Frequency (per week): _____
Delivered by (where/by whom)_____
Progress monitoring: ATTACH

*Intervention Goal #2*_____
Begin date: _____ End date_____
Time (amount per day): _____ Frequency (per week): _____
Delivered by (where/by whom)_____
Progress monitoring: ATTACH

*Intervention Goal #3*_____
Begin date: _____End date_____
Time (amount per day): _____ Frequency (per week): _____
Delivered by (where/by whom)_____
Progress monitoring plan: ATTACH

motivation to show appropriate behavior, which is often reinforced through social interactions and may increase meaningful personal relationships.

## Jun Baseline Data

Ms. Casad then presented Jun's holistic profile to the PLC (see Table 5.9). She reported his strengths and challenges, classroom supports, and AQS score. Jun's strengths include strong computation skills, happy disposition, and peers like him. His greatest challenge was his behavior manifested in (1) showing distractibility by getting up and walking around at random times; (2) displaying lack of response to instruction, both verbal and nonverbal; (3) acting as if in "his own world" by staring or looking dazed. In summary, Jun shows an unusually high level of distractibility and failure with task completion.

Ms. Casad reported on Jun's parents' cultural assets, gained from their telephone conversation. The Hes seemed very interested in helping Jun in any way they could, and were very supportive of the school. Their cultural assets include having confidence in the teacher's advice, demonstrating a positive view of their son and wanting the best for him, holding high expectations for the U.S. school system, having concern for their son's social network, acknowledging Jun's strengths and passions, enacting strategies of de-escalating behavior, and setting boundaries (see Table 5.10).

Involving Jun's parents is essential for his academic development (including cultural-linguistic, cognitive, and socioemotional success). Ms. Casad

**Table 5.9** Holistic Profile: Jun

| Cultural | Linguistic | Social-emotional |
|---|---|---|
| Moved here from China with family. Has one older sister.<br><br>Lives w/ mother, father, sister, and brother.<br><br>Possibly emigrated here for political asylum reasons.<br><br>Strong family connection.<br><br>Want best for their children. | **Home Language Survey:** Mandarin and English.<br>**ELD previous services:** N/A<br>**LAS score English:** Level 2–3<br>**Mandarin:** Level 1<br>**Parent English level:** Father proficient in Mandarin and some English; Mother proficient in Mandarin and little English.<br>**Length of time in U.S. schools:** 2 years<br>**AQS score:** 20 *less acculturated* | Quiet and happy.<br><br>Uninterested, easily distracted, often off task.<br><br>Displays "odd" behaviors (kicking the air and wandering).<br><br>Lacks social skills.<br><br>Difficulty in forming positive interpersonal relationships. |
| **CLASSROOM SUPPORTS Cultural** | **Linguistic** | **Social-emotional** |
| Made connections from Jun's cultural assets to content: connected pioneers' journey to immigrants' journey.<br><br>Wrote classroom book, "About Us." | Dictionary or translator tool.<br>Sheltered instruction:<br>word banks, picture clues, match game, graphic organizers. | Student check-in w/ emotion list.<br>Reflection and journaling.<br>Giving student choice and voice.<br>Clear expectations and positive, direct feedback.<br>Ignore undesired behaviors.<br>Reward positive behavior. |

**Table 5.10** The He's Cultural Assets

| Cultural | Linguistic | Socioemotional |
|---|---|---|
| "Should Jun have repeated third grade?"<br>**Confidence in teacher's advice**<br>"Jun is a happy boy and we don't want any more stress on him."<br>**Positive view of son and wanting best for him**<br>"What do you see happening for Jun in your class?"<br>**Expecting more from U.S. school system than China** | "I should have kept him back in school. If his English is better, he would have higher grades."<br>**Misguided belief about learning English**<br>"He reads aloud to me better than his sister sometimes. When I ask him to translate, he can't tell me what he just read."<br>**Misguided belief about language development and denial of other possible disabilities** | "Does Jun have any friends at your school?"<br>**Concern for son's social network**<br>"Jun has always loved numbers." "We gave him a karate video game and he loved it. He could play for hours."<br>"He reads aloud to me better than his sister sometimes."<br>**Acknowledging Jun's strengths and passions**<br>"After we made him stop playing the video game, he began punching and kicking the air, physical moves he had learned from the game."<br>**Enacting strategies of de-escalating behavior, setting boundaries, and pacifying the condition.** |

reported that the Hes also had concerns about Jun's behaviors at home. Mr. Hill suggested Ms. Casad send home a *Behavior Rating Scale* survey to verify that Jun exhibited similar behaviors at home as at school (see Table 5.11).

Jun's behaviors have been occurring in both contexts, school and home; and have been occurring consistently more than six months, which are two indicators of the possibility of the presence of a high-incidence exceptionality. The results of comparing Ms. Casad's and the He's responses on the survey will give the PLC team important data on behavior patterns, and insights into the possible presence of ADHD. However, behavior characteristics of ADHD can also appear similar to those associated with acculturation (see Table 5.12).

Jun has been identified as having an unusually high level of distractibility and failure with task completion. The PLC wondered if Jun's behavior was due to frustration because instruction was not taught at his instructional level, thus outside of his Zone of Proximal Development (ZPD, Vygotsky, 1987). Mrs. Tellez had helped Ms. Casad create instruction using comprehensible input (i.e., at his ZPD; see Krashen, 1982) by implementing three classroom strategies in large group settings: (1) sheltered instruction strategies (word banks, picture clues, graphic organizers), (2) proximity, and

**Table 5.11** Behavior Rating Scale

Child's name_____ Date_____
Name of person completing this form_____

What class(es) do you teach this child?_____
In a typical day, how many hours do you observe this child?_____

*Instructions: Please circle the number next to each item that best describes the behavior of this child during the past 6 months. (0-never, 1-sometimes, 2-often, 3-always)*

1. Fails to give close attention to details or makes careless mistakes in his/her work 0 1 2 3
2. Fidgets with hands or feet or squirms in seat 0 1 2 3
3. Has difficulty sustaining his/her attention in tasks or fun activities 0 1 2 3
4. Leaves his/her seat in classroom or in other situations in which seating is expected 0 1 2 3
5. Doesn't listen when spoken to directly 0 1 2 3
6. Seems restless 0 1 2 3
7. Doesn't follow through on instructions and fails to finish work 0 1 2 3
8. Has difficulty engaging in leisure activities or doing fun things quietly 0 1 2 3
9. Has difficulty organizing tasks and activities 0 1 2 3
10. Seems "on the go" or "driven by a motor" 0 1 2 3
11. Avoids or is reluctant to engage in work that requires sustained mental effort 0 1 2 3
12. Talks excessively 0 1 2 3
13. Loses things necessary for tasks or activities 0 1 2 3
14. Blurts out answers before questions have been completed 0 1 2 3
15. Is easily distracted 0 1 2 3

TOTAL SCORE

Source: Barkley & Murphy (1998). Copyright 1998 by The Guilford Press

**Table 5.12** ADHD and Acculturation Factors

| ADHD | Acculturation |
|---|---|
| Problems with attention | Heightened anxiety |
| Hyperactivity | Confusion in locus of control |
| Must be maladaptive and present for six months to warrant classification | Withdrawal |
| | Silence, unresponsiveness |
| Can change over time but can be lifelong | Response fatigue |
| Ignoring directions | Code-switching |
| Inattention to detail | Distractibility |
| Fail to complete tasks | Resistance to change |
| Distractible and forgetful | Disorientation |
| Not listening when spoken to directly | Stress-related behaviors (including fidgeting, inability to concentrate, forgetfulness, problems with attention) |
| Difficulty organizing tasks and directives | |
| Fidgets | |
| Runs about or climbs excessively | Post-traumatic responses |
| On the go or driven by motor | Survival guilt |
| Talks excessively | |
| Impulsivity | |
| Interrupts or intrudes on others | |
| Source: Adapted from DSMV manual | Source: Collier (2011, 2013, 2015, 2016) |

(3) making connections from Jun's cultural assets to content (i.e., pioneers' journey to immigrants' journey). However, none have been successful in addressing Jun's attention issue in a sustainable manner. The team now needs to focus an intervention strategy in small-group instructional sessions (i.e., Tier 2 of the RTI process). Mrs. Tellez informed the group that Jun has been in the U.S. two years, and scored 20 on the AQS, termed, *less acculturated*. Students in this category should be receiving assistance not only with the acculturation process, but also with stress reduction and positive coping methods (Collier, 2013).

Collier (2011, 2013) suggests that the team select one of the intervention strategies that in their judgment will best show them if the student responds appropriately given this intervention. Ms. Casad would preview the intervention with Jun, and begin the intervention in a small group with 30-minute instruction occurring daily (or three times a week). The team looked at suggestions from the AQS to help *less acculturated* students (see Appendix I).

## Guided Practice in Classroom Behavior Expectations and Survival Strategies

After eliminating several strategies to help *less acculturated* students that involved native-language or translation supports, the team focused on those targeting *classroom behavior expectations.* They chose *Guided practice in classroom behavior expectations and survival strategies,* with purpose to (1) build transfer skills, (2) develop personal control of situations, (3) improve confidence in school interactions, (4) reduce distractibility, and (5) reduce acting out behaviors (Collier, 2015, 2016). (See Table 5.13.)

**Table 5.13** Guided Practice in Classroom Behavior Expectations and Survival Strategies

| **Purpose of the Strategy** |
| --- |
| 1. Build transfer skills<br>2. Develop personal control of situations<br>3. Improve confidence in school interactions<br>4. Reduce distractibility<br>5. Reduce acting out behaviors<br>6. Develop confidence in cognitive academic interactions |
| **How to implement** |
| In RTI models, this strategy may be done with small groups, in individualized, focused intensive periods of time, or in specially designed individual programs and may be included in the IEP. |
| At Tier 1, this strategy is done with the entire general education classroom population and may be done within an integrated classroom. |
| Older student, peer, or specialist demonstrates how to act in a given school or school culture situation. The situation is explained, in home and community language when possible, and each stage is modeled. Students then practice each stage of the interaction with familiar participants until comfortable and successful in appropriate behaviors. |
| **Research base[1]** |
| Buchanan, L. (1990); Hafernik, J. J., Messerschmitt, D. S., & Vandrick, S. (2002); Rubenstein, I. Z. (2006); Davis, B. M. (2005); Nelson, J. R., Martella, R., & Galand, B. (1998). |
| **What to watch for with ELL/CLD students** |
| Particular social groups and cultures have different expectations of adults and children when it comes to being accountable for task completion. This is a learned difference between cultures. The teacher needs to be aware that the expectations in an American school may need to be taught directly to CLD students and not just assumed to be understood. |
| One way to introduce the idea of behavior and strategies specific to your classroom is to ask students about how their parents have them behave at home or with learned playing games. This can then be expanded to the idea of acting appropriately in a classroom. |
| Demonstrate all of the desired behaviors and strategies. Some role-play may be helpful. Examples of bad behaviors may be used with caution. |

Sources: Collier (2013, 2015, 2016)

1 Sources cited in Collier (2013)

The team agreed to meet in six weeks to review and analyze (1) data collected on both Rosa and Jun's behavioral interventions and (2) FBAs, which will determine the need for Behavioral Intervention Plans. For Jun, interventions include (1) Sheltered English strategies (called accommodations on assignments), (2) Guided practice in classroom behavior expectations and survival strategies, and (3) comparing the *Behavior Rating Scale* from home and school. Ms. Casad would record progress on Intervention Tracking Sheets (see Table 5.8), and felt very supported and confident with clear plans to support Rosa and Jun. After the meeting, she stayed and talked with Mr. Hill about (1) ways to monitor students' interventions and (2) Trent, one of her students experiencing Specific Learning Disability.

## Specific Learning Disability (SLD)

Specific Learning Disability is defined by the Individuals with Disabilities Education Improvement Act (2004) as:

> A disorder in one or more of the basic psychological processes involved in understanding or in using language, spoken or written, which manifest itself in the imperfect ability to listen, think, speak, read, write, spell, or do mathematical calculations. Such terms includes conditions as perceptual disabilities, brain injury, minimal brain dysfunction, dyslexia, and developmental aphasia. This term does not include learning problems that are primarily the result of visual, hearing, or motor disabilities, of mental retardations, of emotional disturbance, limited English proficiency, or of cultural factors, environmental or economic disadvantage.
>
> (34 C.F.R. §300.7(c)(10)ii)

Students experiencing SLD often show challenges with attention, memory, metacognition, and organization. Mr. Hill explained the additional two levels of instructional differentiation that are most often delivered to students needing intensive support: (1) accommodations and (2) modifications. Trent required *accommodations* in the classroom, which are defined as changes in course content, teaching strategies, standards, test presentation, location, timing, scheduling, expectations, student responses, environmental structuring, and/or other attributes which provide access for a student with a disability to participate in a course/standard/test, which DO NOT fundamentally alter or lower the standard or expectations of the course/standard/test (IDEA, 2004). Mr. Hill referred Ms. Casad to a list of general accommodations

**Table 5.14** Testing and Classroom Accommodations

Flexible or visual schedule
Small-group size
Visual aids
Amplification
Large print
Spelling aids: Audio Dictionary
Alternate means of response
Writing utensil, special pencil, or pencil grip
Dictation
Extended time
Frequent breaks
Preferential seating
Adaptive or special furniture
Visual organization
Place keeper
Graphic organizer
Assistive technology (e.g., assistive listening device, audio materials)
Bilingual dictionary
Opportunity to respond orally
Math aids: number line, fraction bar or circle, calculator
Positive reinforcement system

Sources: Reprinted from Martin & Hauth (2015), p. 140. Adapted from *Curriculum/Classroom Accommodations and Modifications*, Fairfax County Public Schools 140. Copyright 2015 Council for Exceptional Children. Virginia Department of Special Services.

(see Table 5.14). *Modifications* are high impact strategies that affect curricular expectations of students and DO fundamentally alter or lower the standard or expectations of the course/standard/test (IDEA, 2004). They alter the content of curriculum, as well as the ways in which students are taught, and require adjustments in the structure and content of the educational program that affect the level of curricular mastery expected of students (Collier, 2015). Examples include: different/separate curricula, giving step-by-step directions, visual schedules, providing physical supports or prompts as needed by the student, Assistive Technology (AT) and Augmentative and Alternative Communication (AAC), which are devices that incorporate the individual's full communication abilities and may include any existing speech, vocalizations, gestures, manual signs, and aided communication.

They agreed that both Trent and Jun needed similar accommodations on their assignments. Accommodations listed in Trent's IEP include (1) break task into small steps using words, FIRST, NEXT, LAST; (2) seat near instruction; (3) frequent checks for understanding. Jun would also benefit from these supports, as they created comprehensible input (Krashen, 1982) necessary for language development. The next day, Ms. Casad planned a math lesson on perimeter adding behavior objectives for Rosa, and these accommodations for Jun and Trent (see Table 5.15).

Table 5.15 Math Perimeter Lesson Plan

| Common Core State Mathematics Standard | Behavior Objectives (Rosa) | Accommodations (Jun and Trent) |
|---|---|---|
| Solve real-world and mathematical problems involving perimeters of polygons, including finding the perimeter given the side lengths, finding an unknown side length. | | |
| **Student friendly objective:** I will find the perimeter of shape when given the side lengths and find an unknown side length when needed. | I will complete Self-Assessment behavior chart at the end of the class. I will participate fully and stay on task. | I can explain the steps for finding the perimeter of a shape. "I found the perimeter by ___." |
| **Academic vocabulary:** (1) perimeter, (2) feet/foot, (3) measure/measurement, (4) equal, (5) opposite **Everyday vocabulary:** fence, garden | | Students will create mini-dictionary on perimeter for academic vocabulary words with 4-square graphic organizers |
| **Materials needed:** ActiveBoard flipchart, objectives, ruler, work pages, math journals, and paper. | Behavior supports: (1) Thermometer, (2) Self-Assessment | Sentence frame and mini-dictionary |
| **Connect to cultural assets:** Yesterday I spent time in my garden. Teacher shows picture of her garden. Tell story of going out to the garden and seeing that deer had eaten my flowers and veggies! I need to build a fence. I have never built a fence before! Show a picture of a fence. | Create motivation for participation—call on students to share: Do you have gardens at home? Have you ever seen or worked in a garden? How am I going to figure out how much fence I need to build? | |
| **EXPLICIT MODEL "I DO"** Take student ideas and create steps for finding the perimeter: **First**, find the length of each side of the shape—talk about the word measure, measurement, feet and foot (have a ruler to show a foot). **Next**, write an equation and add the sides together to find the total. **Last**, label your answer and write a sentence with your answer. side 1 + side 2 + side 3 + side 4 = total We can find the perimeter of many things! Doorway, around the ActiveBoard, the edge of a book | I will participate fully and stay on task. | Check for understanding Fill out three-box graphic organizer with first, next, last. Write definition of perimeter: the total distance around the edge of a shape. Teacher explains: I found the perimeter by ___. |

(Continued)

**Table 5.15** (Continued)

| Common Core State Mathematics Standard | Behavior Objectives (Rosa) | Accommodations (Jun and Trent) |
|---|---|---|
| **GUIDED PRACTICE "WE DO"** Let's do another one together. Here is another shape. Let's find the perimeter together. What is my first step? Next steps … | Listen to peers | Students complete problem together in small group verbally stating, "First____, next____, last____." "We found the perimeter by _____." |
| **INDEPENDENT PRACTICE "YOU DO"** Complete page with six perimeter problems. Explain expectations of showing work using an equation, labeling the answer and writing the answer in a sentence. | Use Thermometer if needed | Allow students to complete reduced number of problems. |
| Ask students go home and look for an object (desk, bed, table, etc.) they can find the perimeter of. Find the perimeter and come back and report. | Complete Self-Assessment of Behavior | |

## Conclusion

Ms. Casad is developing four critical dispositions, resulting in successful cross-cultural communication with and understanding of diverse families' experiences: (1) cultural empathy, (2) open-mindedness, (3) social initiative, and (4) flexibility (van der Zee & van Oudenhoven, 2000). She can empathize with the feelings and behaviors of CLD families (i.e., *cultural empathy*). She is becoming more *open-minded* by demonstrating an unprejudiced attitude toward different cultural norms (i.e., Mrs. Ramirez's belief in the school's job to educate Rosa). As a culturally competent teacher, she is creating inclusive communities where diverse families feel part of their children's educational experience.

In the past, Ms. Casad sought a classroom that was quiet and structured, one in which she controlled the climate of student response. She sought to eliminate disruptive behaviors, which resulted in power struggles because she did not allow for student self-monitoring of voice or choice. Ms. Casad could now increase her scores on both statements on the *Self-Assessment of Cultural Competence* scale: (1) I am aware of different communication/behavior patterns among different groups and (2) I understand learning varies among individuals and does not follow one pattern (see Reflection Activity #1 in Chapter 1).

By rejecting a traditional view of punitive behavior management and viewing Rosa's behaviors through a culturally responsive lens, Ms. Casad is taking social initiative and being flexible in challenging situations, which requires adjusting her behavior to meet Rosa's specific needs. By reflecting on her belief of "knowing what to do," she realized she only knew one aspect of one student, but realized there were always other possibilities and explanations. This reflection on being a "lifelong learner" will help Ms. Casad and the team move forward with culturally responsive analyses, and follow appropriate steps to meet students' needs.

Misplacement and overrepresentation of ELLs in special education is often based on inadequate training of educators and limited perspectives when working with CLD students. By presenting students' holistic profiles and viewing data from a culturally responsive perspective, Ms. Casad and the PLC team designed whole-class strategies to support student strengths, and interventions matched to present levels of academic and behavioral needs.

In the next chapter, authors provide a culturally responsive analyses of FBAs and interventions implemented with Rosa and Jun. Looking at data through a cultural lens provides in-depth and appropriate interpretation of actions, resulting in students taking responsibility for their behaviors, and moving beyond behavior management (extrinsic motivation) to student empowerment (intrinsic motivation). Together, these data will provide evidence to better determine difference from disability, and guide teams to decide if referral for special education services is appropriate.

## Reflection Activities

### Reflection Activity #1: Parent Involvement Plan
Read ways to create Parent Involvement Plans (PIP) below and then create one yourself. The main Objective and Goals of a PIP are:

To engage, unify, and empower the ELL families at _____ School.

- ◆ **Goal #1:** Increase family *attendance* at _____by 25%.
- ◆ **Goal #2:** To increase family *engagement* at _____ by 25%.
- ◆ **Goal #3:** To *empower* parents to become leaders within the ELL community.

Imagine that a new immigrant family has moved into the neighborhood your school serves. What is already in place to make this family feel welcome?

What programs does the school offer that would inspire and challenge their children? What still needs some work? Parent involvement starts with the school: The ideas and energy come from the schools and government mandates. Schools try to "sell" their ideas to parents. School staff and public institutions might feel they know what the problems are and how to fix them, and determine the criteria to use in evaluating success. Parent engagement, however, begins with the parents: Ideas are elicited from parents by school staff in the context of developing trusting relationships. They emerge from parent/community needs and priorities. Questions to consider:

How can we get more families to come to these meetings?
How can we provide better access to meetings?
What content would be most interesting and meaningful for them?
How can we motivate and empower our diverse communities?

### ELL Family Engagement Plan

◆ Strengthen home-school partnerships;
◆ Recognize and build upon your ELL parents' strengths;
◆ Harness the energy and ideas of staff, parents, and students in shaping those partnerships;
◆ Mobilize and empower staff to become teacher leaders;
◆ Engage school-wide staff members beyond the ELL/bilingual departments;
◆ Learn how to advocate for and allocate resources on behalf of ELL families;
◆ Encourage all participants to keep trying new, creative approaches until they find what works.

### Strategies

If you do not yet know this information about your ELLs, find out:

◆ What languages they speak (which may be at least two or three!);
◆ If families who speak the same language, such as Spanish, come from different countries or different regions within the same country;
◆ The educational background of families and the school system of their countries;
◆ If any of your ELLs are migrants, refugees, or students with interrupted formal education;
◆ If your families have experienced war or another traumatic event such as a natural disaster.

In order to learn more about your ELL families, start with your ELL/bilingual educators. These individuals are an important resource whose experience working with ELL students and families can benefit the entire school community—and they will appreciate the opportunity to share their expertise. Find out what resources are available from the district and community. This may include helpful background information as well as a network of interpreters. Enlist a knowledgeable staff member, community member, or parent. If you find such a person, examine his/her background as it relates to what you need. For example, you may know a Somali young adult who is bilingual but doesn't remember Somalia. He may be more helpful as an interpreter than as a liaison for Somali families who have just arrived in the U.S. Ask the families. You may want to include some questions in your Home Language Survey or a very basic questionnaire that ELL parents fill out with an interpreter during student enrollment.

### Important Steps to Take to Incorporate ELL Families

◆ Integrate cultural traditions of your ELL families throughout the school.
◆ Show that you value families' native languages.
◆ Find ways to communicate with ELL parents.
◆ Make the enrollment process manageable for ELL parents, and accessible all year.
◆ Provide opportunities for parents to learn more about important topics and skills.
◆ Look for ways that ELL parents can help with children's schoolwork.
◆ Think outside the box about parent engagement.

Building bridges between the school and the parents takes a vision that involves careful planning. When the school climate is welcoming and conducive to parents stepping foot on the campuses and feeling genuinely welcomed and received as partners in the education of their children, then we may begin to see increased involvement of our ELL families. When parents begin to participate, the children's academic achievement increases, teachers teach better, and more students continue to the end of their academic career and graduate (see links for examples of Parent Involvement Plans in Breiseth, Robertson, & Lafond, 2011).

## Reflective Activity #2: Valuing Behavior From a Culturally Responsive Perspective (Scharf, 2016)

Choose one of the two activities to complete: (1) Design a thoughtful classroom setup from a culturally responsive perspective or (2) Design an appropriate culturally responsive behavior management system.

1. **Culturally Responsive Classroom:** Design a thoughtful classroom setup and structure from a culturally responsive perspective that

honors student experiences, establishes norms for shared inquiry and dialogue, creates social-emotional learning safety in your classroom, and allows you to analyze behavior from a culturally based perspective.

Consider some key principles of a culturally responsive perspective of behavior that supports and models the values of cultural differences:

a.  Belief in the dignity of every person.
b.  Community building practices.
c.  Equity and fairness built from empathy and understanding.
d.  Respect for cultural and linguistic differences.
e.  Respect for the safety and inclusion of all individuals and groups.
f.  Establish norms for shared inquiry and dialogue.

  ◆ Think about how you set up your classroom structure: Does it honor your student's experiences, cultural differences, language differences, and behavioral norms of CLD students?
  ◆ What can you change tomorrow to make your teaching and your classroom culture more culturally responsive?
  ◆ What steps will you take to make this change?
  ◆ To help you plan, finish this sentence, "To honor my students' cultural backgrounds within my classroom culture, I will . . ."
  ◆ List challenges you might face in using one of the strategies. Identify supportive allies in your building.
  ◆ Remember that this work is not in addition to what you already do; rather, it should frame what you currently do so that you can be more culturally inclusive in your work with students.

2.  **Culturally Responsive Behavior Management System:** Design an appropriate culturally responsive behavior management system into your behavioral management practices. You will need to reflect on your own personal cultural assets and consider your students' cultural assets while doing this. And remember that this work is not in addition to what you already do; rather, it should frame what you currently do so that you can be more inclusive in your work with students.

There are three primary aspects to consider when designing this:

a.  All students and teachers must commit to creating a safe, inclusive community where all students and teachers are respected.

b.   Disciplinary incidents must be treated as opportunities for growth, restitution, and community building (not just "punishment").

c.   Behavior management practices must address issues of fairness, equity, and cultural awareness.

Following are some strategies to consider when designing a culturally responsive behavior management system.

◆   Student-generated agreements and contracts establish shared ownership of classroom norms.

◆   Zero indifference (not zero tolerance) means never letting disrespectful conduct go by as though nothing has happened, but does not require automatic suspension, expulsion, or other punishments that take kids out of class.

◆   Restorative justice emphasizes building community, repairing harm, and restoring relationships rather than simply punishing those who have engaged in misconduct.

Also consider that as a culturally responsive teacher, you can:

a.   Adopt social-emotional and cultural lenses in which to view behaviors.

b.   Know your students and develop your own cultural competence.

c.   Plan and deliver effective Culturally Responsive Instruction.

d.   Move the paradigm from punishment to development.

e.   Resist the criminalization of school behavior.

f.   Move from a behavioristic perspective to a more culturally responsive perspective.

*Remember that this work is not in addition to what you already do; rather, it should frame what you currently do so that you can be more culturally inclusive in your work with students.

# Bibliography

Artiles, A. J., & Klingner, J. K. (Eds.). (2006). Forging a knowledge base on English Language Learners with special needs: Theoretical, population, and technical issues. *Teachers College Record, 108*, 2187–2438. [Special issue].

Artiles, A., Kozleski, E. B., Trent, S. Osher, D., & Ortiz, A. (2010). Justifying and explaining disproportionality, 1968–2008: A critique of underlying views of culture. *Exceptional Children, 76*, 279–299.

Artiles, A. J., & Ortiz, A. (2002). *English Language Learners with Special Education Needs*. Washington, D.C.: Center for Applied Linguistics.

Aud, S., Fox, M. A., & KewalRamani, A. (July 2010). *Status and Trends in the Education of Racial and Ethnic Groups, (NCES 2010–2015): U.S. Department of Education, National Center for Education Statistics.* Washington, D.C.: U.S. Government Printing Office.

Barkley, R. A., & Murphy, K. R. (1998). *Attention-Deficit Hyperactivity Disorder: A Clinical Workbook* (2nd ed.). New York: The Guilford Press.

Breiseth, L., Robertson, K., & Lafond, S. (2011). A guide for engaging ELL families: Twenty strategies for school leaders. *Colorín Colorado.* Retrieved from: www.colorincolorado.org/sites/default/files/Engaging_ELL_Families_FINAL.pdf

Bradley, R., Danielson, L., & Doolittle, J. (2005). Response to Intervention. *Journal of Learning Disabilities, 38*(6), 485–486.

Brown, J. E., & Doolittle, J. (2008). A cultural, linguistic, and ecological framework for Response to Intervention with English Language Learners. *Teaching Exceptional Children, 40*(5), 66–72.

Burr, E., Haas, E., & Ferriere, K. (2015). *Identifying and Supporting English Learner Students with Learning Disabilities: Key Issues in the Literature and State Practice (REL 2015–086).* Washington, D.C.: U.S. Department of Education, Institute of Education Sciences, National Center for Education Evaluation and Regional Assistance, Regional Educational Laboratory West. Retrieved from: http://ies.ed.gov/ncee/edlabs

Collier, C. (2011). *Seven Steps to Separating Difference from Disability.* Thousand Oaks: Corwin Press.

Collier, C. (2013). *Acculturation Quick Screen AQS III.* Ferndale, WA: CrossCultural Developmental Education Services.

Collier, C. (2015). *Seven Steps to Separating Difference from Disability Workbook.* Thousand Oaks: Corwin Press.

Collier, C. (2016). *But What Do I Do? Strategies from A to W for Multi-Tier Systems of Support.* Thousand Oaks: Corwin Press.

Ford, A., Davern, L., & Schnorr, R. (2001). Learners with significant disabilities: Curricular relevance in an era of standards-based reform. *Remedial and Special Education, 22*(4), 214–222.

Gargiulo, R., & Metcalf, D. (2010). *Teaching in Today's Inclusive Classrooms.* Belmont, CA: Wadsworth/Cengage Learning.

Herrera, S. G., Cabral, R. M., & Murry, K. G. (2013). *Assessment Accommodations for Classroom Teachers of Culturally and Linguistically Diverse Students* (2nd ed.). Boston: Pearson.

Individuals with Disabilities Education Act Amendments of 1997, P.L. 102–119, 20 U.S.C. § 1400 et seq. http://idea.ed.gov/

IRIS. (n.d.). *Response to Intervention (RTI) Processes.* Vanderbilt University. Retrieved from: https://iris.peabody.vanderbilt.edu/module/rti01-overview/

Krashen, S. (1982). *Principles and Practice in Second Language Acquisition.* Oxford, UK: Pergamon Press.

Kushner, M. I., & Ortiz, A. A. (2000). The preparation of early childhood education teachers for English Language Learners. In *New Teachers for a New Century: The Future of Early Childhood Professional Development* (pp. 124–154). Washington, D.C.: U.S. Department of Education, National Institute on Early Childhood Development and Education.

Mackenzie, J. Z. (2010). *Empowering Spanish Speakers.* Tucson: Summerland Corporation.

Martin, C. C., & Hauth, C. (2015). *The Survival Guide for New Special Education Teachers: Curriculum/Classroom Accommodations and Modifications.* Fairfax County Public Schools 140, Council for Exceptional Children, Virginia Department of Special Services.

Rogoff, B., Paradise, R., Arauz, R. M., Correa-Cavez, M., & Angelillo, C. (2003). Firsthand learning through intent participation. *Annual Review of Psychology, 54,* 175–203.

Saenz, L. M., Fuchs, L. S., & Fuchs, D. (2005). Peer-assisted learning strategies for English Language Learners with learning disabilities. *Exceptional Children, 71*(3), 231–247.

Scharf, A. (2016). Critical practices for anti-bias education. *Teaching Tolerance.* Retrieved from: www.tolerance.org/magazine/publications/critical-practices-for-antibias-education/classroom-culture

Skiba, R. J. (2013). Reaching a critical juncture for our kids: The need to re-assess school-justice practices. *Family Court Review, 51*(3), 380–387.

van der Zee, K. I., & van Oudenhoven, J. P. (2000). The Multicultural Personality Questionnaire: A multidimensional instrument of multicultural effectiveness. *European Journal of Personality, 14*(4), 291–309.

Vincent, C. G., Sprague, J. R., & Tobin, T. J. (2012). Exclusionary discipline practices across students' racial/ethnic backgrounds and disability status: Findings from the Pacific Northwest. *Education and Treatment of Children, 35*(4), 585–601.

Vygotsky, L. S. (1987). *The Collected Works of L.S. Vygotsky* (Vol. 1). R. W. Rieber & A. S. Carton (Eds.). New York: Plenum Press.

# 6

# Weighing Evidence: Challenges Due to Intrinsic or Extrinsic Conditions?

## Introduction

In Chapters 3, 4, and 5, we saw that both Rosa and Jun did not respond to high quality classroom instruction (i.e., culturally responsive pedagogy); therefore, the Professional Learning Community team determined appropriate interventions to support student strengths (see Figure 6.1). Now in Chapter 6, readers are invited to the Student Study Team (SST) compiled of additional experts to discuss Rosa and Jun's progress to those interventions and other data sources (e.g., Functional Behavior Assessment, Portfolios, Self-Assessments, and observations). The team's two objectives are to evaluate students' (1) learning environment through cultural responsive behavior analyses (i.e., view difficulties as located in external environment as alternative explanation) and (2) acculturation level of *integration* into schooling norms.

Informal and formal language assessments (i.e., in listening, speaking, reading, writing) help with putting together many pieces of the complex puzzles of Rosa and Jun. Now the team must decide if student learning and behavior problems are primarily due to (1) language learning and cultural factors (i.e., external) or (2) a disabling condition (i.e., internal).

Team members decide that Rosa's challenges are due to cultural factors, and her responses to interventions (Peer Learning, Portfolio, and Self-Assessment), are adequate to resolve her challenges. The team also determines that Jun

**Figure 6.1** Flowchart: Meeting Student Needs

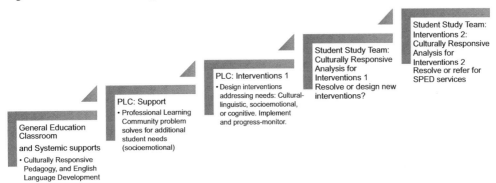

needs additional interventions that ensure adequate opportunities to learn. Thus, they need more data on specific cognitive and social contexts to determine if his learning challenges are due to intrinsic, biological factors, which warrant referral for special education services.

There are two end-of-chapter reflective activities:

1. Reflecting on the entire process and investigating the pieces of the puzzle for each student.
2. Describing and applying your understanding of analyzing the learning environment through cultural responsive behavior analyses.

## Effective Student Study Teams

Once students begin receiving interventions, the team now becomes a "Student Study Team" (SST), sometimes referred to as the "Multi-Disciplinary Team" (MDT), as new members join to problem solve student needs (see Figure 6.1). Jennings (2009) explains that the effectiveness of problem-solving educational teams (i.e., SST, MDT, or "prereferral teams") is a combination of (1) the level of effort the team members put forth, (2) the amount of knowledge and skills each member brings, and (3) the appropriateness of the strategies chosen, implemented, and analyzed. An effective team leader describes the task(s) members are expected to accomplish in concrete terms in a specific time frame. Mrs. Tellez volunteered to be the leader (i.e., case manager) who will document team tasks, questions, actions, and decisions. Administrators often serve on problem-solving teams, and are often needed to approve funding to support chosen interventions; however, some teachers expressed fear of being seen as incompetent, and felt greater satisfaction when principals were not team leaders (Sindelar, Griffin, Smith, & Watanabe, 1992). Teams proceed more effectively when given (1) space for meetings, (2) release time, (3) clerical support, (4) access to the school's information such as Positive Behavior Intervention Support, and (5) staff training (Jennings, 2009).

## Beginning the Puzzle of Rosa

SST team members now include (1) Betty Wilson (other fourth grade teacher), (2) Lori Casad, (3) John Hill (SPED teacher), (4) Angelica Tellez (ELD teacher), (5) Ronald Call (Title 1 Specialist), and (6) Karin Mola (school psychologist). Mrs. Mola and Mr. Call joined the team, as they needed additional expertise in analyzing Rosa's progress to interventions, which were designed to increase her socialization with peers and ability to self-manage behaviors. Mrs. Tellez began the meeting by explaining the objective ways to analyze Rosa's progress through cultural, linguistic, cognitive, and socio-emotional lenses documented on the form, *Baseline Holistic Profile* (see Table 6.1), which was projected on a large screen.

Information was already filled in rows: (1) Rosa's file review with strengths and challenges, (2) classroom supports, and (3) caregiver input (from parent meeting). After summarizing this information, the team decided to first discuss the Functional Behavior Assessment (FBA) that Mr. Hill had conducted, which would serve as a baseline assessment (see Table 6.2).

**Table 6.1** Rosa's Baseline Holistic Profile

| STEPS to Determine Difference from Disability | Cultural-Linguistic | Social-Emotional | Cognitive |
|---|---|---|---|
| **Ch. 2 File Review Strengths and challenges** | **Strengths:** Strong self-esteem, bilingual, resilient. Attends catechism classes. Kinesthetic learning style. **Challenges:** Left family and friends when moved from Mexico. Crossed border on inner tube. Brothers may be in gangs. Wants to stay in ELD. | **Strengths:** Strong verbal and nonverbal communication. Independent, hard worker, leadership skills. **Challenges:** Lacks social skills due to independence. Difficulty in forming interpersonal relationships. Shows physical aggression and emotional outbursts. | **Strengths:** Average grades on report cards. At grade level in reading/ELA. **Challenges:** Math. Often does not finish her work due to behavior problems. |

| Chs. 3 and 4 Classroom Supports | ◆ Made connections from Rosa's cultural assets to content. ◆ Wrote classroom book, "About Us." ◆ Activities to build understanding of "difference" (e.g., conversation starters, write letter to racism). ◆ Oral language development, "tell a friend." ◆ Bilingual books. | ◆ Activities to build empathy: ◆ student check-in with emotion list. ◆ Reflection and journaling. ◆ Giving choices. ◆ Clear expectations and positive feedback. ◆ Classroom meetings for respect. ◆ Reward positive behavior: Kindness cards. ◆ Kindness Week. ◆ Taught sentence frame, "I respectfully disagree because . . ." | ◆ Word bank. ◆ Realia. ◆ Manipulatives, graphic organizers. ◆ Post objectives. |
|---|---|---|---|
| Chs. 4 and 5 Caregiver Input | ◆ Strong belief in storytelling and oral tradition. ◆ Supporting native-language development. ◆ Humble, collaborative, accesses available resources (religious, dedicated Catholic). | ◆ Positive view of daughter. ◆ Strong confidence in role as mother. ◆ Enacts strategies of ignoring, de-escalating behavior, and avoiding power struggles. ◆ Acknowledges Rosa's fierce independence and strong will. | ◆ Trust in school. ◆ Lack of confidence in academic abilities. ◆ Strong belief in school's job to educate Rosa. |
| Chs. 5 and 6 Interventions #1 and Progress | **Peer modeling Strengths: Challenge:** | **Self-Assessment of behavior Strengths: Challenge:** | **Portfolio progress Strengths: Challenge:** |
| Ch. 6 Additional Data | **Interview w/ Rosa Strengths: Challenges:** | **FBA Strengths: Challenges:** | ? |
| Ch. 6 Data Suggests (Cultural Analysis) | | | |
| Decide: (1) Resolve, or (2) New Interventions | | | |
| Decide: (1) Resolve, (2) Refer to SPED, or (3) 504 Plan | | | |

**Table 6.2** Functional Behavior Assessment—Rosa's Math Perimeter Lesson

| Antecedent | Behavior | Consequence |
|---|---|---|
| During Explicit Instruction Ms. Casad said, "write an equation and add the sides together to find the total." | Yells, "this is dumb!" | Teacher ignored the outburst. |
| Student next to Rosa said something in Spanish to her (with teasing voice). | Stands up with angry look on face and says something mean in a low voice (teacher didn't hear exact words). | Privately, teacher reminded Rosa about behavior objectives and Thermometer. |
| Teacher told everyone to work with the person next to her. | Throws her paper off her desk, stands up, and walks around room | Teacher asked Rosa if everything was okay and if she would like to work alone. |
| Teacher asked students to go home and look for an object (desk, bed, table) to find the perimeter. | Rosa blurts out, "No way I do this at home!" | Teacher says, "Sure you can Rosa, we can all do that." |
| Teacher explained that assignment was due at end of class time. | Blurts out negative comment to teacher (soft voice). | Teacher told Rosa to raise hand if she had something to say. |

## Rosa's FBA

Mr. Hill reminded team members that FBAs were used to describe and identify patterns of student behaviors, and then directed their attention to the *Behavior* column on the FBA form. He began by reporting that he observed five classroom interactions, in which Rosa displayed emotional outbursts in all five. "Rosa appeared to be able to control the volume of the outbursts, as her voice varied between soft, medium, and loud. Two out of the five interactions were paired with physical movements such as standing up, throwing paper, and walking away. Each of the five behaviors displayed were short in duration, a few seconds long, although I was not able to time them accurately." Then he directed their attention to the *Antecedent* column, and continued, "An antecedent is an event or action that occurred immediately before the behavior (i.e., outburst). In four of the five antecedents, Ms. Casad had given students the following directives such as: (1) write an equation, (2) work with the person next to you, (3) look for an object at home to find the perimeter, and (4) finish the assignment before the end of class."

## Behavior Analyses: Silence or Empower

"We are here to discover patterns of how others' words or actions (i.e., antecedents) prompted Rosa's behaviors, and what message(s) she may be communicating to us with them." Mr. Hill explained that behaviors are typically

Table 6.3 Two Lenses of Behavior Analyses

| Behaviorist | Culturally Responsive |
|---|---|
| Power<br>Control<br>Right and wrong<br>Unacceptable and punitive<br>Positive and negative<br>Focus on reducing or increasing<br>Assume problem is located internally | Egalitarianism<br>Tied to individual's cultural norms<br>Liberation or redirection<br>Understanding social factors<br>Educating and reassuring<br>Assume problem is located in external<br>environment |

analyzed from a traditional behavioristic lens (i.e., medical model) that views problem behaviors in isolation, and located within an individual. This lens seeks to remedy isolated behaviors by increasing positive behaviors and decreasing negative behaviors, or extinguishing them (i.e., school suspension). He continued, "When we analyze Rosa's behaviors from a culturally responsive perspective, we will understand her behaviors as important communication, and seek multiple explanations for those behaviors. From this perspective, we will assess the learning environment as part of her challenges. These two differing perspectives often create a dichotomy." He listed two columns on the whiteboard (see Table 6.3) and continued. "All behavior is a form of communication, including those labeled as 'problem behaviors.' If we can discover the underlying message that Rosa's behaviors are communicating, we can create more effective instructional and environmental interventions" (Donnellan, Mesaros, & Anderson, 1984, cited in Lawrence-Brown & Sapon-Shevin, 2014). By viewing Rosa's behaviors as meaningful, we presume she is a competent member of society. This lens also may reduce educators' desires to suspend students like her from school. Research shows that Hispanic students were more likely than White students to be suspended for minor misbehaviors, particularly non-compliance (Skiba, Horner, Chung, Rausch, May, & Tobin, 2011).

Mrs. Tellez thanked Mr. Hill for explaining the different lenses to view Rosa's behaviors. All members agreed that it was important to understand ways to support Rosa to be a contributing member of a democratic society, instead of alienating or silencing her. She suggested the team now hear about Rosa's progress in response to the interventions, which will add clues to messages her behaviors are communicating. Directing their attention back to Rosa's Baseline Holistic Profile (see Table 6.1) in the row labeled *Interventions #1*, she passed out three more puzzle pieces (i.e., data sources): (1) Self-Assessment behavior reports (see Tables 6.4 and 6.5, quantitative sum of rating scales), (2) Peer modeling reports (see Table 6.6, qualitative data), and (3) Portfolio progress (see Table 6.7).

**Table 6.4** Rosa's Self-Assessment of Behavior

| Objectives | *S WK 1 | **T 1 | S WK 2 | T 2 | S WK 3 | T 3 | S WK 4 | T 4 | S WK 5 | T 5 | S WK 6 | T 6 | Total S | Total T |
|---|---|---|---|---|---|---|---|---|---|---|---|---|---|---|
| #1 I showed respect to myself, others, and property | 30 | 22 −8 | 28 | 23 −5 | 32 | 30 −3 | 34 | 35 −1 | 38 | 38 −0 | 40 | 38 −2 | 202 | 186 DIF 16 |
| #2 I handled my anger in appropriate manner— Thermometer | 20 | 13 −7 | 18 | 12 −6 | 26 | 17 −9 | 27 | 20 −7 | 30 | 25 −5 | 30 | 26 −4 | 157 | 113 DIF 44 |
| #3 I stopped unkind behavior the first time staff member or student asked | 25 | 18 −6 | 24 | 17 −6 | 27 | 22 −5 | 30 | 30 −0 | 36 | 35 −1 | 35 | 35 −0 | 177 | 157 DIF 20 |

*S= Student.     **T= Teacher.

Each box is a total score of 15 ratings (3 periods per day x 5 days/week), total possible=45

RATING SCALE:  3—Yes, all of the time
2—I had some minor problems in choosing appropriate behaviors
1—I had some major problems
0—I had severe challenges

Student Reflection:

Teacher Comments:

Table 6.5  Results of Self-Assessment: Rank-Ordered

| Objective #1: I showed respect to myself, others, and property | TOTAL STUDENT 202 | TOTAL TEACHER 186 | DIFFERENCE 16 |
|---|---|---|---|
| Objective #3: I stopped unkind behavior the first time asked | 177 | 157 | 20 |
| Objective #2: I handled my anger in appropriate manner | 157 | 113 | 44 |

Table 6.6  What I Learned From My Peer Mentor

| Date | Week 1 (2x week) | Week 2 | Week 3 | Week 4 | Week 5 | Week 6 |
|---|---|---|---|---|---|---|
| **In soccer I learned** | Shooting the ball at the goal. To dribble ball. | Heading can hurt! Girls are good at soccer. | Some kids do not know rules. Some kids are bossy and don't pass ball. | You need to pass the ball to get up the field. Call to player you passing. | I am really good! I know to fake people out! | I love soccer! I want to be on team. |
| **I learned to be a sixth grader . . .** | You can be boss of the school. You can have lots of friend. | You have to study all the time. You go to middle school next. | Nothing. | People are nice to you. You can talk about soccer game in school. | Soccer is the best. You have to practice all the times. | You need to make good grades to play on middle school team. |

# Success With Showing Respect to Self, Others, and Property

Ms. Casad began explaining the intervention, Self-Assessment behavior reports (See Table 6.4), by describing steps taken after the Professional Learning Community team adjourned two months ago. She had met with Rosa and Mrs. Ramirez (Rosa's mother) to brainstorm ways to help Rosa succeed in school. Together they discussed ways they could support Rosa to control her outbursts, and find ways for healthy expression of emotions. After much discussion, Rosa expressed her ability to succeed with three behavior objectives: (1) I showed respect to myself, others, and property; (2) I handled my anger in an appropriate manner (e.g., used Thermometer Scale); and (3) I stopped unkind behavior or inappropriate comments the first time staff member or student asked. Mrs. Ramirez agreed to use similar language and positive reinforcement at home for consistency. Ms. Casad explained the process to

Table 6.7  Rosa's Portfolio Work Samples

NAME: Rosa Ramirez    Term:    FALL    WINTER    SPRING

| Cultural-Linguistic Social Studies and Science Assignment | Progress | Reading/ELA Assignment | Progress | Math Assignment | Progress | Social-Emotion Behavior | Progress |
|---|---|---|---|---|---|---|---|
| *Oregon Trail* vocabulary dictionary | 4/5 words correct and pictures. Great details. | Reading Log | I like the book, *Esmerelda Rising* also. Read three out of four nights two weeks in a row. | Perimeter dictionary | Messy writing but accurate definitions. | Kindness Cards | 18 earned in 1 week. Rosa helped many students! |
| States of Matter CLOZE paragraph | 8/10 Demonstrates understanding! | Dialogue Journal | Rosa saw how Esmerelda learned to change her opinion of her father. | Perimeter word problems | 2/5 correct. Needs more effort. | Self-Assessment Daily Summary | Increased ability to respect self and others. Needs to use Thermometer more often. |
| Vapor? Liquid? Solid? Reflection | Strong reflection with good questions. | Self-Assessment and Peer Assessment | Looks like you have a different opinion than your peer. | Angles and measurement chapter quiz | 7/10 Great effort! I see you really studied. | Emotions List and reflection | I see you chose "frustrated" again today. I'm glad you can express this emotion. |
| *Oregon Trail Dinner Party* Journal entry | I like how you took the perspective of the tribal chief! | *Oregon Trail* Comprehension question | 3/5 Answered where and when correct, missed why? | Angles word problem | 2/4 correct. Rosa left room and did not finish assignment. | Class meetings Respect Agreements reflection | I agree this word respect is not very clear, and it helps to write examples. |
| Student Choice *Oregon Trail essay, "Effects on American Indians"* | Self-assessed: "I am better at writing. I like the chief." | Student Choice *Esmerelda Rising*: Compare and contrast essay. | Self-assessed: "I like Esme. She is like me. I don't see my father either. She lived in Mexico too." | Student Choice *Measurement and Perimeter homework* | Self-assessed: I like using measurement tape. My bed perimeter is 15 feet! | Student Choice *Conversation Starters Activity* | Self-assessed: "Jennie asked me what my name means. I said red, but it can mean pink. I don't like pink." |

Rosa of rating herself for each objective at the end of each class period, and then she, herself, would rate Rosa. Ms. Casad modeled the process of assessing an example behavior through an explicit "think-aloud," ensuring Rosa understood the tool. Together, they decided to eliminate the self-assessment process during lunch, realizing this would be too difficult.

Mr. Call (Title 1 Specialist) helped design this tool, and began explaining the scoring codes (see Table 6.4). "Each box has a potential total score of 45 (3 class periods per day with 3 possible points per period, 3x3=9, multiplied by 5 days per week, 9x5=45 total points per week). For *Objective #1* (I showed respect to myself, others, and property) Rosa's total score was 202, and Ms. Casad's was 186. Quantitatively, this objective received the highest scores from both of them, so was the most successful. This objective also showed the smallest difference between Rosa and Ms. Casad's scores, which is further evidence of its success. There were two ways of analyzing this tool with quantitative measures: (1) compare Rosa's scores (to each other) every week to determine if scores increased as weeks progressed and (2) compare Ms. Casad's and Rosa's scores to each other to determine if they became closer in range. In analyzing data in this manner, *Objective #3* was also successful (see Table 6.5). Finally, *Objective #2* (I handled my anger in appropriate manner) received the lowest total scores and had the greatest discrepancy among scores.

## Need Time to Learn the Intervention Before Measuring It

Mrs. Tellez asked team members for questions or comments. Most questions were directed to Ms. Casad about the implementation process (i.e., reliability and validity of intervention). She replied, "At first it was difficult to remember to pay attention to details of Rosa's behaviors, but then, I found that the three objectives helped direct my attention. I could not record during my explicit instruction, but observed Rosa during guided practice (i.e., group work) and independent practice, which was the last 30 minutes of each period (e.g., reading, math, and English language arts) before lunch. Rosa and I needed to operationally define 'respect' in *Objective #3*, because that term was too ambiguous for both of us, and we needed concrete examples. We also needed to determine the difference between a rating of '2' (i.e., I had some minor problems in choosing appropriate behaviors) and rating of '1' (I had some major problems). After a while, we finally felt confident in our scores by week 3. If we implement more interventions, my suggestion is that we build in time to practice and learn the intervention before measuring it." Mrs. Wilson spoke, "Looks like this Self-Assessment built Rosa's intrinsic motivation, which is very positive. Lori, sounds like you also learned about the difficulty in assessing behaviors, but found a consistent method, great work!"

## Peer Learning Successful

Mrs. Mola replied, "Very insightful observations Lori, thank you for your valuable feedback and metacognitive suggestions, which we will make for all faculty implementing future interventions." She then asked Ms. Casad to report on Peer modeling (see Table 6.6). Ms. Casad began, "By pairing Rosa with a strong sixth grade peer mentor, this intervention was aimed at developing Rosa's social and physical skills, which may provide an outlet for her emotional outbursts. In looking at the response report (summary of 6 weeks) you can see Rosa's descriptions of her own learning (see Table 6.6). First, she began with simple and basic assessments (weeks 1–2). Then, after a week of frustration (week 3), her comments gained some detail and a positive outlook (weeks 4–5). Finally, at the end of the soccer unit, she expressed confidence and a desire to be on a soccer team (week 6). She also gained knowledge of the academic success necessary to play on the middle school team. I would definitely call that progress!" Ms. Casad beamed with excitement. Mrs. Wilson replied, "Yes, again we see Rosa as motivated! She also saw a reason for performing well in school. That is progress!"

The team further discussed the benefits of combining Peer modeling with physical activity, and assessed the intervention as a success. Mrs. Tellez congratulated Ms. Casad on her intensified efforts to support Rosa. She emphasized the cultural competence, including advocacy and professional growth Ms. Casad was demonstrating. "I would love for you to share your experiences at the next staff meeting. Let's now look at Rosa's Portfolio progress form, to see if Rosa's academics were being positively impacted by the success of the socioemotional interventions."

## Culture and Cognition Linked: Relevant Literature Builds Cognition

Team members viewed Rosa's Portfolio progress form (see Table 6.7), which was not considered an intervention, but a progress-monitoring tool that provided a picture of Rosa's academic performance in a summary format. Looking over the tool, Mr. Call shared his observation, "The data in the *Student Choice* row is so telling. I can see Rosa chose assignments in which she felt she really had learned something. Look at the 'Compare and contrast essay' for *Esmerelda Rising*. It appears Rosa connected with the main character and how she felt about her father. By selecting and reading literature that Rosa made cultural connections with (Self: Text-to-Self, and Social Capital:

**Table 6.8** Rosa's Holistic Profile and Progress

| STEPS to Determine Difference from Disability | Cultural-Linguistic | Social-Emotional | Cognitive |
|---|---|---|---|
| **Chs. 5–6: Interventions #1 and progress** | **Peer modeling Strengths:** *Rosa learned* (1) rules of soccer, (2) confidence, (3) social rules of team sports—working together, (4) sixth graders must earn good grades to play. **Challenge:** Frustration working with others. | **Behavior Self-Assessment Strengths:** Strong progress with two objectives (1) I showed respect to myself, others, and property. (2) I stopped unkind behavior the first time asked. Built Rosa's intrinsic motivation. **Challenge:** Using tools to handle anger in appropriate manner. | **Portfolio progress Strength:** Chosen assignments showed Rosa's connection to (1) character's grief and resilience, (2) table peer in *Conversation Starters Activity*. **Challenge:** Math |

Text-to-World), her cognitive processes expanded in both literal and figurative reading comprehension. Great choice of recommending this book to Rosa! I see that relevant literature provided Rosa a connection to a strong female character, as well as a healthy outlet for her emotions." He continued, "It also looks like she made some social connections to Jennie in the *Conversation Starters* Activity." Ms. Casad replied, "Yes, now that you mention it, I do see Rosa and Jennie say hello to each other."

Mr. Call commented, "I see Rosa did the math perimeter homework even though she felt angry about it during the FBA observation. So . . . she may have had initial reservations about completing it at home, but she did it! I see her inability to control her outbursts, yet persistence with academics. She seems so resilient!" Mrs. Mola spoke next. "That is good progress; however, it looks like Rosa is still struggling with most math assignments." Team members were again directed to Rosa's Holistic Profile and Progress (see Table 6.8) to fill in progress in the box, *Portfolio progress*. Progress was now filled in for the entire row of Interventions. "Let's now look back at how the FBA might provide insight into math progress."

## Behavior as Need for Help, and Need for Control

Mrs. Mola reminded the team about looking for ways the antecedents and behaviors formed a pattern. "In four of the five antecedents, Rosa was asked to perform an action (1) write an equation, (2) work with the person next to you, (3) look for an object at home to find the perimeter, and (4) finish the assignment before the end of class. These four antecedents could be divided into two categories of Rosa's perceived levels of *internal and external control* she had over situations. Considering the background knowledge about Rosa, I will posit hypotheses that may explain some of her behaviors in response to Ms. Casad's directives."

## Internal Control

"One example of internal control is one's ability (i.e., individually) to access content knowledge of finding perimeter (1) to write the correct equation and (2) finish the assignment before the end of class. In the independent practice of the lesson, Rosa needed to write the correct equation by locating numbers of four sides of an object, then compute the addition correctly to obtain the correct answer, and repeat this several times to finish the assignment in a finite amount of time. If Rosa could not perform these steps independently, she would fail." Mrs. Wilson spoke up, "Rosa might feel overwhelmed with the tasks, may feel pressure not to fail, and need for possible additional support." The team agreed that Rosa's message of emotional outbursts may be a plea for help for additional tools (e.g., list of steps, copy of perimeter formula, additional practice before individual performance, positive feedback, check-in after each step, or additional time). With these tools, she may feel control over cognitive processes (i.e., knowledge, attention, memory, reasoning, problem-solving, and decision-making) to perform math problems by herself, which demonstrated motivation for success.

## External Control

Mrs. Mola continued, "In assessing the external learning environment as part of Rosa's challenge, she may not feel control over the other two directives (i.e., *External control*) (1) work with the person next to you and (2) look for an object at home to find the perimeter of. Data show that Rosa has difficulty with peer relationships, so working with someone else probably places additional pressure on her. Lori, I know sometimes you give Rosa the choice to work by herself. How has this strategy worked?" Ms. Casad responded, "Usually I remember to tell her she can work by herself if she chooses, but I am inconsistent with reminding her. I can try to remind Rosa every morning." Mrs. Mola agreed, "Great Lori, I think this consistency of offering her choice will empower Rosa to feel she has some control and responsibility over her actions, yet maintain her motivation." Next, they considered Rosa's home life and voice.

# Cultural-Linguistic Analyses, Combined With Socioemotional Factors

### Trauma From Crossing the Border

Mrs. Tellez directed attention to the Cultural-Linguistic column and *Rosa's Voice* (see Appendix G) to gain a better understanding of her *cultural self* (i.e., self, family and social capital, see Chapter 1, Tables 1.2 and 1.3) that may explain her behaviors. Team members looked under *File Review* and mentioned (1) Rosa and her mother came to the U.S. on inner tubes, (2) left friends and family there, and (3) Rosa's brother was in a gang. They agreed that all these were sources of extreme stress. Mrs. Tellez said, "No wonder she is angry! I think anger is an appropriate emotion for Rosa to be feeling. I am sure she appreciates the socioemotional supports in the classroom, and wonder if her mother is receiving any support. Rosa must be experiencing trauma, grief, and loss in both her external and internal environment."

### Sociopolitical Context

Mrs. Tellez continued, "When looking at all data sources, one seemed to be missing, the sociopolitical context. In the current political environment, people in authority were demonizing immigrants, especially those from Mexico (e.g., referring to them as murderers and rapists). Another problem was the current federal administration rule threatening those with DACA status (Deferred Action for Childhood Arrivals, September 5, 2017 announcement). These factors can create internal and external struggles for Rosa, contributing to strong emotions. Some factors are in our control, and some are not. Let's look at some factors we can control, like here at school. The fourth grade faculty are doing so much to challenge racism and discrimination, but let's look at the topic of expectations."

### Stereotype Threat

Another possibility of why Rosa may be angry is that she may feel that others hold low expectations of her, which she could internalize, and hold for herself. She may feel that she does not have opportunities to show how bright she is, and not appropriately challenged. We see she has many strengths, such as her natural leadership skills and quickness to pick up on new things. Research shows that often educators from the dominant culture have low expectations of those with minority status, which in turn influences the individual to have low expectations of themselves (i.e., *Stereotype threat*; see Steele, 1997; Steele & Aronson, 2005). Another result of both discrimination and Stereotype threat is *Internalized racism*, a view in which the dominant group's culture is seen as normal, while the subordinate group is seen as inferior. Looking to the larger society to construct a sense of self, members of the subordinate group find negative images that serve to colonize and recolonize them.

(Speight, 2007, p. 130)

"If Rosa is experiencing these phenomena, she may lack trust (1) for people in the dominant culture, (2) for those in authority, and (3) in herself; therefore, she may perform poorly. In hearing Rosa's voice, we see evidence of this: *'I needed to learn more English to be more like a white person. . . . It was all in English so I just felt stupid in there. . . . Here everyone thinks I am just stupid. . . . Some teachers don't understand that they treat you mean. I have tried to be nice to the other students in my classes, especially the white students but they only laugh at my bad English. I am nice to them and they are mean to me so I am mean back now and have to let them know I am as smart as they are, so I fight them to make them understand.'*

"In addition, there may be low expectations for girls from Mexico, from Mexicans themselves, and others (Mackenzie, 2010), which increases Rosa's challenges." Mrs. Tellez asked Ms. Casad to meet, reflect, and discuss their expectations of Rosa together.

## Holistic Support

Based on all data sources, the team created a plan for Rosa's success, and agreed to continue the current supports, with additional math tools. They decided that Rosa had responded to these interventions, and predicted that with additional time and consistency, her case would "resolve" (see Figure 6.1). Mrs. Tellez summarized the plan in three levels (1) *self and cultural assets*, (2) *intensive classroom support*, and (3) *school and district-wide support*.

### Self and Cultural Assets

Rosa was experiencing trauma and grief (combination of cultural-linguistic and socioemotional), which was the cause of most of her anger and emotional outbursts, with additional causes not considered here (e.g., father's separation, brother in gang). Rosa's confident dispositions will help her self-manage emotions, as well as challenge stereotype threats and internalized racism. She needed support in navigating complex identities within the acculturation process, for she was navigating Funds of Knowledge (i.e., family's cultural assets; Moll, Amanti, Neff, & González, 2005) and Funds of Identities (i.e., individual agency; Moll, 2014) that may manifest in integration, assimilation, rejection, or deculturation (Padilla, 1980; Collier, 1987, 2013). The team was here to assess and guide Rosa's integration process into academic success.

## Intensive Classroom Support

The team would continue to support Rosa's cognitive, academic, and socioemotional contexts for continued success by (1) navigating appropriate expectations of her, (2) placing Rosa in leadership roles with additional responsibilities, (3) continuing Self-Assessment of Behavior with focus on utilizing the Thermometer Scale (and other de-escalation techniques such as mindfulness), and (4) providing math instructional accommodations (e.g., list of steps, copy of formulas, additional practice before individual performance, check-in after each step, choice of working with peer or alone, and additional time) (i.e., change antecedents). Ms. Casad would need to experiment to see which tool Rosa responds to, one(s) that will not substantially change or alter the objectives, standards, or outcomes of math assignments (i.e., classroom accommodation). If Rosa demonstrates need for more intensive math supports that do significantly alter or change the objectives, standards, or outcomes (i.e., modification), then the team will need to re-evaluate her progress and need for *specially designed instruction* (i.e., purpose of IEP). Mr. Hill also agreed to conduct another FBA in math class to see if Rosa's behaviors change in response to the change of antecedents. On Rosa's Holistic Profile and Progress, team members filled in progress in rows Additional Data and Decide Plan: Resolve or New #2 Interventions (see Table 6.9).

## School and District-Wide Support

Team members pledged to mitigate sociopolitical environments by making stronger stances to oppose policies that alienate CLD children/families. They agreed to advocate with administrators, parent and community organizations to create a strong, vocal, action-oriented message of inclusion and support for ALL families, as a "sanctuary city" (i.e., a city that limits its cooperation with the national government effort to enforce immigration law. Leaders of sanctuary cities want to reduce the fear of deportation and possible family break-up among people who may be here illegally; Wikipedia). With support in these three areas, Rosa may learn to trust those with appropriate authority, and her peers, which will help her demonstrate positive behaviors and communication as a meaningful member of a democratic society.

**Table 6.9** Rosa's Holistic Profile and Progress

| STEPS to Determine Difference from Disability | Cultural-Linguistic | Social-Emotional | Cognitive |
|---|---|---|---|
| **Additional data (observations FBA and interview)** | **Interview w/ Rosa Strengths:** Strong self-esteem, confidence. **Challenges:** Doesn't feel "white" peers like her. She doesn't like them. | **FBA Strengths:** Confident in self-expression and advocacy skills. **Challenges:** Emotional, outbursts following antecedents: Teacher asked (1) write an equation, (2) work with the person next to you, (3) look for an object at home to find the perimeter, and (4) finish assignment before end of class | |
| **Data suggests (cultural analyses)** | May be experiencing<br>◆ stereotype threat<br>◆ internalized racism (low expectations from others and herself)<br>◆ trauma, grief, and loss | ◆ May feel overwhelmed with lack of control over tasks asked to perform,<br>◆ may feel pressure not to fail | May need to feel more control (choice to work alone) and math tools |
| **Decide plan: Resolve or new #2 interventions** | (1) navigate appropriate expectations of Rosa, (2) place Rosa in leadership roles with additional responsibilities | (3) continue Self-Assessment of Behavior Objective #2: utilizing the Thermometer Scale (and other de-escalation techniques such as mindfulness) MAINTAIN AND RESOLVE | (4) provide math accommodations (list of steps, formulas, additional practice before individual performance, check-in after each step, additional time) |

## Commitment to Student Success

At the end of the meeting, team members acknowledged Ms. Casad's intensified efforts to support Rosa, including (1) increased cultural competence and advocacy, (2) professional growth in becoming a teacher leader, and (3) learning about intervention implementation (e.g., reliability and validity). She also learned to view the importance of (4) silencing or empowering Rosa through behavior management techniques, (5) collaborating with Mrs. Ramirez to use similar language and positive reinforcement at home, and (6) consistency, reflection, and commitment to difficult tasks.

## Intervention Responses for Jun

The SST met the following week to discuss Jun's progress to classroom interventions. Mrs. Tellez again volunteered to be the leader, and explained the meeting's objective was to analyze Jun's progress through cultural, linguistic, cognitive, and socioemotional lenses documented on the form, Baseline Holistic Profile (see Table 6.10). An additional member was added to the team, Mrs. Rowan, the district Autism Specialist, as members thought Jun may possibly be experiencing High-Functioning Autism.

**Table 6.10** Jun's Holistic Profile

| STEPS to Determine Difference from Disability | Cultural-Linguistic | Social-Emotional | Cognitive |
|---|---|---|---|
| **Ch. 2 File Review Strengths and Challenges** | **Strengths**<br>Lives w/ mother, father, sister, and brother.<br>**Challenges**<br>Moved here from China with family.<br>Possibly emigrated here for political asylum reasons.<br>Family holds high respect of teachers.<br>**LAS score**<br>**English:** Level 2–3<br>**Mandarin:** 1<br>**Length of time in U.S. schools:** 2 years<br>**AQS score:** 20 less acculturated | **Strengths**<br>Appears happy.<br>Likes to be by himself.<br>Independent.<br>Non-competitive.<br>Kinesthetic learner.<br>Likes to play video games.<br>Likes math.<br>**Challenges**<br>Easily distracted, often off task.<br>Kicks the air and wanders around.<br>Lacks social skills.<br>Difficulty in forming positive interpersonal relationships. | **Strengths**<br>Math computation<br>**Challenges**<br>English Language Arts |
| **Chs. 3 and 4 Classroom Supports** | Made connections from Jun's cultural assets to content: connected pioneers' journey to immigrants' journey<br>Wrote classroom book, "About Us."<br>Assistance with acculturation process | Dictionary or translator tool.<br>Sheltered instruction: word banks, picture clues, match game, graphic organizers. | Student check-in with emotion list.<br>School survival and adaptation assistance (peer).<br>Clear expectations and positive, direct feedback.<br>Ignore undesired behaviors.<br>Reward positive behaviors. |
| **Chs. 4 and 5 Caregiver input** | **Parent English level:** Father proficient in Mandarin and English. Mother proficient in Mandarin and some English.<br>**Strengths**<br>Positive view of son and want best for him.<br>Acknowledge Jun's strengths and passions.<br>**Challenge**<br>Misguided belief about learning English and language development. | **Strengths**<br>Concern for son's social network.<br>Enacts strategies of de-escalating behavior, and setting boundaries.<br>**Challenge**<br>Pacifying behaviors. | Confidence in teacher's advice.<br>Expecting more from U.S. school system than China. |

Information was already filled in rows: (1) Jun's file review with strengths and challenges, (2) classroom supports, and (3) caregiver input (from parent meeting). After summarizing this information, Ms. Casad reported Jun's strengths: appears to be happy, likes to be by himself, independent, non-competitive, likes to play video games, and is near grade level in math. His greatest challenge was his behavior, specifically (1) showing distractibility by getting up and walking around at random times and (2) displaying lack of response to instruction, both verbal and nonverbal. In summary, Jun showed an unusually high level of distractibility and failure with task completion. The team decided to first discuss results of the intervention implemented over six weeks (1) *Guided practice in classroom behavior expectations* (see Chapter 5 for reasons chosen), (2) Sheltered English strategies, monitored with classroom Portfolio. Last, Mr. Hill would describe the (3) Functional Behavior Analysis, and (4) present the comparison of *Behavior Rating Scales* from Jun's parents (i.e., home) and school. In conclusion, after considering all data sources, the team would create hypotheses that may explain Jun's behaviors, and decide if he demonstrated responses, or needed additional interventions (see Figure 6.1).

## Guided Practice in Classroom Behavior Expectations

Ms. Casad began describing the intervention, which she reminded team members was chosen from the Acculturation Quick Screen (AQS, Collier, 2013), due to Jun's *less acculturated* status. This was designed as a tool for a teacher or peer to model expected behaviors in group or independent work during reading class. Ms. Casad and Mr. Call spoke with Jun about including his input in the tool, but Jun appeared not to understand. They spoke with Jun's father who helped determine appropriate *Behavior Objectives* that could be reinforced at home (1) looking with attention at speaker during interactions, (2) indicating comprehension (verbally or nonverbally), and (3) demonstrating appropriated body language (as defined by contextual expectations) (see Table 6.11). Discussion ensued about intervention fidelity, and Ms. Casad replied she was fairly consistent in implementation and assigning ratings (i.e., validity and reliability). Mr. Call had twice observed and rated Jun in the intervention sessions to establish consistent ratings (i.e., inter-rater reliability). The team defined "progress" as "ratings will increase from week two through week six." Ms. Rowan described characteristics of students on the Autism spectrum as having difficulty with those objectives. She would need to observe Jun in the classroom and on the playground to gather more information on determining if he may be experiencing High-Functioning Autism. She added, "Neurotypically developing students would usually show some type of response to one

**Table 6.11** Jun's Guided Practice in Classroom Behavior Expectations

Description: Teacher or peer models expected behavior for group work or independent work during morning reading period. Mark with tallies.

| Behavior Objectives | TUE WK1 | TH WK1 | TUE WK2 | TH WK2 | TUE WK3 | TH WK3 | TUE WK4 | TH WK4 | TUE WK5 | TH WK5 | TUE WK6 | TH WK6 |
|---|---|---|---|---|---|---|---|---|---|---|---|---|
| Jun looks with attention at speaker during interactions | 0 | 1 | 1111 | 1 | 111 | 0 | 11 | 11 | 1 | 111 | 0 | 1 |
| When called on, Jun indicates comprehension (verbally or nonverbally) | 1 | 0 | 1 | 111 | 1 | 0 | 11 | 0 | 111 | 1 | 11 | 0 |
| Demonstrates appropriate body language (as defined by expectations) | 1 | 0 | 11 | 111 | 11 | 1 | 0 | 11 | 1111 | 0 | 11 | 1 |

of those objectives." Based on the definition of progress, and data analysis, the team decided that Jun did not show progress to the intervention.

## Portfolio

Ms. Casad next described the accommodations she provided for Jun in English Language Arts and Social Studies classes: (1) more time to complete assignments, (2) break assignments into small sections, (3) work with a peer, (4) frequent checks for comprehension (see Table 6.12). She explained that even with the instructional accommodations, Jun did not seem to show comprehension in (1) the Oregon Trail unit, (2) Kindness Week activities, or (3) classroom meetings discussions of respect. Jun also appeared to have difficulty choosing assignments to include in the Portfolio for "Student Choice," which should be a fairly easy task.

## Specific Learning Disability

Team members commented on Jun's math strengths, which placed him close to peers near grade level. Mr. Hill added, "This pattern of strengths in mathematics, and significant challenges in other areas is typical of students experiencing Specific Learning Disability (SLD).

"Other characteristics of SLD include being socially withdrawn, difficulty concentrating, following directions, interpreting facial expressions, and understanding social situations; all which extend beyond the classroom (Klingner, Hoover, & Baca, 2008). Therefore, it makes sense to think that neurotypical developing students will demonstrate some type of social engagement, ability to concentrate and follow directions, correctly interpret facial expressions, and understand social situations (Farnsworth, 2016)." These clues were in line with Ms. Rowan's observations. However, Mrs. Tellez said it was too early to make these connections, with more data to still present. She pointed to the Flowchart (Figure 6.1) and reminded team members that the SST process needs to be very thorough, and they could not rush into making evaluative decisions yet. After all, they were finding so many pieces to Jun's puzzle.

## Behavior Rating Scales

Ms. Casad expressed frustration: "No matter what I have tried with him, he rarely did what was expected!" Mrs. Wilson offered comfort: "I'm sure it is frustrating for you, and may be for his parents as well. Let's see how Jun's classroom behavior compared with that at home (see Table 5.11). Mr. Hill

Table 6.12 Jun's Portfolio Work Samples

NAME: Jun He   Term:   FALL   WINTER   SPRING

| Cultural-Linguistic Content areas | Progress | Reading | Progress | Math Assignment | Progress | Social-Emotion Behavior | Progress |
|---|---|---|---|---|---|---|---|
| *Oregon Trail* **vocabulary dictionary** | Copied two definitions 2/5. | **Reading Log** | Observed reading, *Magic Treehouse* (grade 2 level), appears engaged, has not taken any Accelerated Reader tests yet. Did not turn in homework log. | **Perimeter dictionary** | Copied definitions, meticulous printing | **Kindness Cards** | Jun earned 2 in 1 week. Low number compared to most students in class. |
| **States of Matter CLOZE paragraph** | 3/10 correct Looks like he guessed. | **Dialogue Journal** | Jun copies sentences out of book. | **Perimeter word problems** | 4/5 correct, great work! | **Guided practice in classroom behavior expectations** | No pattern, inconsistent. |
| **Vapor? Liquid? Solid? Reflection** | Wrote 2 sentences; unclear ideas. | **Self-Assessment and Peer Assessment** | Did not complete. | **Angles and measurement end of chapter quiz** | 8/10 great understanding. | **Emotions List** | Chooses random emotions, doesn't appear to understand |
| *Oregon Trail Dinner Party Journal entry* | Took same perspective as example. | *Oregon Trail Comprehension questions* | 1/5 correct. | **Angles word problems** | 3/4 correct. Did not label answers. | *Respect Agreements reflection* | Did not turn in. |
| **Student Choice** Oregon Trail essay, "Effects on American Indians" | "I am good. Indian good." | **Student Choice** *Written book report.* | Completed sentence starters. | **Student Choice** *Angles homework* | 5/6 correct, meticulous drawing of angles. Great attention Jun! | **Student Choice** | Did not make choice |

presented the two Rating Scales, which received similar scores, but differed on many items. The Hes (Jun's parents) and Ms. Casad assigned four items the same ratings, which showed Jun (1) does respond when spoken to directly, (2) will listen one-on-one, and (3) can engage in leisure activities or doing fun things quietly, and (4) does not talk excessively. He exclaimed, "So there were a few patterns in common between home and school! These ratings indicate that Jun can direct his attention in these contexts, thus, probably does not experience Attention Deficit Hyperactivity Disorder (ADHD), nor Attention Deficit Disorder (ADD). However, other commonalities among the two scales showed (1) difficulty sustaining attention, (2) fidgeting, (3) difficulty organizing tasks, and (4) losing things." Ms. Rowan wondered aloud about ways Jun interacted with peers, as it is in these contexts where students experiencing Autism have challenges. She agreed to observe Jun the following week.

## FBA Results

Mr. Hill passed out Jun's FBA and directed the team to the *Behavior* column, (see Table 6.13). He reported (1) Jun got out of his chair six times over a ten-minute period and looked around the classroom; (2) walked toward the

Table 6.13 Functional Behavior Assessment—Jun

| Antecedent | Behavior | Consequence |
|---|---|---|
| Teacher giving instruction. | Jun gets out of chair multiple times (8) over a 10-minute period and just looks around the classroom. | Teacher ignored for 2 minutes. Then asked Jun to stay in seat just like the other students while she was giving instructions. |
| Teacher giving instructions and other students listening and asking questions. | Jun begins walking toward door but turns around and kicks the air and does Karate chops. | Teacher ignored. |
| Teacher circulating around room to help students individually. | Wanders around his desk staring at ceiling. | Teacher asked Jun to stay seated and keep working on assignment and that she would be with him in a minute. |
| Teacher asked Jun if he understood instructions, and if he could show her his work he had already done. | Responds to question with bizarre or "odd" response that has nothing to do with topic and makes classmates laugh. | Teacher told Jun to (in a loud and stern voice) to sit down and that she would be with him in a minute. She then told the class not to laugh when he speaks like that. |
| Teacher asked students to work in assigned groups, three students to a group. | Moves to corner by himself during "group" work. | Teacher let Jun work by himself but explained to him that he could work with his group if he liked. |

door but turned around, kicked the air, and performed Karate chops; and (3) moved to a corner by himself during "group" work. Antecedents: teacher (1) giving instructions, (2) circulating around room to help students individually, and (3) asking if Jun understood instructions. The team discussed how behaviors could be connected to antecedents; however, they did not see any connections, nor did they see patterns in the consequences given (i.e., Ms. Casad ignored him, or told Jun to get back in his seat).

## What About Jun's Language Development?

Mrs. Tellez reminded the team that they had not yet discussed Jun's language development. She had some real concerns about both his native and English Language Development. On the state exam, the English Language Proficiency Assessment (ELPA) given to him in the beginning of the year (five months earlier), Jun scored level 3 (e.g., Intermediate). She read the ELPA21 Intermediate Level 3 descriptor, *Student would be developing in all areas of language and was working on producing and expanding simple and compound sentences; composing brief narratives or informational texts, including a few details.* However, she questioned this score, and had many work samples to show Jun was performing between a level 1 and 2 on the Language Acquisition Scales (see Chapter 2, Table 2.3). Therefore, she decided to give Jun the Woodcock-Muñoz Language Survey III (WMLS III), in English, an additional standardized language assessment to compare with the ELPA. (See www.hmhco.com/hmh-assessments/bilingual/wmls-iii for more information on the WMLS III.)

On the WMLS III, Jun scored in Level 1, *Initial Development* level, in English, the preproduction stage of language learning, in which students required substantial instructional assistance in the classroom. The *Initial Development* level indicates that Jun's receptive and expressive skills are very limited and he has minimal comprehension and speech. Mrs. Tellez added that Jun typically struggles to understand simple conversations, even when topics are familiar. His spoken language often consists of single words or familiar phrases.

## Language Discrepancies

Jun lived in an entirely Mandarin-speaking home until age 6. At age 6, most typically developing children have command of syntax and pragmatics in their native language and still have difficulty with plurals and verb tenses.

On Jun's native-language assessment given in grade 3, he scored in the Beginning Language Acquisition Stage (i.e., Stage 1; see Jun's NLP Appendix D and Table 2.3), which indicate his expressive skills in Mandarin are very limited and he has minimal comprehension and speech. This score indicated atypical first language development. Ms. Casad said that Jun's writing samples did not show progress in the past five months, and all her students showed some progress. He also was unable to write more than one sentence. "Some days he can write two complete sentences, and on other days, he cannot write more than two words. You just never seem to know when he is going to have a good day or not."

Mrs. Tellez pointed out the significant difference in Jun's ELPA and the WMLS results (both consisting of reading, writing, speaking, and listening sub-tests) to determine language proficiency. She informed the team that when these discrepancies in language assessments exist, additional data is needed. Although these two standardized language assessments are great indicators for language proficiency, data triangulation is important (i.e., collecting data from a minimum of three sources). She suggested an additional language assessment that could measure and compare Jun's native language and English proficiency, the Bilingual Verbal Analogies Test (BVAT). The district would need to hire a certified interpreter who spoke fluent Mandarin, and train him/her to administer and score the assessment. Fifteen percent of IDEA (2004) funds pay for such services, as Valley District does not have access to these services. The team agreed and filled in progress for Jun's Profile and Progress in the rows for (1) Intervention #1 and (2) Additional Data (see Table 6.14).

## Cultural Analyses: Explanations for Behaviors

Now that all data was presented, team members could begin discussing cultural analyses as explanations for behaviors. Mr. Hill reminded them of the reauthorization of IDEA's (2004) the *exclusionary clause* which emphasizes that a child cannot qualify for Special Education Services if learning difficulties are a result of environmental (i.e., lack of quality instruction, lack of opportunity) or linguistic and cultural difference. Therefore, the ultimate question they must consider, "Is Jun's learning and behavior problems primarily due to (1) *language learning and cultural factors* (i.e., external) or (2) *a disabling condition* (i.e., internal)?" (Collier, 1987, 2013). According to these two areas, discussion began on hypotheses for Jun's behaviors and lack of progress.

Table 6.14 Jun's Holistic Profile and Progress

| STEPS to Determine Difference from Disability | Cultural-Linguistic | Social-Emotional | Cognitive |
|---|---|---|---|
| Chs. 5 and 6 Intervention #1 and Progress | **Sheltered English Strategies Strengths** Handwrites meticulously. Copies off texts accurately. Can fill in sentence frames. **Challenges** Self-expression | **Guided practice in classroom behavior expectations Strengths** Was able to mimic peers occasionally. **Challenges** *No progress | **Portfolio** *Accommodations:* (1) Additional time to complete assignments, (2) break assignments into small sections, (3) work with a peer, (4) frequent checks for comprehension **Strengths** Math **Challenges** Writing more than one sentence in English. Choosing emotions. Choosing assignments. |
| Ch. 6 Additional data | **Language Acquisition Assessments Strengths** Performed well on standardized test (ELPA). **Challenges** Performed low on (1) WMLS, (2) in-class assignments, and (3) Curriculum-Based Measurements. | **Behavior Rating Scale Strengths** Responds when spoken to directly. Listens one-on-one. Engages in leisure activities or doing fun things quietly, and does not talk excessively. **Challenges** Difficulty sustaining attention. Fidgets. Has difficulty organizing tasks, and loses things. | **FBA Strengths** Sat down when teacher asked him to. **Challenges** Responds to question with odd response and off topic. Kicks the air and Karate chops. |

# Language Learning and Cultural Factors

## Culture

Mrs. Mola mentioned that Jun may have been exposed to trauma, depending on reasons he came to the U.S., or during his journey, which may explain atypical behaviors as response to trauma. "According to the data (see Table 6.14), it appears that Jun has a very 'normal' home with a sister, brother, mother, and father. However, he could be displaying anxiety from the trauma of immigration. Ms. Casad, when you spoke with the parents, did they indicate any political or cultural factors that could be influential?" Ms. Casad said that they did not mention seeking asylum or other cultural factors that may create trauma. "Something interesting that came up in a different discussion with Jun's mother was that she was malnourished when pregnant with him, which could greatly impact his cognitive and social/emotional development." Mrs. Mola agreed this physical pre-natal condition would definitely have great impact on Jun's development and an important piece of the puzzle; however, she thought Mrs. He's condition during pregnancy cannot be considered a cultural factor, but a true disabling condition.

Mrs. Tellez replied, "Yes, pre-natal physical conditions definitely contribute to the presence of intrinsic disabilities. Let's look back at his *cultural self* (i.e., self, family and social capital; see Chapter 1, Tables 1.2 and 1.3) to see his dispositions." Under *File Review*, they saw that Jun has been in the U.S. 2 years, and demonstrates independence and non-competitiveness. Therefore, he could be negotiating Eastern communal cultural values with Western values of independence (similar to Rosa negotiating Funds of Knowledge with Funds of Identities). She continued, "It seems as this could be the case for any immigrant or CLD student. So, at some point, all ELLs must negotiate their identities, and decide how far they will climb into or out of the melting pot. This becomes an equalizer of experience for ELLs, with outcomes that vary in quality and quantity depending on many factors (e.g., length of time in U.S., purpose for coming, power relationships, resident status, amount of agency, etc.). Finding out reasons for arrival in the U.S. would add another critical piece to Jun's puzzle. The main question asked here is, is Jun's rate of acculturation typical? In order to answer, we need several years of data to compare with. Most CLD students will acculturate gradually over several years and at a steady rate relative to length of time, type and amount of instruction, and level of assistance with transition. However, those who do not show change year-to-year may have some unidentified difficulty or be having some other destabilizing stressful experience (Collier, 2013). Jun scored in the category *less acculturated* on the Acculturation Quick Screen (AQS III; Collier, 2013), and still needed time for integration into schooling norms."

## Language

Mrs. Tellez then reminded members of the length of time ELLs may spend in each stage of Language Acquisition (see LAS Chapter 2, Table 2.3). "According to the chart, and time spent in the U.S. (2 years), Jun should be in Stage 3 Intermediate (1–3 years in U.S. schools), depending on (1) if Jun received high *quantity and quality of native and English language instruction*, (2) if Jun has *typical cognitive ability*, (3) if Jun has a *risk-taking personality* (see Fillmore, 1991), (4) if he is *motivated* to learn English, (5) if he has *access to English resources* (e.g., books, television, internet, native speakers, etc.), (6) and if the *structure of English is similar to Mandarin* (i.e., structure of shallow vs. deep orthographies). Much of these data were missing puzzle pieces. One way to gauge typical from atypical development was to compare his progress to *true peers*."

# True Peers

In order for data to be valid and reliable, the evaluation of ELL progress needs to be compared to "true peers." True peers are defined as students who have the same or similar levels of language proficiency, acculturation, and educational backgrounds (Brown & Doolittle, 2008). Using true peers as a comparison requires collecting information usually not part of progress monitoring with English-only students, for normative growth rates (normed on English-only speakers) are established. If an ELL does not match the growth of his/her true peers, instruction should be intensified. Upon being compared to two "true peers" (from other fourth grade classes at their school), Jun's peers have adapted to their school environment without behavioral concerns or needing additional interventions. Jun's true peers' reading levels and fluency in English are one year behind other fourth graders, and their comprehension of English is currently at grade level (see Table 6.15). Although Jun can decode almost as proficiently as his native English-speaking peers at grade level, his comprehension level is at or equivalent to Kindergarten level. Jun also lags significantly behind in oral language development (i.e., verbal expression).

The team considered all data and found no consistent or predictable patterns of behavior, and behaviors were not connected to antecedents. Positive Behavior Interventions Supports were also ineffective for Jun. He is a likable student and did not have intentions of malevolence. The team needed to listen to Jun's voice, and had not been utilizing his strengths, which would focus on Kinesthetic learning, playing video games, and math. However, these may require more than accommodations, and may require *specially designed instruction* found in an Individualized Education Plan. They decided

Table 6.15 True Peers

| Name and (Length of Time in U.S.) | Reading Fluency Level (oral) | Reading Comprehension | Behaviors | ELPA Scores | |
|---|---|---|---|---|---|
| Jun (2 yrs) | grade level | Kindergarten level | Distracted, walking around, kicks air | 3 | Seldom demonstrates skills |
| Alex (2 yrs) | grade level | 3rd grade | Typical | 3.4 | Mostly 3s: Demonstrates skills |
| Maria (2.5 yrs) | Almost at grade level | 3rd grade | Typical | 3.1 | Mostly 3s: Demonstrates skills |

on implementing more interventions (see Figure 6.1) to test the hypothesis that Jun's learning challenges were due to an intrinsic disabling condition.

## Opportunities to Learn

Jun shows challenges in all three areas of development (1) linguistic, (2) socio-emotional, and (3) cognitive. The results of Jun's native-language assessment (see Appendix D) demonstrated atypical native-language development (e.g., missing command of syntax, semantics, and pragmatics), which is negatively impacting his English development. The team needs to ask Jun's parents if he has a history of oral language delay, which will give an insight into psychological processes, as an intrinsic disability will be evident in the native language (Ford, 2005). Accurate language assessments are needed to offer a glimpse of students' processing skills, and one piece in the larger picture of a comprehensive evaluation to distinguish typical or atypical language development. Based on observations in peer groups, we see that he has not developed social skills as compared to similar peers. Based on current data in three areas (linguistic, socioemotional, and cognitive), we hypothesize that Jun demonstrates signs of the presence of a disability. However, (1) further assessments in all three areas and (2) additional time to show progress are needed to verify this hypothesis. The *focus is on giving Jun adequate opportunity to learn, before assuming his challenge is a disabling condition.*

## Holistic Support and Plan

### Cognition

1. Implement an intervention for six weeks, then administer a Dynamic assessment, which examines what ELLs can do, and not what they know. Procedure: teach Jun a task at his performance level (see Table 2.3—Stage 2). For example, explicitly teach him how to locate characters' names in a text, give him time to practice and generalize, then assess. This process of monitoring him during and after learning a task is effective for ELLs because it does not depend on background experiences (Klingner, Sorrells, & Barrera, 2007).
2. Jun's parents stated concerns about his behaviors, and that Mrs. He had experienced malnutrition during pregnancy. The team needed additional puzzle pieces on Jun's *physical and cognitive development* including answers to the following: a. Did Jun regularly attend school in China or were there gaps in his education? b. Describe his

education in China (preschool, kindergarten, and grade 1), c. Did other teachers have concerns about him? d. Describe his pregnancy and delivery, e. Describe Jun's health and developmental milestones including age crawled, walked, talked, illnesses, etc., f. Is there a family history of learning difficulties? g. Does he usually learn new skills quickly or slowly? Answers will provide clues on cognitive development and possible presence of an Intellectual Disability.

## Linguistic

3.  Administer the Bilingual Verbal Analogies Test (BVAT), which will yield additional data to view patterns of specific factors affecting typical and atypical development.
4.  Observe Jun in peer groups and audiotape speech to collect and analyze language samples, which provide clues on language development (e.g., pragmatics), and cognitive development (e.g., executive functioning skills needed to plan and carry out social tasks) (Farnsworth, 2016).
5.  Ask parents the following: a. reasons for arrival in the U.S., b. if Jun received high quantity and quality of native-language instruction, c. if he has a risk-taking personality and is motivated to learn English, and d. if he has access to English language resources (e.g., books, television, internet, native speakers).

## Socioemotional

6.  The Autism specialist will conduct an observation of Jun engaged in typical activities and routines (Bagnato, McLean, Macy, & Neisworth, 2011) on the playground and in the classroom to assess his social skills. Social and cognitive skills develop simultaneously in neurotypical individuals, as people see the need to belong to social groups. Rogoff (2003) emphasizes that one concept of participating in a social group is that students learn to participate in later situations according to how they did in previous ones. Seeing connections between situations involves support from a more skilled participant. For students to generalize appropriately across experiences, apprenticeship helps in deciding which strategies relate to each other, and which approaches fit different circumstances. Students experiencing cognitive or sensory disorders (i.e., Autism Spectrum Disorder or Intellectual Disability) show atypical social development, and are challenged in effective ways to participate in social groups.

## Conclusion

Readers were invited to the Student Study Team (SST) to explore their objectives of evaluating Rosa's and Jun's (1) learning environment through cultural responsive behavior analyses (i.e., view difficulties as located in external environments as alternative explanation) and (2) acculturation level of *integration* into schooling norms. You also saw informal and formal language assessments as important pieces of the complex puzzles! In analyzing all data, the team considered if student learning and behavior problems are primarily due to (1) language learning and cultural factors (i.e., external) or (2) a disabling condition (i.e., internal). Members decided Rosa's challenges were due to cultural factors, and her responses to interventions were adequate to resolve challenges. The team determined that Jun was not responding to interventions and he needs additional interventions that ensure adequate opportunities to learn. Thus, the team needs more data on specific cognitive and social contexts to determine if learning challenges are due to intrinsic, biological factors, which warrant referral for Special Education services.

## Reflection Activities

### Reflection Activity #1: Discovering Details of Identity

Ms. Casad was learning so much about the process of determining difference from disability! In comparing responses to interventions from Rosa and Jun, she was starting to grasp the process of putting pieces together to form a complete puzzle. She saw the importance of native-language development, and how it correlated to English Language Development. Even though she now knew the amount of effort and skills needed to ensure students' needs were met, she occasionally wondered about the lengthy and detailed process. Why was it so important to discover the different puzzle pieces in culture, language, cognition, and socioemotional areas? Describe reasons you think each one is important, and what you have learned about each student.

### Reflection Activity #2: Behavior as Nature or Nurture?

Describe your understanding of analyzing the learning environment through cultural responsive behavior analyses (i.e., view difficulties as located in external environment as alternative explanation) and (2) acculturation level of *integration* into schooling norms. Then choose one student you know who is receiving special education services, and apply these two principles to him/her. You may have to investigate more to explain their (1) difficulties as located in external environment and (2) acculturation level of *integration* into schooling norms.

# Bibliography

Bagnato, S. J., McLean, M., Macy, M., & Neisworth, J. T. (2011). Identifying instructional targets for early childhood via authentic assessment: Alignment of professional standards and practice-based evidence. *Journal of Early Intervention, 33*, 243–253.

Brown, J. E., & Doolittle, J. (2008). A cultural, linguistic, and ecological framework for Response to Intervention with English Language Learners. *Teaching Exceptional Children, 40*(5), 66–72.

Collier, C. (1987). Comparison of acculturation and education characteristics of referred and nonreferred culturally and linguistically different children. In L. M. Malare (Ed.), *NABE Theory, Research and Application: Selected Papers, 1987* (pp. 183–195). Buffalo, NY: State University of New York at Buffalo.

Collier, C. (2013). *Acculturation Quick Screen AQS III.* Ferndale, WA: CrossCultural Developmental Education Services.

Donnellan, A. M., Mesaros, R. A., & Anderson, J. L. (1984). Teaching students with autism in natural environments. What educators need from researchers. *Journal of Special Education, 18*, 505–522.

Farnsworth, M. (2016). Differentiating second language acquisition from Specific Learning Disability: An observational tool assessing dual language learners' pragmatic competence. *Young Exceptional Children.* Advance online publication. doi: 10.1177/1096250615621356

Fillmore, L. W. (1991). When learning a second language means losing the first. *Early Childhood Research Quarterly, 6*(3), 323–346.

Ford, K. (2005). *Fostering Literacy Development in English Language Learners.* Retrieved from: www.colorincolorado.org/article/12924/

Jennings, M. (2009). *Before the Special Education Referral: Leading Intervention Teams.* Thousand Oaks: Corwin Press.

Klingner, J. K., Hoover, J. J., & Baca, L. M. (2008). *Why Do English Language Learners Struggle with Reading? Distinguishing Language Acquisition from Learning Disabilities.* Thousand Oaks: Corwin Press.

Klingner, J. K., Sorrells, A. M., & Barrera, M. T. (2007). Considerations when implementing Response to Intervention with culturally and linguistically diverse students. In D. Haager, J. Klingner, & S. Vaughn (Eds.), *Evidence-Based Reading Practices for Response to Intervention* (pp. 223–244). Baltimore, MD: Paul H. Brookes.

Lawrence-Brown, D., & Sapon-Shevin, M. (2014). *Condition Critical: Key Principles for Equitable Education.* New York: Teachers College Press.

Mackenzie, J. Z. (2010). Empowering Spanish Speakers. Tucson: Summerland Corporation.

Moll, L. (2014). Funds of identities: A new concept based on the Funds of Knowledge approach. *Culture & Psychology, 20*, 31–48.

Moll, L., Amanti, C., Neff, D., & González, N. (2005). Funds of Knowledge for teaching: Using a qualitative approach to connect homes and classrooms. In *Funds of Knowledge: Theorizing Practices in Households, Communities, and Classrooms* (pp. 71–88). Mahwah, NJ: Lawrence Erlbaum Associates.

Oregon Department of Education. (2015). *ELPA 21*. Retrieved from: www. Oregon.gov/ODEode.frontdesk@ode.state.or.us

Padilla, A. M. (1980). The role of cultural awareness and ethnic loyalty in acculturation. In A. M. Padilla (Ed.), *Acculturation: Theory, Models and Some New Findings* (pp. 47–84). Boulder: Westview Press.

Rogoff, B. (2003). *The Cultural Nature of Human Development*. New York: Oxford University Press.

Sindelar, P. T., Griffin, C. G., Smith, S. W., & Watanabe, A. K. (1992). Prereferral intervention: Encouraging notes on preliminary findings. *Elementary School Journal, 92,* 245–258.

Skiba, R. J., Horner, R. H., Chung, C. G., Rausch, M. K., May, S. L., & Tobin, T. (2011). Race is not neutral: A national investigation of African-American and Latino disproportionality in school discipline. *School Psychological Review, 40*(1), 85–107.

Speight, S. (2007). Internalized racism: One more piece of the puzzle. *Counseling Psychologist, 35*(1), 126–134.

Steele, C. M. (1997). A threat in the air: How stereotypes shape intellectual identity and performance. *American Psychologist, 52*(6), 613–629.

Steele, C. M., & Aronson, J. (2005). Stereotypes and the fragility of academic competence, motivation, and self-concept. In A. J. Elliot & Carol S. Dweck (Eds.), *Handbook of Competence and Motivation* (pp. 436–455). New York: Guilford Press.

Wikipedia. "Sanctuary City" Definition. Retrieved from: https://en.wikipedia. org/wiki/Sanctuary_city

# 7

# Discussion and Final Thoughts

## Discussion

Authors of this text have focused on the general education teacher's role in the referral process for determining differences from disabilities among CLD/ELL students. Now that you are informed about the complexities of this process, you can appreciate the amount of dedication and difficulty required for working through this process. The general education teacher's role in accurately implementing this process is crucial for providing the best services and opportunities for CLD/ELL students. Yes, it is a long and complex process, but students from Culturally and Linguistically Diverse backgrounds and those who don't speak English, enter our schools with the same expectations from their teachers as any other student; they come to our schools for an education. Coming to our schools from a different culture and not having command of the language used in that school has already put these students behind their peers in many ways, but to have an exceptionality along with those differences makes it nearly impossible to perform at the same rate as their peers without the support of culturally responsive teachers. Understanding what to look for and how to find information for determining if your CLD/ELL student has a disability can only improve his or her opportunities and possibilities. In gaining that understanding and knowledge, you are able to provide them with the support they need for reaching their full potential. Isn't this really what all teachers want for all students?

As mentioned in the beginning of the text, the very first step in the process of becoming an effective teacher for those who are different than ourselves is to begin reflecting on who we are as cultural individuals, and developing an understanding of why we do what we do. Beginning to understand our own *cultural self* is possibly the most critical step in this entire process, because as you have seen, having an understanding of what makes you the cultural being you are, essentially knowing your Funds of Knowledge and "cultural assets," the more likely you are going to provide culturally appropriate instruction to all of your students. While you are developing a better understanding of your *cultural self*, you are also simultaneously building a better understanding of your students. We showed you how important it is to develop a Holistic Student Profile, which is a step toward getting to know your students and what makes them who they are as individuals with specific needs.

There are many puzzle pieces to answering the complex question, "How do I determine differences from disabilities with my ELL/CLD students?" Collaboration with professionals is a good place to start and a very effective way to obtain results that help answer that question. Collaborating with education specialists is a key part of the process that is often overlooked when attempting to answer this question alone. Collaboration helps with finding important data about your students that one individual may not be aware of. Specialists can help with reviewing cumulative files to explain the many perspectives on students' lives when developing the Holistic Student Profile. Collaborating with the ELD specialist helps with finding out if the student is demonstrating typical or atypical English Language Development, which requires investigating (1) English and native-language proficiency levels in listening, speaking, reading, writing (i.e., phonetics, syntax, semantics, pragmatics); (2) factors affecting students' language acquisition (e.g., motivation, exposure to target language, personality, etc.); (3) behaviors demonstrated in each stage of second-language acquisition; and (4) effective instruction. One must also understand the need for a variety of authentic language and performance assessments in drawing an accurate picture of ELLs' language and cognitive skills, which include observations in peer groups that reveal social and language development (Farnsworth, 2016). Practitioners must also collaborate with the SPED teacher to understand (1) characteristics of high-incidence categories (ADHD, SLD, and ED), (2) eligibility determinations, as well as (3) reasons CLD/ELL students are difficult to accurately assess. Another critical step is for educators to advocate for ethical practices that determine difference from disability, which requires discipline, courage, intentional reflection, and collection of various types of data (Farnsworth, 2016).

## Possible Outcomes for Rosa

In examining the process of determining if Rosa needed special education services, there could have been multiple outcomes. The authors concluded the scenario at the end of Chapter 6 with the Student Study Team (SST) deciding that Rosa was responding to interventions, therefore, not requiring special education services, and would receive continued classroom support. Let's look at some possible outcomes for Rosa if the process was carried out improperly. If the team did not recognize Rosa's strengths, properly monitor her progress with sufficient time, and analyze multiple data sources from a culturally responsive perspective, they could have decided to refer her for special education services under the Emotional Disturbance (ED) category. After all, she did display several characteristics of a student with ED such as impulsiveness, aggression, anxiety, acting out or fighting, difficulty in learning, and poor coping skills. This could have been another misplacement that happens all too often when educators make quick judgments or assumptions that are often misinformed and misunderstood. It is critical that educators do not make quick decisions that result in missed opportunities for students. Rosa did display several characteristics of someone experiencing ED, but effectively working through the process enabled the team to find the best solution for her without referral for special education services.

Another possibility for Rosa could have been placing her on a 504 Plan.

Rosa fits the two requirements for a 504 Plan in that she (1) displays many learning and attention concerns and (2) has several characteristics of a student with an exceptionality, i.e., ED, but not to the level of meeting set criteria for that category under IDEA.

To qualify for a 504 Plan, there are two requirements:

1.  A child has any disability, which can include many learning or attention issues.
2.  The disability must interfere with the child's ability to learn in a general education classroom. Section 504 has a broader definition of a disability than IDEA. That's why a child who doesn't qualify for an IEP might still be able to get a 504 Plan. Section 504 defines a person with a disability as someone who:
    ◆   Has a physical or mental impairment that "substantially" limits one or more major life activity (such as reading or concentrating).
    ◆   Has a record of the impairment.
    ◆   Is regarded as having an impairment, or a significant difficulty that isn't temporary. For example, a broken leg isn't an impairment, but a chronic condition, like a food allergy, might be.

(See the following for more in-depth information regarding the 504 Plan: https://ed.gov/about/offices/list/ocr/504faq.html and www.washington. edu/doit/what-difference-between-iep-and-504-plan).

If Rosa's behaviors fit most of the criteria for ED, why didn't the SST place Rosa on a 504 Plan? The team decided that Rosa showed positive progress with emotion management and academics, and that the "impairment" was a result of cultural factors located in her environment. Rosa learned appropriate behavior in the time frame given, thus, deeming the behaviors she displayed as temporary. A 504 Plan restricts support services the classroom teacher can provide. The benefits of keeping Rosa with a culturally responsive classroom teacher and her peers with continued use of specific support interventions was decided as the best outcome for her.

Another possibility for Rosa could have been to treat her as a "behavior problem" with malevolent intent, and push her through the system as quickly as possible with devastating consequences (i.e., school-to-prison pipeline). If Rosa did not have a teacher like Ms. Casad and had not been taken through the entire process to determine the underlying causes of her behavior, she could have easily been overlooked and not considered worth the effort. This is a common result for CLD/ELL students when educators do not recognize their own biases or discomfort in working with diverse students who possess different cultural assets than themselves. The teaching force is still primarily composed of White, middle-class, monolingual women (like Ms. Casad), who often perpetuate the status quo (Sleeter, 2015), by not knowing their cultural identity or realizing their cultural biases. However, Ms. Casad went the full distance with Rosa, investing time, energy, work, and patience, which greatly affected Rosa's educational and social/emotional outcomes. Viewing Rosa's strong dispositions as strengths, and building on them for success, will positively influence her cognitive, linguistic, and social/emotional development.

## Possible Outcomes for Jun

Based on data collected for Jun, the SST could have decided a referral to special education services for any of the following categories, SLD, ADHD, or possibly Autism. Jun displayed several characteristics in all of these categories. However, referring him before the entire process was completed would have been based on insufficient data. If he was referred and found eligible for any of these categories, the result may have been another misplacement unable to meet his cognitive, cultural, linguistic, and social/emotional needs. Educators can and often do make assumptions based on experience, student observations, and patterns of behaviors or academic performance that a student is experiencing an exceptionality. When making assumptions such as this without sufficient information, we are doing a disservice to our students and ourselves as educators. It is crucial to have a well-informed data-driven case before making a decision to refer for special education services, as you have seen with César and Rosa. Once the team has decided to refer a student for special education service, the next step is to determine eligibility.

Regardless if a district utilizes RTI or other methods to determine eligibility for special education services, there is always an evaluation team (i.e., classroom teacher, ELL teacher, special education teacher, school nurse, speech language pathologist, occupation therapist, psychologist, and medical doctor in some cases) that conducts a comprehensive evaluation of the child (including medical, physical, psychological, language, etc.). The evaluation team must also include families as part of the decision-making process, and ensure that students will receive the best possible instruction available regardless of their differences or abilities.

After all data has been gathered, the team discusses the results of the evaluation and tests two hypotheses: (1) the ELL's learning or behavior problems are primarily due to language learning and cultural factors and (2) the student's problems are primarily due to a disabling condition (Collier, 2010). Baca and Cervantes (2003) state that an appropriate evaluation must include the establishment of school-based support teams to evaluate students in their own environment using a bilingual, nondiscriminatory evaluation process, which necessary to test these two hypotheses.

At the end of Chapter 6, the team concluded with recommending additional interventions for another six weeks with Jun (see Figure 6.1; last step). After that time, the team might determine that Jun showed little progress in the areas of language development, cognitive and academic development, and social/emotional development. Since he continued to show little progress and not respond at the level expected or near the same rate as his peers, a referral could be made for Jun to receive special education services.

## Does Jun Have Specific Learning Disability (SLD)?

If we compare Jun with a student experiencing SLD such as Trent, who was found eligible for SPED services under SLD, we see many similarities between them. Initially it was considered that Jun showed similarities of a student with SLD. Because of those similarities, the SST suggested many of the same accommodations for classroom instruction and assessment for Jun as are written in Trent's IEP. It was after weeks of implementing those specific interventions that the SST realized Jun required more assistance, and additional interventions top provide more opportunities to learn before making a referral. Jun's case is very complex since he is experiencing multiple factors in cognitive, linguistic, and social-emotional development, which extend beyond the factors of SLD.

The exclusionary clause that IDEA (2004) (www.naset.org/2522.0.html) added to the category of SLD does exactly that, exclude a child to qualify for SLD if learning difficulties are a result of environmental (i.e., lack of quality instruction, lack of opportunity) or linguistic and cultural difference. This is an important addition; however, it still provides little guidance to school personnel in determining a language difference from an intrinsic disability. Therefore, a comprehensive evaluation including both formal (i.e., standardized) and informal (i.e., nondiscriminatory) assessments is necessary to view the wide range of students' language abilities (including quantity and quality of language instruction), and gaps in learning (i.e., lack of opportunity including absences and previous schooling) to help test the two hypotheses mentioned above.

Exclusionary factors are aspects of the student's background and/or experience, which might influence a student's performance, which must be considered before a student can qualify for SLD. The SST or multi-disciplinary team must rule out causes such as visual, hearing, or motor disabilities, cognitive or emotional disabilities, cultural factors, environmental or economic disadvantages, and limited English proficiency as the primary reason for a student's difficulty before that student can become eligible to receive services under SLD.

> In accordance with the SLD rule, a student may not be found to have a specific learning disability if the IEP team determines any one of the exclusionary factors listed in the rule is the primary reason for the student's insufficient progress and/or inadequate classroom achievement. The exclusionary factors are: environmental or economic disadvantage; limited English proficiency; cultural factors; other impairments; lack of appropriate instruction in reading, math or any of the eight achievement areas being considered within SLD [Wis. Admin. Code § PI 11.36(6)(d) 1.].

(p. 31)

What about the possibility that Jun was experiencing Attention Deficit Disorder/Attention Deficit Hyperactivity Disorder (ADD/ADHD) or Autism Spectrum Disorder (ASD)? These two disabilities are difficult to distinguish and are often confused. They overlap and have similar characteristics, but you should know that ADHD is not considered a disability under IDEA;

however it does fall under the category for Other Health Impairment (OHI). Students with ADHD are eligible for an IEP under OHI. They can also be placed on a 504 Plan with accommodations. Autism Spectrum Disorder is a category under IDEA and students found eligible can qualify for an IEP (see Department of Education, https://sites.ed.gov/idea/ for more on similarities and differences of ADHD and ASD).

Jun demonstrates many characteristics of both ADHD and ASD. He has difficulties in paying attention, concentrating, and being impulsive which may suggest ADHD. He also struggles with social skills and communication, as do many students experiencing ASD. However, closely analyzing the data collected throughout the entire process, including the final weeks of additional interventions, we see that Jun shows more evidence of a student experiencing an Intellectual Disability (ID). The compiled data from multiple sources, starting in the beginning of this process to the final stage showed that Jun is not making progress or responding in any of the areas of cognitive development, linguistic development, or social/emotional development and would benefit from additional support beyond what is in place for him.

Characteristics of students with ID have been associated with a negative influence on academic achievement. Students who are mildly intellectually disabled and who are poor readers share a deficit in phonological language skills similar to other students with disabilities (e.g., SLD) (Fletcher, Blair, Scott, & Bolger, 2004). Students with intellectual disabilities are also often significantly delayed in general oral language skills. Students with mild intellectual disabilities are characterized by general delays in cognitive development that influence the acquisition of language and academic skills. Moreover, while these students can learn some information that is part of the general education curriculum, they learn more slowly than do typical students. Deficits in specific cognitive skill areas also contribute to this delay. Three of the most important cognitive skill deficits exhibited by students with mild intellectual disabilities are related to attention, memory, and generalization (McLeskey, Rosenberg, & Westling, 2013). Jun displayed all of these characteristics.

The authors chose this case (Jun) intentionally to bring out the complexities of determining a difference from a disability. Jun has his differences and it is very likely he also has a disability. However, that will need to be determined through a comprehensive evaluation by a team of experts. They will determine if Jun is eligible for special education services under the category of Intellectual Disability (ID). The data collected by Ms. Casad and the PLC and SST teams will be used to evaluate and determine if Jun's learning and behavior problems are primarily due to language learning and cultural factors or if they are primarily due to a disabling condition.

## In Conclusion

We have shown in this discussion and throughout the text that the general education teacher's role in this process is absolutely necessary and critical. That role includes the essential parts of the puzzle when determining differences from disabilities, i.e., developing your *cultural self*, making attempts to understand your CLD/ELL students as individuals with specific needs, collaborating with other educators, learning how ELLs acculturate into a new learning environment, extending your knowledge about language and how it is acquired, listening to your students and their families, extending your knowledge about special education and high-incidence exceptionalities, and implementing effective interventions to meet ELL student needs.

Most teachers want to be more involved in their students' education and are naturally caring individuals, but have not had the proper training to carry out a referral process and determine differences from disabilities. Many general education teachers have also not been trained or have only received minimal education on second-language acquisition or best practices for ELL students in their classrooms.

The authors suggest more professional development is needed for general education teachers specifically in the areas of acculturation, language acquisition, and collaborating with ELD/SPED teachers. Without proper training and knowledge of these three specific areas when attempting to determine differences from disabilities, overrepresentation of ELLs and students from culturally diverse backgrounds misplaced in special education will undoubtedly continue.

Although the case study students' names in this book are fictitious, their stories are not. Their stories have displayed the reality of ways ELLs and students from Culturally and Linguistically Diverse backgrounds can reach their potential and become a vital part of society. Regardless of the outcome of this process, we still have a responsibility to teach our CLD/ELL students like César, Rosa, Jun, and Trent, with or without disabilities.

## Bibliography

Baca, L., & Cervantes, H. T. (2003). *The Bilingual Special Education Interface* (4th ed.). Upper Saddle River, NJ: Pearson.

Collier, C. (2010). *Seven Steps to Separating Difference and Disability for Diverse Learners*. Thousand Oaks, CA: Corwin.

Farnsworth, M. (2016). Differentiating second language acquisition from Specific Learning Disability: An observational tool assessing dual language learners' pragmatic competence. *Young Exceptional Children.* Advance online publication. doi: 10.1177/1096250615621356

*Fletcher,* K. L., Blair, C., Scott, M. S., & Bolger, K. E. (2004). Specific patterns of cognitive abilities in young children with mild mental retardation. *Education and Training in Developmental Disabilities, 39*(3), 270–278.

*McLeskey,* J. L., Rosenberg, M. S., & Westling, D. L. (2013). *Inclusion: Effective Practices for All Students* (2nd ed.). Boston: Pearson.

National Association of Special Education Teachers. (2006/2007). *Introduction to Learning Disabilities.* Retrieved from: www.naset.org/2522.0.html

Sleeter, C. (2015). *White Bread: Weaving Cultural Past into the Present.* Boston: Sense Publishers.

# Appendix A: Trent's Full IEP

## Part B: Oregon Standard Individualized Education Program

To be used in conjunction with Individualized Education Program, Part A: IEP Guidelines for Completion

### Demographics

| | | |
|---|---|---|
| _____Trent Jones__<br><br>Student | Valley School District<br><br>Resident District | April 25, 2016<br><br>IEP Meeting Date |
| | *Valley Elementary* | April 25, 2016 |
| Gender: __X_ M ___ F<br>Date of Birth (mm/dd/yy | Grade: 4 | Annual IEP Review Date |
| 03/13/2006 | | April 26. 2017<br><br>Amendment Date |
| ___xxxxxxxx_____<br><br>Secure Student Identifier (SSID) | ___Mr. Hill_____<br><br>Case Manager | _____xxxxxx_____<br><br>Most Recent (re)<br>Evaluation Date |
| _____90_____<br><br>Primary Disability Code &<br>Category | Secondary Disability Code &<br>Category—OPTIONAL | __April 25, 2019 __<br><br>Re-Evaluation Due Date |

### Meeting Participants

| | | |
|---|---|---|
| __Trent_____<br><br>Student | _____Karrie_(mother)___<br><br>Parent/Guardian/Surrogate | _Joshua (father)_____<br><br>Parent/Guardian/Surrogate |
| _____Mr. Hill_____<br><br>Special Education Teacher/<br>Provider | _____<br><br>Special Education Teacher/<br>Provider | _____Mrs. X_____<br><br>District Representative |

_____Ms. Casad_____        _____        _____Mrs. X_____

General Education Teacher        General Education Teacher        Individual Interpreting Instructional Implications of Evaluations

_____N/A_____        _____        _____

Agency Representative, if appropriate        Other        Other

*NOTE: If required team member participates through written input or is excused from all or part of the IEP meeting, attach documentation of parent's and district's agreement to participate by written input or excuse.*

A district provided interpreter was used for this meeting: YES, NO X.

Name _____

## Procedural Safeguard Notification *34 CFR 300.504(a)*

Parent was provided the special education procedural safeguards in his/her native language or other mode of communication

YES_X___ NO_____ *April 25, 2016*

If student is of transition age, he/she was provided the special education procedural safeguards in his/her native language or other mode of communication

YES_____ NO_____, N/A.

(*) To note required team members?

## Special Factors

In developing each student's IEP, the IEP team must consider        *(34 CFR 300.324):*

| A. Does the student exhibit behavior that impedes his/her learning or the learning of others? | *34 CFR 300.324(a)(2)(i)* |
|---|---|
| _____ YES | __X___ NO |
| *If YES, the IEP addresses the use of positive behavioral interventions and supports, and other strategies, to address that behavior(s).* | |

| B. Does the student have limited English Proficiency? | | 34 CFR 300.324(a)(2)(ii) |
|---|---|---|
| _____ YES    English Language Level_____ | | ___X__ NO |
| *If YES, the IEP team must consider the language needs of the student as those needs relate to the student's IEP* | | |

| C. Is the student blind or visually impaired? | | 34 CFR 300.324(a)(2)(iii) |
|---|---|---|
| _____ YES | | ___X__ NO |
| *If YES, Braille needs are addressed in the IEP, or an evaluation of reading/writing needs is completed and a determination is made that Braille is not appropriate* | | |

| D. Does the student have communication needs? | | 34 CFR 300.324(a)(2)(iv) |
|---|---|---|
| __X___ YES | | _____ NO |
| *If YES, the IEP addresses communication supports, services, and/or instruction* | | |

| E. Is the student deaf or hard of hearing? | | 34 CFR 300.324(a)(2)(iv) |
|---|---|---|
| _____ YES | | __X___ NO |
| *If YES, the IEP addresses the student's language and communication needs, opportunities for direct communication with peers and professional personnel in the student's language and communication mode, academic level, and full range of needs, including opportunities for direct instruction in the student's language and communication mode.* | | |

| F. Does the student need assistive technology devices or services? | | 34 CFR 300.324(a)(2)(v) |
|---|---|---|
| __X__ YES | | _____ NO |
| *If YES, the IEP addresses assistive technology devices or services.* | | |

| G. Does the student require Accessible Instructional Materials (large print, Braille, audio or digital text) | | 34 CFR 300.210(b)(3); 300.172(b)(4) |
|---|---|---|
| _____ YES | | __X___ NO |
| *If YES, alternate format(s) is/are identified in the IEP* | | |

## Present Levels of Academic Achievement and Functional Performance

In developing each student's IEP, the IEP team must consider                    *(34CFR 300.324):*

| | |
|---|---|
| Student's overall strengths, interests, and preferences: | *34 CFR 300.324 (a)(1)(i)* |

Trent is kind and loving 4th grade student who has confidence in his skills to learn. He has a good sense of humor and is very helpful. He is good at public speaking and is creative, and enjoys art and building things. He likes baseball and P.E. and enjoys games that involve excitement and competition.

| | |
|---|---|
| Input from parent(s) in the areas of academic achievement and functional performance, including concerns for enhancing the education of their child: | *34 CFR 300.324(a)(1)(ii)* |

Mom is concerned about Trent continuing to make progress. She feels he needs to work on comprehension and reading skills. She does not want him to get lost in the system.

Present level of academic achievement (i.e., reading, writing, mathematics, etc.), including most recent performance on State or district-wide assessments:

· Strengths of the student
· Needs of the student
· How the student's disability affects involvement and progress in the general education curriculum
*34 CFR 300.320(a)(1); 300.324(a)(iii)*

Narrative and supporting data:

Results of state-wide and district-wide assessments:

OSAT Reading: Valley Elementary. S 2015 Rit: 2370 Performance level: DN Benchmark: 2 Exemption: none

OSAT Math: Valley Elementary. S2015 Rit: 2370 Performance level: DN Benchmark: 2 Exemption: none

OSAT Science: Valley Elementary. S2015 Rit: 219 Performance level: DN Benchmark: 2 Exemption: none

DIBELS: Valley Elementary. Initial Sound: Letter Naming: Phonemic Segmentation: Nonsense Words: Oral Reading Fluency: 89 Mid-Year 2015–2016

DIBELS: Valley Elementary. Initial Sound: Letter Naming: Phonemic Segmentation: Nonsense Words: Oral Reading Fluency: 87 Fall 2015–2016

Star Reading: Valley Elementary. S2015 Grade Equivalence: 2

Star Math: Valley Elementary. S2015 Grade Equivalence: 4

Ravens: Valley Elementary. F2010 Percentile: 15

Reading:

On 9/19/15 in a classroom setting and taken individually on a Chromebook, Trent took an iReady assessment (district-wide assessment used for reading and math) in the following areas: Phonological awareness and high-frequency words. Trent scored in the 1st grade level for phonics, 3rd grade level for vocabulary, 4th grade level for literature comprehension and 3rd grade level for informational text. Trent is able to understand organization and basic features of texts, decode regularly spelled one-syllable words with short vowels. Trent is also able to identify characters and some details from 2nd grade texts, and explain what the text says and support inferences made about the text. Trent is also able to recognize characters and story elements in a story such as setting, plot, problem, and solution in 3rd grade level texts. Trent will continue to work on reading and comprehension in text at the 3rd grade level. Trent will continue to work on recognizing characters and story elements at the 3rd grade level.

Math: N/A

Written Language:

On 9/19/15 in a classroom setting and taken individually and handwritten, Trent responded to a narrative writing prompt asking him to describe his dream home if money were not an issue. Trent spelled 46/87 words correctly, and is able to demonstrate basic organizational skills in his writing. He stayed on topic throughout his entire response. Trent's sample had 1/9 sentences written completely (containing subject, verb, and object). Trent will continue to work on writing complete sentences (containing subject, verb, and object), while checking for punctuation errors at the 2nd grade level.

How the student's disability affects involvement and progress in the general education curriculum.

Trent's disability in Specific Learning Disability affects his ability to make progress at the same rate and speed as his same grade nondisabled peers. Due to organizational issues, Trent struggles with multi-step tasks and will benefit from a specially designed instruction and accommodations. He also requires specially designed instruction in academics to make progress in the classroom.

Present level of functional performance (not limited to, but may include communication, social skills, behavior, organization, fine/gross motor skills, self-care, self-direction, etc.), including the results of initial or most recent formal or informal assessments/observations:
· Strengths of the student
· Needs of the student
· How the student's disability affects involvement and progress in the general education curriculum
*34 CFR 300.320(a)(1)*

Narrative and supporting data:
Attendance:
Not an area of concern

Behavior Skills:
Not an area of concern

Communication:
SLP will provide present levels

Fine/Gross Motor Skills:
Not an area of concern

Life Skills:
Not an area of concern

Social Skills:
Not an area of concern

Study Skills:
As of 10/13/2016 Trent is passing the majority of his subjects. He is currently not passing in Language Arts. Trent will continue to work on completing assignments and turning them in when they are due. Trent will ask for help when needed from his teachers.

How the student's disability affects involvement and progress in the general education classroom.

Trent's disability in Specific Learning Disability affects his ability to make progress at the same rate and speed as his same grade nondisabled peers. Due to memory issues, Trent struggles with multi-step tasks and will benefit from a specially designed instruction and accommodations. He also requires specially designed instruction in academics to make progress in the classroom.

## Annual Academic and Functional Goals and Objectives

| Goal Area: Reading-Literature | *34 CFR 300.320(a)(2)(i)* |
|---|---|

Annual Goal: Expressions and Equations
Reading Literature: Trent will increase answering questions and identify parts of story (beginning, middle, ending, plot, and resolution) of texts from a 2nd grade level to a 2.5 grade level 4 out of 5 opportunities as measured by weekly class assignments by June 2017.

Objectives:
Trent will identify parts of story to support the main idea of a text 4 out of 5 opportunities.

Trent will determine the central idea of a story and write a three sentence summary of the story 4 out of 5 opportunities.

Trent will recognize parts of a story (e.g., how setting shapes the characters or plot) 4 out of 5 opportunities.

Writing-Planning/Editing

Trent will use pre-writing strategies (outline) in 3 out of 4 opportunities and edit (organize sentences to match characters) his writing from a 2nd grade level to a 2.5 grade level in 3 out of 4 opportunities as measured by a monthly writing prompt by June 2017.

After a writing prompt, Trent will edit writing samples from a 2nd grade level to a 2.5 grade level with 80% accuracy as measured by a monthly writing prompt.

Objectives:
Trent will produce complete sentences with writing that targets the purpose of the story 3 out of 4 opportunities.

Trent will develop writing by planning, outlining (organization) 3 out of 4 opportunities.

Trent will use technology (Chromebook) to assist his writing 3 out of 4 opportunities.

Expressions and Equations

Related Content Standard(s), if applicable:
Reading
Writing
Mathematics: N/A

How progress will be measured:
Work Sample
Curriculum Based Measures
Weekly Class Assignments
Teacher Observations

How progress will be reported, including frequency: 34 CFR 300.320(a)(3)(i)
At the end of each grading period (quarter).

| Progress Towards Goal | *34 CFR 300.320(a)(3)(ii)* |
|---|---|

Date of Progress: __6_/_10__/_2016__
Narrative and supporting data:

## Services

The IEP team must identify and provide appropriate services to enable the student:

- ◆ To advance appropriately towards attaining the annual goals *34 CFR 300.320(a)(4)(i)*;
- ◆ To be involved in and make progress in the general education curriculum and to participate in extracurricular and other nonacademic activities *34 CFR 300.320(a)(4)(ii)*;
- ◆ To be educated and participate with other children with disabilities and nondisabled children in extracurricular and other nonacademic activities *34 CFR 300.320(a)(4)(iii) & 300.107.*

| Specially Designed Instruction *34 CFR 300.39* | Anticipated Amount and Frequency | Anticipated Location | Starting Date | Ending Date | Provider | Role Responsible for Monitoring |
|---|---|---|---|---|---|---|
| Math—N/A | | | | | | |
| Reading | 14 hours per month | Special Ed. Setting | 09/06/2016 | 04/25/2017 | Special Ed. Teacher | |
| Written Language | 4 hours per month | Special Ed. Setting | 09/06/2016 | 04/25/2017 | Special Ed. Teacher | |
| **Related Services** *34 CFR 300.34* | **Anticipated Amount and Frequency** | **Anticipated Location** | **Starting Date** | **Ending Date** | **Provider** | **Role Responsible for Monitoring** |
| Communication | 1 hour per month | Special Ed. Setting | 09/06/2016 | 04/25/2017 | Sp/Lang. Specialist | |
| Social/Behavior | 7 hours per Year | Special Ed. Setting | 09/06/2016 | 04/25/2017 | Sp/Lang. Specialist | |
| **Supplementary Aids/Services; Accommodations** *34 CFR 300.320 (a)(4)(i)–(iii)* | **Anticipated Amount and Frequency** | **Anticipated Location** | **Starting Date** | **Ending Date** | **Provider** | **Role Responsible for Monitoring** |
| Break task into small steps | Multi-Step Projects/ Tasks | Reg/Special Ed. Setting | 4/26/2016 | 4/26/2017 | | |
| Seat Near Instruction | Independent Work | Reg/Special Ed. Setting | 4/26/2016 | 4/26/2017 | | |

| Frequent Checks for Understanding | Instruction | Reg/Special Ed. Setting | 4/26/2016 | 4/26/2017 | | |
|---|---|---|---|---|---|---|
| **Supplementary Aids/Services; Modifications** *34 CFR 300.320 (a)(4)(i)–(iii)* | **Anticipated Amount and Frequency** | **Anticipated Location** | **Starting Date** | **Ending Date** | **Provider** | **Role Responsible for Monitoring** |
| Team determined none needed | | | | | | |
| **Program Modifications/ Supports for School Personnel** *34 CFR 300.320 (a)(4)(i)–(iii)* | **Anticipated Amount and Frequency** | **Anticipated Location** | **Starting Date** | **Ending Date** | **Provider** | **Role Responsible for Monitoring** |
| Consultation to Regular Education Teacher | | | | | | |

## Nonparticipation Justification *34 CFR 300.320(a)(5)*

Describe the extent (including amount), if any, to which the child will not participate with nondisabled children in the regular classroom and in extracurricular and other nonacademic activities: Trent is removed to a special education setting for specially designed instruction for Reading—8 Hours per month, Written Language—4 Hours per month, Communication—1 Hour per month, Social/Behavior Skills—7 Hours per year.

Provide explanation justifying the removal, if any: Trent's disability in Specific Learning Disability affects his ability to make progress at the same rate and speed as his same grade nondisabled peers. Due to organization issues, Trent struggles with multi-step tasks and will benefit from specially designed instruction and accommodations to assist with this. Trent also requires specially designed instruction in academics to make progress as well.

# Appendix B: Emotion Words List

Instructions: Complete the following statement using all of the emotion words below that you are feeling. *"Right now I feel . . ."*

| | | | | |
|---|---|---|---|---|
| Joyful | Tenderness | Helpless | Defeated | Rageful |
| Cheerful | Sympathy | Powerless | Bored | Outraged |
| Content | Adoration | Dreading | Rejected | Hostile |
| Proud | Fondness | Distrusting | Disillusioned | Bitter |
| Satisfied | Receptive | Suspicious | Inferior | Hateful |
| Excited | Interested | Cautious | Confused | Scornful |
| Amused | Delighted | Disturbed | Grief-stricken | Spiteful |
| Elated | Shocked | Overwhelmed | Helpless | Vengeful |
| Enthusiastic | Exhilarated | Uncomfortable | Isolated | Disliked |
| Optimistic | Dismayed | Guilty | Numb | Resentful |
| Elated | Amazed | Hurt | Regretful | Trusting |
| Delighted | Confused | Lonely | Ambivalent | Alienated |
| Calm | Stunned | Melancholy | Exhausted | Bitter |
| Relaxed | Interested | Depressed | Insecure | Insulted |
| Relieved | Intrigued | Hopeless | Disgusted | Indifferent |
| Hopeful | Absorbed | Sad | Pity | Trust |
| Pleased | Curious | Guilty | Revulsion | Afraid |
| Confident | Anticipating | Hurt | Contempt | Nervous |
| Brave | Eager | Lonely | Weary | Disinterested |
| Comfortable | Hesitant | Regretful | Bored | Disoriented |
| Safe | Fearful | Depressed | Preoccupied | Disgraced |
| Happy | Anxious | Hopeless | Angry | Uncomfortable |
| Love | Worried | Sorrow | Jealous | Neglected |
| Lust | Scared | Uncertain | Envious | Awkward |
| Aroused | Insecure | Anguished | Annoyed | Frustrated |
| Tender | Rejected | Disappointed | Humiliated | Exasperated |
| Compassionate | Horrified | Self-conscious | Irritated | |
| Caring | Alarmed | Shamed | Aggravated | |
| Infatuated | Shocked | Embarrassed | Restless | |
| Concern | Panicked | Humiliated | Grumpy | |

# Appendix C: Rosa's AQS III Scoring Form

**Date:** *October 15*
**NAME/ID#:** *Rosa*    **SCHOOL:** *Valley Elementary*
**DATE OF BIRTH:** *May 1st*    **SEX:** *Female*    **GRADE:** *4th*
**AGE AT ARRIVAL IN U.S.:** *6 years old*
**LANGUAGE(S) SPOKEN AT HOME:** *Spanish*

Table C.1  AQS

| CULTURAL/ENVIRONMENTAL FACTORS | Information | Scores |
|---|---|---|
| 1. **Time in United States/Canadian schools** | Date from passport, 3 years | 3 |
| 2. **Time in Your School/District** | Two years | 2 |
| 3. **Time in ESL or Bilingual ELL Education** | Two years | 2 |
| 4. **Home/Native-Language Proficiency** | Speech emergence to intermediate fluency, limited academic | 3 |
| 5. **School/English Language Proficiency** | High speech emergence to intermediate fluency, limited academic | 3 |
| 6. **Bilingual Balance** | Can understand peers most of the time, but does not show understanding of content vocab | 3 |
| 7. **Ethnicity/Cultural Identity** | Hispanic/Latina | 2 |
| 8. **% in School Speaking Student's Language/dialect** | 13% | 5 |
| | **AQS III Score Total:** | 23 |

| | |
|---|---|
| 1. **Time in U.S./Canadian schools:** Less than 180 days (1 yr/good atten) instruction = 1 Between 190–360 days (2yrs/good atten) of instruction = 2 Between 370–540 days (3yrs/good atten) of instruction = 3 | Between 550–720 days (4 yrs/good atten) of instruction = 4 Between 730–900 days (5 yrs/good atten) of instruction = 5 More than 920 days of instruction = 6 |
| 2. **Time in Your School/District:** Less than 1080 hours (1 yr/good atten) instruction = 1 Between 1090–2160 hours of instruction = 2 Between 2170–3240 hours of instruction = 3 | Between 3250–4320 hours (4 yrs/good atten) of instruction = 4 Between 4330–5400 hours of instruction = 5 More than 5500 hours of instruction = 6 |
| 3. **Time in ESL or Bilingual ELL Program** Less than 360 hours of direct instruction = 1 Between 360 and 500 hours of direct inst. = 2 Between 500 and 800 hours of direct inst. = 3 | Between 800 and 1080 hours of direct instruction = 4 Between 1090 and 1440 hours of direct instruction = 5 More than 1450 hours of direct instruction = 6 |

| 4. **Home/Native-Language Proficiency** | |
|---|---|
| Does not speak language, preproduction = 1<br>Early production to speech emergence = 2<br>Speech emergence to intermediate fluency, limited academic = 3 | High intermediate fluency, moderate academic fluency = 4<br>Advanced intermediate social & academic fluency = 5<br>Advanced social & academic fluency = 6 |
| 5. **School/English Language Proficiency** | |
| Does not speak language, preproduction = 1<br>Early production to low speech emergence = 2<br>High speech emergence to intermediate fluency, limited academic = 3 | High intermediate fluency, moderate academic fluency = 4<br>Advanced intermediate social & academic fluency = 5<br>Advanced social & academic fluency = 6 |
| 6. **Bilingual Balance** | |
| Essentially monolingual = 1<br>Primarily one, some social in other = 2<br>Limited academic either language, moderate social both =3 | Good social both, basic academic one, intermediate academic other = 4<br>Most academic in one, intermediate academic in other = 5<br>Bilingual in social and academic language = 6 |
| 7. **Ethnicity/cultural identity** | |
| American Indian, Native American, Alaska. Native, Indigenous Populations or First People = 1<br>Hispanic/Latino/Chicano, South or Central America or Caribbean = 2 | African American, Black, Roma/Gypsy, African, East Asian or Pacific Islander = 3<br>West Asian or Middle Eastern = 4<br>Eastern European, former Soviet Bloc = 5<br>Western European, Scandinavian = 6 |
| 8. **Percent in School Speaking Student's Language or Dialect** | |
| 81%–100% of enrollment = 1<br>66%–80% of enrollment = 2<br>50%–65% of enrollment = 3 | 30%–49% of enrollment = 4<br>15%–29% of enrollment = 5<br>0%–14% of enrollment = 6 |

# Appendix D: Jun's NLP

### ASSESSMENT OF NATIVE LANGUAGE PROFICIENCY
#### ENGLISH FOR SECOND LANGUAGE LEARNERS (ESLL)

**General Information**

Students Name _____  Date _____  Duration of Interview _____
School _____  Grade: _____  Interviewer's Name _____
Language: Being Assessed *Mandarin*  Place of Interview *school library*
    Need to be Assessed _____
Number of years of schooling completed _____  Number of Students in interview group  1
in Native Country      Assessee     Others

**Performance Rating Scale** (Circle your choice)     **Proficiency**

| NATIVE LANGUAGE PERFORMANCE CRITERIA | Good | Fair | Poor |
|---|---|---|---|
| RESPONDS TO SIMPLE QUESTIONS AND/OR INSTRUCTIONS<br>Indicators: 叫什么名字<br>今年多大 | 3 | 2 | (1) |
| GIVES ORAL DIRECTIONS<br>Indicators: 告诉老师你要用电话<br>告诉公车司机你要下车 | 3 | 2 | (1) |
| DESCRIBES PEOPLE, PLACES, OBJECTS OR ACTIONS<br>Indicators 家中有什么人？<br>在课室有什么特色 | 3 | 2 | (1) |
| SHARES INFORMATION, EXPERIENCES OR OPINIONS<br>Indicators: 最爱吃零食是什么？ | 3 | 2 | (1) |
| Score: | | | |

**COMMENTS:**
broken sentences, has a 10 year old sister.
    Doesn't know much about father's job.
    phone number   Seems to be friendly.
(Additional comments may be written on the back of this sheet.)

**Assessment of Student's Native Language Proficiency**     Circle number

| Score: | If Total is: | | Level |
|---|---|---|---|
| This Rater _____ | 20 and above: | Proficient: | 3 |
| Other Rater _____ | Between 14-19: | Marginally proficient: | 2 |
| Total _____ | 13 and less: | Non-proficient: | (1) |

**COMMENTS ON ANY DIFFERENCES IN SCORES BETWEEN THE TWO RATERS:**
Writing sample
Don't know all letters!

**Figure D.1** Jun's NLP

# Appendix E: Jun's AQS III Scoring Form

**Date:** *October 12*
**NAME/ID#:** *Jun*          **SCHOOL:** *Valley Elementary*
**DATE OF BIRTH:** *April 6th*   **SEX:** *Male*          **GRADE:** *4th*
**AGE AT ARRIVAL IN U.S.:** *7.5 years old*
**LANGUAGE(S) SPOKEN AT HOME:** *Mandarin*

| CULTURAL/ENVIRONMENTAL FACTORS | Information | Scores |
|---|---|---|
| 1. **Time in United States/ Canadian schools** | Date from passport, two years | 2 yrs |
| 2. **Time in Your School/District** | One year | 1 |
| 3. **Time in ESL or Bilingual ELL Education** | Two years | 1 |
| 4. **Home/Native-Language Proficiency** | NLP answers mostly 1s | 1 |
| 5. **School/English Language Proficiency** | Three | 3 |
| 6. **Bilingual Balance** | Can understand peers most of the time, but does not show understanding of content vocab | 3 |
| 7. **Ethnicity/Cultural Identity** | China | 3 |
| 8. **% in School Speaking Student's Language/dialect** | 7% | 6 |
| **AQS III Score Total:** | | 20 |

| | |
|---|---|
| 1. **Time in U.S./Canadian schools:**<br>Less than 180 days (1 yr/good atten) instruction = 1<br>Between 190–360 days (2yrs/good atten) of instruction = 2<br>Between 370–540 days (3yrs/good atten) of instruction = 3 | Between 550–720 days (4 yrs/good atten) of instruction = 4<br>Between 730–900 days (5 yrs/good atten) of instruction = 5<br>More than 920 days of instruction = 6 |
| 2. **Time in Your School/District:**<br>Less than 1080 hours (1 yr/good atten) instruction = 1<br>Between 1090–2160 hours of instruction = 2<br>Between 2170–3240 hours of instruction = 3 | Between 3250–4320 hours (4 yrs/good atten) of instruction = 4<br>Between 4330–5400 hours of instruction = 5<br>More than 5500 hours of instruction = 6 |

**3. Time in ESL or Bilingual ELL Program**
Less than 360 hours of direct instruction = 1
Between 360 and 500 hours of direct inst. = 2
Between 500 and 800 hours of direct inst. = 3
Between 800 and 1080 hours of direct instruction = 4
Between 1090 and 1440 hours of direct instruction = 5
More than 1450 hours of direct instruction = 6

**4. Home/Native-Language Proficiency**
Does not speak language, preproduction = 1
Early production to speech emergence = 2
Speech emergence to intermediate fluency, limited academic = 3
High intermediate fluency, moderate academic fluency = 4
Advanced intermediate social & academic fluency = 5
Advanced social & academic fluency = 6

**5. School/English Language Proficiency**
Does not speak language, preproduction = 1
Early production to low speech emergence = 2
High speech emergence to intermediate fluency, limited academic = 3
High intermediate fluency, moderate academic fluency = 4
Advanced intermediate social & academic fluency = 5
Advanced social & academic fluency = 6

**6. Bilingual Balance**
Essentially monolingual = 1
Primarily one, some social in other = 2
Limited academic either language, moderate social both = 3
Good social both, basic academic one, intermediate academic other = 4
Most academic in one, intermediate academic in other = 5
Bilingual in social and academic language = 6

**7. Ethnicity/cultural identity**
American Indian, Native American, Alaska. Native, Indigenous Populations or First People = 1
Hispanic/Latino/Chicano, South or Central America or Caribbean = 2
African American, Black, Roma/Gypsy, African, East Asian or Pacific Islander = 3
West Asian or Middle Eastern = 4
Eastern European, former Soviet Bloc = 5
Western European, Scandinavian = 6

**8. Percent in School Speaking Student's Language Or Dialect**
81%–100% of enrollment = 1
66%–80% of enrollment = 2
50%–65% of enrollment = 3
30%–49% of enrollment = 4
15%–29% of enrollment = 5
0%–14% of enrollment = 6

# Appendix F: Collaborating With Families of English Language Learners, the "Sharing Basket" Project

> "There is no joy in possession without sharing."
>
> —*Erasmus*

*Objective*: The objective of this project is to have the parents model the appropriate role of "Show and Tell." In our school, we call it the "Sharing Basket" (an actual basket is sent home with the child when it is their turn to share). A letter and an email will be sent home to the families explaining how the "Sharing Basket" works. Guidelines for appropriate items to share will be given as examples.

*Rationale*: To send the message to all our children and families that we are all special and unique. No two children or two families are the same or have the same *story*. I want to prepare the children for the "Sharing Basket" so that they can think about items that are special to them. I also want to know what they find interesting and for them to learn more about their families. In turn, the other children, families, and teachers get to know more about each other. We will also document where the items are from, on a map.

*Implementation Plan*: The letter/email will be sent home in English and Spanish. There will be a two-week time frame where the parents are welcome to share at drop off, pick up, or schedule a time that suits their own schedule.

*Measurement Tool*: Items/stories to be shown/relayed—i.e.:-photos, books, tales of ancestors, elderly family members, mementos, etc.

## Sharing Basket—Parent Project (Letter Home in English)

Dear Families,

We would like to say a big *Thank you* to all the families that filled in and brought back the family photograph albums. It is wonderful to see the children sharing their family photographs with all their friends and with the staff.

We feel we know you all and your child a little bit better. The children are very proud of their wonderful families and their faces just glow.

Families are really important to the children and for the teachers to understand the child, it is important for them to know their families. Every child is unique and special and so are their families. Learning about the whole child is important to unlocking interests and ways of learning. Family cultures, traditions, beliefs, etc. all have a wonderful impact on the child's educational journey.

We would like to start a "Sharing basket" with the intent of learning about the child's interests and letting them discover their own special uniqueness by sharing stories, treasures, things that fascinate them, family treasures, and adventures.

To begin this project we would love for you, the parents, to model how to use the "Sharing Basket" before the children get to bring the baskets home.

Here are some examples of some things you can share:

◆ A photo of a special holiday/vacation, family member, pet, etc.;
◆ A scarf, article of clothing, fabric with a special attachment;
◆ A book, poem, letter that is meaningful to you;
◆ An ornament or statue from a different country;
◆ An art piece or drawing you like or have done;
◆ Something from when you were a child;
◆ A story about your child or a grandmother from another country;
◆ A memory of a special place;
◆ A special talent you have, or your job;
◆ A shell you picked up, that reminds you of something special . . . (you got married on the beach!).

The list is endless so we would love for you to let your imagination run free.

The baskets will remain at school because we hope to have a few parents per day sharing. Sharing time can be at Drop off or Pick up during the next two school weeks—Monday 2nd Nov. to Thursday 12th Nov. If you would prefer a time during the school day just check with a teacher beforehand. If you are unable to attend but have something to share, we would love for you to write a note explaining the article and your teacher can read it to the children.

We are also hoping to put up a map of the world and pinpoint places that relate to our stories, articles, and families.

Thank you all so much and we are so excited to learn more about each other. (The teachers are also going to join in).

## Compartiendo Basket—Proyecto de Padres (Spanish Translation)

Estimadas familias

Capitán Shell, profesor de Jenifer y me gustaría decir un gran agradecimiento a todas las familias que llenaron y trajeron los álbumes de fotos familiares. Es maravilloso ver a los niños que comparten sus fotos familiares con todos sus amigos y con el personal. Sentimos que todo usted y su hijo, conocemos un poco mejor. Los niños están muy orgullosos de sus maravillosas familias y sus rostros apenas resplandor.

Las familias son muy importantes para los niños y para los profesores a comprender al niño, es importante para ellos saber sus familias. Cada niño es único y especial y también lo son sus familias. Aprender sobre todo el niño es importante para desentrañar intereses y formas de aprendizaje. Culturas familiares, tradiciones, creencias, etc. todos tienen un impacto maravilloso en el viaje educativo del niño.

Nos gustaría comenzar una "cesta Compartir" con la intención de aprender acerca de los intereses del niño y dejar que ellos descubren su propia singularidad especial por compartir historias, tesoros, cosas que les fascinan, tesoros de la familia y de aventuras.

Para empezar este proyecto nos encantaría que ustedes, los padres, para modelar cómo utilizar el "Compartir Basket" antes de que los niños reciban para llevar las cestas casa.

Estos son algunos ejemplos de algunas cosas que usted puede compartir:

- Una foto de un día de fiesta/vacaciones, miembro especial de la familia, mascotas, etc.;
- Una bufanda, prenda de vestir, telas con un accesorio especial;
- Un libro, un poema, carta que es significativo para usted;
- Un ornamento o una estatua de un país diferente;
- Una pieza de arte o dibujo que te gusta o lo ha hecho;
- Algo de cuando eras un niño;
- Una historia acerca de su hijo o una abuela de otro país;
- A la memoria de un lugar especial;
- Un talento especial que tiene, o su trabajo;
- Una cáscara que recogió, que te recuerda a algo especial . . . (que se casó en la playa!).

La lista es interminable, así que me encantaría para que usted deje su imaginación vuele libremente.

Las cestas permanecerán en la escuela porque esperamos tener unos padres por compartir días. Tiempo para compartir puede ser a dejar o recoger durante los próximos dos semanas- escuela segundo Lunes noviembre al jueves 12 de noviembre Si prefiere un tiempo durante el día escolar acaba de comprobar con un maestro de antemano. Si no pueden asistir, pero tienen algo que compartir, nos encantaría para que usted escriba una nota explicando el artículo y el profesor puede leer a los niños.

También esperamos que aguantar un mapa del mundo y punto pin lugares que se relacionan con nuestras historias, artículos y familias.

Agradecimiento a todos mucho y estamos muy emocionados de aprender más unos de otros. (Los maestros también van a participar).

Gracias!!!

# Appendix G: Rosa's Story

At the age of 6, Rosa and her mother crossed the Rio Grande on an inner tube to come to the United States. She is a very high-strung and spirited young girl who is unrestrained when telling you *exactly* how she feels. Although during the first interview Rosa told me that she didn't want to hurt my feelings by talking about gringos. I assured her that my feelings were not hurt and she continued in her usual manner.

Rosa is average in size for her age and has long dark brown hair. During her grade school years, she came to school every day wearing a dress with ribbons or bows in her hair. She is very much a tomboy, and by the end of the day her clothes were soiled and her hair disheveled from playing so energetically during the day. Numerous times during recess Rosa would have a boy down on the ground slapping him until he cried. I would frequently have to physically pull Rosa off several kids during these fights. Most of the fights were due to other kids calling her "wetback" or that she didn't speak very much English and that she was "stupid."

Rosa is the youngest of three and has two older brothers. One of her brothers is in a local gang and one of them was in jail at the time of our interviews. This appeared to bother her because she brought it up several times throughout the interviews. Her parents are separated. She lives with her mother and one brother. She only sees her father occasionally. Rosa has a strong accent when she speaks English and prefers to speak Spanish.

After a series of tests, it was decided that Rosa would go to ELD for core subject areas and Language Arts. Rosa's first years of school in the United States were pull-out for ESL and placed in the lowest reading groups for her grade level.

## Rosa's Story

I first came right here at 6 years old in a big . . . like a tire. Like, how do you call it? An inner tube, yeah. Just me and my mom, we were the only ones [crossing]. We sneaked across the river in the inner tube and then we had to run. It was during the day. It was not that hard to pass at day. It was hard to cross the river though. I was scared. You had to pay like a hundred dollars to pass it. And then they [Border Patrol] catch [caught] us and we had to go back and pass again. We didn't say our real name [when we were caught].

We said our fake names. Then they took pictures of us . . . if you get caught, they [smugglers] will pass you again. Just two times and that is it. I don't want to pass by the river again. (Yo no quiero pasar por el río de nuevo.)

Just for two years I was in Mexico for school, first grade and kinder. (En México yo estúve en el kinder garden y el primer año de primaría.) I completed first [grade] over there [Mexico] but the secretary in grade school when I first got here messed up. She put me in first when I was supposed to go to second. Really the whole school messed up, I think. They didn't test me in the beginning. They just told my mom I was going to be in first grade again. My mom didn't know, she said okay. Al princípio yo estaba miedosa porque todos hablaban inglés. Yo no sabía nada del lenguaje en inglés cuando yo llegue aquí. Yo no sabía escríbir o decir algo. Yo no quisé ir a la escuela, porque yo no sabía nada, pero cuando comencé aprender inglés, yo quisé ir a la escuela. En ese momento, yo estaba pensando lo que necesítaba aprender para ser como un gringo. (At first it was scary because everybody was speaking English. I didn't know any English when I first came here. I didn't know how to write it or say it or anything. I didn't want to go to school because I didn't know nothing, but then when I started to learn English I want[ed] to go. I was thinking that I needed to learn more English to be more like a white person.) I thought that I had to act like the whites too. So they could like me. But then I realized that they wouldn't like me however I am. I don't need to learn more English for them to like me. I don't care if they like me. I just thought I was never going to learn it [English]. I know that I am smart at reading and math too, I don't like math as much as reading so I don't do the math work very good.

Algúnos maestros no entienden que ellos te asustan y amenazan con sus actitudes. Por esta ráson yo me quisé salír de la escuela en el octavo grado. (Some teachers don't understand that they treat you mean.) I have tried to be nice to the other students in my classes, especially the white students but they only laugh at my bad English. I am nice to them and they are mean to me so I am mean back now and have to let them know I am as smart as they are, so I fight them to make them understand.

Like [my science teacher] because he would always sit us in the back and we didn't know what to do. Or he would explain to us one time and we didn't understand nothing and he didn't explain to us anymore. He didn't want to explain to us. He said, "I have to explain it in English and then I have to explain it in Spanish and it is too hard. We don't have time to do that". Like he was mean. And he say, "I don't know how to speak in Spanish, to translate it and all that" and he is Mexican too, but he doesn't like to speak it I think. That is their job but some don't want to explain. We are learning English in ESL, well that is what she [ESL teacher] says. I am doing it [English] dumb so I can stay in that class. I don't want to get out either because I don't want to be with the gringos [white people]. I won't ever get out of ESL. I want to stay in ESL. I told [my ESL teacher] that I don't want to get out. If we pass the test then we have to get out. I just put whatever answer. . . . My mom says to speak English and to get a good job because she doesn't want me to be cleaning houses and the bathrooms. She wants me to get a good job. That is why she brought me over here, to learn English and to graduate and get a good job.

Soy pura Mexicana [I am pure Mexican]. See that is the way that I feel. That I have to be true to myself. I felt real bad when I was with the gringos and that is why I never want to be with the gringos. But I wish at least they could treat us the same like them.

# Appendix H: When I Feel Angry, I Can Make Choices. I Can Handle My Anger in Good Ways!

## When I feel angry, I can

1. Get away from the person who is making me mad. If I am at home, I can go to another room.

At school, I can ask to go to a quiet spot in my classroom.

2. Tell Mom, Dad, teachers, sisters, and kids that I feel angry. My voice can be upset, but I need to use nice words.

3. Ask to take a five minute break from an upsetting job or job that I do not like to do.

4. Squeeze and pound play dough or any squishy, soft thing.

5. Count to five and take five deep breaths and then blow them out.

When I feel angry, there are things that I can do and things that I can not do! I can not hit, kick, or hurt myself. I can not stomp or pound things.

If I remember to do some of the 5 things when I feel angry, I can start to feel better and not so angry.

# Appendix I: Strategies and Examples for Less Acculturated Students (Collier, 2013, 2016)

**Strategies for Families of Less Acculturated students (on AQS):**

Cross-cultural counseling for families
Family-centered learning activity
Guided practice w/ service personnel from school/government agencies
Home activities
Survival strategies for parents/families
Videotapes and booklets about schools, communities, social service providers, laws

**Strategies for Less Acculturated Students**

Bilingual aide, peers, and texts
Consistent sequence
Content modification
Context embedding
Cross-cultural counseling
Demonstration
Experience-based learning
Guided practice and planned interactions with different speakers
Guided practice in classroom behavior expectations and survival strategies
Guided practice in cognitive learning strategies
Guided practice in constructive quality interactions
Guided reading and writing in home and community language
Language games with L1/L2 match
Leveled readers if literate in L1
Peer/school adaptation process support
Rest and relaxation techniques
Scaffolding
Sheltered cognitive learning strategies
Sheltered interactions
Sheltered language
Word walls and labels in both languages
Wordless picture books

## Example Strategy #1: Guided Practice in Constructive Quality Interactions

1. Purpose of the strategy
   a. Build transfer skills
   b. Build awareness of appropriate school language and rules for academic and social behaviors

    c. Develop confidence in school language and rules for academic and social interactions

    d. Develop personal control of situations

    e. Reduce response fatigue

2. How to do it

    a. At Tier 1, this strategy may be done within an integrated classroom.

    b. In RTI models, this strategy may be done with small groups, in individualized, focused intensive periods of time, or in specially designed individual programs and may be included in the IEP.

    c. Peer or specialist demonstrates how to act or speak in a given school culture situation. The situation is explained in home and community language when possible, and each stage is modeled. Representatives of school language and rules who are familiar to the learners come into the classroom and role-play the situation with the instructor. Students then practice each stage of the interaction with these familiar participants until comfortable with the interaction.

3. Research base: Carrigan (2001), cited in Collier (2013, 2016).

4. What to watch for with ELL/CLD students

    a. Learning to survive and thrive in a new environment is challenging for anyone. This can be especially difficult for ELL and CLD learners and their families as they learn to interact in a new language and with new social rules and expectations.

    b. Bring in people from the community with whom the participants are comfortable first. Gradually expand the interaction circle as folks become more confident.

    c. Small social support groups within school and within the community can provide a "safe" group within which to ask questions and learn ways to succeed at tasks or in solving problems.

## Example Strategy #2: Rest and Relaxation Techniques

1. Purpose of the strategy

    a. Enhance ability of students to learn new things

    b. Develop self-monitoring skills

    c. Reduce anxiety and stress responses

    d. Reduce culture shock side effects

2. How to do it
   a. At Tier 1, this strategy may be done within an integrated classroom.
   b. In RTI models, this strategy may be done with small groups, in individualized, focused intensive periods of time, or in specially designed individual programs and may be included in the IEP.
   c. Relaxation techniques are shown in video or demonstration form with an explanation in home and community language when possible. Students discuss when they might need to use these techniques.
3. Research base: Allen, Klein, & Skiba (1997), and Thomas, P. (2006) cited in Collier (2013, 2016).
4. What to watch for with ELL/CLD students
   a. Heightened anxiety, distractibility, and response fatigue are all common side effects of the acculturation process and attributes of culture shock.
   b. ELL and CLD students need more time to process classroom activities and tasks. Building in rest periods will provide thinking and processing breaks in their day.

38071118R00111

Made in the USA
Lexington, KY
03 May 2019